A SPIRITUAL TRILOGY

I WAY BEYOND THE RIVER
II THE WALLS CAME TUMBLING DOWN
III IT CAME TO PASS

ANNE URNE

FIRST EDITION

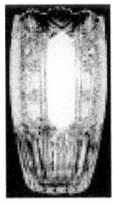

BOIS PUBLISHING
OKLAHOMA CITY, OKLAHOMA

Copyright © 2003 by Anne Urne
All rights reserved.

BOIS PUBLICATIONS
5411 Colfax Place
Oklahoma City, Oklahoma 73112

Cover Photographer: David W. Hudson

Printed in the United States of America
First Printing: April 2003
Second Printing: September 2011
10 9 8 7 6 5 4 3 2

ISBN 0-9727967-0-3 $21.00

Library of Congress Cataloging-in-Publication Data

Urne, Anne
    A Spiritual Trilogy

Library of Congress Control Number 2003091290

ACKNOWLEDGMENTS

It is no coincidence that this 3-volume book was the result of the collaboration of 3 persons. My daughter, Michelle, niece, Christine, and I shared personal experiences, emotions, struggles, victories, insights and revelations as we journeyed together in our search for inner peace and true happiness. What we discovered was too wonderful not to share!

INTRODUCTION

The three books contained in this trilogy will take you on a spiritual journey that will literally turn your life around. Your journey will begin in *Way Beyond the River* by making a turn in the direction of your heart's desire to find long hidden talents and gifts. In *The Walls Came Tumbling Down* you will be astonished at the invisible roadblocks that inhibited spiritual growth when your journey takes you to the depths of the soul where truths are revealed and knowledge is attained. *It Came to Pass* will propel you into new dimensions where you will discover the place where dreams do come true. Your individual God-given talents and gifts have been waiting there for you all the time. You will enter into the holy place where the supernatural power of God is manifested to perform His will in your life. God's will is the desire of your heart and this journey takes you to your heart's desire which is your destiny.

I Way Beyond the River	13
II The Walls Came Tumbling Down	135
III It Came to Pass	249

♥ ♥ ♥

Then the Lord answered me and said:
Write down the vision upon the tablets,
so that one can read it readily.
For the vision still has its time,
presses on to fulfillment,
and will not disappoint.
If it delays, wait for it,
it will surely come,
it will not be late.

HABACUC 2:3-4

PROLOGUE

*Go stand and speak in the temple to the people
all the words of this life.*

Acts: 5:21

This scripture was mystically conveyed to Anne as she awoke to hear a man's voice clearly asking, *What are your initials?* She replied, "A C T," to which the voice immediately responded, "5 2 1."

Anne's last name began with the letter T. It was during her spiritual journey that she was given the new last name, *Urne*.

This book is the result of a personal spiritual journey that began ten years ago when Anne determined to read the Bible from cover to cover. Miracles and revelations convinced her that time spent in daily Bible reading, study and meditation were the most important part of every day. She devoted each morning to reading seven chapters in succession and would record the date of each completed Bible reading. She quit counting after twenty entries when she ran out of room for her log on the blank pages at the back of her Bible.

In her search for answers to mysteries that presented from the scriptures, Anne embarked on a wondrous spiritual journey.

The answers her soul searched for came in an almost mystical way as she came upon information contained in ancient stories of *The Book of Adam and Eve, The Testament of Reuben* and scriptures excluded from the Bible known as apocrypha. She found books that had been out of print for years that contained riveting prophecies. She read books on Eastern and Jewish spiritualism and then thrilled to the discovery of Western spiritualism.

In her continuous search for spiritual knowledge she finally discovered the Christian mystics. She knew she had struck gold when she discovered St. Therese of Lisieux, St. Teresa of Avila and St. John of the Cross.

At last she had found comrades in her pursuit of spirituality through Jesus. Up to this time she felt completely alone on a path that ran between Christian beliefs and spirituality that omitted Jesus.

Mysticism was the terminology applied to the practice of these saints and Anne recognized it immediately. She was not alone in her spiritual quest for truth. She had been practicing mysticism for years in her prayer and meditation life, and at long last she found a friend who understood her in St. Therese.

Anne was convinced that our spiritual nature was a relatively unknown identity waiting to be found within us, and she was just as adamant that a journey into the spiritual realm could only be traveled safely with Jesus. Jesus was her door to all spiritual investigation and her guide was always the Holy Spirit.

A Spiritual Trilogy contains three books written in succession as Anne's journey progresses through the stages of body, soul and spirit.

These books contain new and potentially controversial ideas about famous biblical figures and the roles they have played both physically as well as spiritually.

Anne unfolds her fascinating answers to spiritual mysteries that she discovered in lost books and ancient stories, as well as from prophesies, dreams and witnesses. It is an adventure that will awaken your inner self.

Once awakened you may discovery your new name. Your spiritual journey is a personal path to discover your own truth.

BOOK I

DEDICATION

My wonderful husband is my leader, guide, hero and my true love. Our life together has been one exciting adventure after another. I watch in awe as he operates in a cool, slow, calm manner that defies these hectic times. His wisdom is a treasure, his charm a delight and his sense of humor a joy. After all the time and study I spent finding out the importance of making a turn, I am taken aback at one of Al's humorous remarks. Every once in awhile he looks at me and just shakes his head, saying, "Where did I make a wrong turn!" He always makes me laugh when he does this, but after reading my own book, I say to him, "How did you know it was the wrong turns that caused all the problems? How do you always seem to know the answer before the question is even asked?" This book is all about a *turn*. Now, as I recall his question to me, I wonder . . . did he know all along what it took me so long to find out? "That's what I love about you, darling. I never get a step ahead of you!"

WAY

BEYOND

THE

RIVER

WAY BEYOND THE RIVER CONTENTS

Chapter 1	17
Begin Your Journey	
Chapter 2	23
Opposites and the Theft of Your Gifts	
Chapter 3	33
Significance of Two	
Chapter 4	39
Journey to the Light	
Chapter 5	49
What is Death?	
Chapter 6	63
The Presence of God	
Chapter 7	71
Tragedy	
Chapter 8	75
Expect a Blessing	
Chapter 9	79
The Revelation of Abel	
Chapter 10	95
Mystery of Iniquity	
Chapter 11	105
Understanding the Time	
Chapter 12	117
Destiny	
Conclusion	129

CHAPTER 1

BEGIN YOUR JOURNEY

This story must begin at the end. And, yet just as God describes Himself as the Alpha and Omega, beginning and the end, we learn that as we reach the end – there are only more exciting beginnings. We are children of God on a journey in a strange land. The spiritual self that is our real self is caught up in this body of flesh and when we arrive in this world, there are so many things we must learn. There is indeed a journey we each shall make.

In preparing for a journey it is useful to check a map. As an explorer on an expedition, I have charted the directions that I discovered in my soul's quest for its destiny. I have been on a wondrous journey with God, traveling through my own spiritual awakenings as I searched for the inner peace and fulfillment that comes with understanding God's love. This understanding is imparted to us by His Holy Spirit of whom it is written, *the Spirit of truth - will teach you all the truth.*

A Map of God's Great Plan

JOURNEY FROM DARKNESS TO LIGHT

NATURAL BIRTH		BAPTISM		SPIRITUAL BIRTH
DARK	R	GRAY	J	LIGHT
Satan Rules	E D	Flesh Rules	O R D	Holy Spirit Rules
Egypt	S	Wilderness	A N	Promised Land
Bondage	E	*Confusion*	R	*Freedom*
ENMITY	A	THE LAW	I V	LOVE
In Sin		Sin Recognition	E R	Without Sin

◀ *GOING BACKWARD* ↔ *GOING FORWARD* ▶

Discover God's will for your life and turn away from the lies and stumbling blocks that lead you in the wrong direction. Model your journey after the Exodus from Egypt to the Promised Land. Turn in the right direction.

Looking at the map from left to right you can see that we begin our journey in darkness when we enter this world a physical being. Our destination is heaven and we must become spiritual beings to enter into our heavenly homes.

To better understand the complexity of our spiritual and physical bodies we should look at the story of Adam and Eve.

Adam and Eve were created in God's image inhabiting spiritual bodies or bright natures. When Adam ate the forbidden fruit his spiritual light was darkened. Sin entered in and the fall from Paradise resulted. But God instantly implemented an ingenious plan to save them from catapulting into complete spiritual darkness by capturing them in a body of flesh in mid-fall. He saved both spirit and soul in a body of flesh until His salvation plan would bring all of us home.

God described spiritual darkness as being the same as death in the *Book of Adam and Eve*. He cast Satan and his treasonous angels into this darkness when they rebelled. God also had a salvation plan from the very beginning to bring us back into the light and into the bright nature of our spirit man. His salvation plan is perfect and we are saved by His grace not our own works. Grace is the favor of God and a gift that cannot be purchased.

As we grow, we are schooled in the way of the world and learn survival skills for our fleshly bodies. Yet, at the same time, we become aware of inner desires that are so deep inside they are difficult to discern. We desire to know who we are and what we are destined to do in this life. This quest begins our journey.

As spiritual beings, we are instinctively or intuitively drawn to learn about the God who created us. We learn that we are created in His image and our journey is complicated by our very own complexity. We are spiritual persons and we have a soul that dwells in a body of flesh. Is that confusing? I should think so. Even when we think we have it — we get even more confused. Most describe the soul as the emotions or mind. The spirit man is harder to grasp. To me, the spirit is my real person; it looks like me and has my personality and individual traits.

The map indicates the three stages of our journey. It begins with our natural birth into the world. The soul is in darkness, cut off from the light of God due to the fall of mankind from the Garden of Eden. Our initial state is considered to be in sin and darkness, not through our fault. but because of the calculated deceit of Satan whereby he deceived Eve and caused Adam to be disobedient when he partook of the apple. Through cunning and deceit, Satan caused the fall of mankind from heaven bringing us under his dominion and power.

The second stage is symbolized by crossing the Red Sea which symbolizes baptism. As we pass through this water to become children of God through the washing away of sin, we cross over to the first stage of our journey. Here we come into a lighter, but gray area. This is the wilderness or desert dry area where we begin to learn more about the God who created us and His Son.

Jesus the Son of God saved our soul from death by making the supreme sacrifice for the sin of mankind. by submitting His flesh upon the cross unto death. He was pure and uncontaminated by sin. So, just as Satan tricked Adam into falling into his power, Satan was overcome when Jesus entered into the prison of darkness, shining with the light of God's glory. He conquered the enemy and won the victory and set the captives free!

Even though the victory has been won, the devil continues to the bitter end to deceive God's children. You have read that Jesus is the door and the only door to our freedom. The reason is that Jesus opened the door of that prison. He bent the bars of brass and broke the gates of iron as it is written of Him in Psalms. The prisoners saw him and believed. Here is the key to the door: Believe in Jesus who is that door. He alone opened it and He alone has the keys!

As long as Satan can turn us away from Jesus, we continue on as prisoners. The joy is that we have the power to choose who to believe. The travesty is that by our own God given power of choice, the devil continues to seduce us into making the wrong choice.

This second stage of our journey is still ruled by our flesh. It is no wonder! The flesh is all we have known, and now we must learn about our spiritual person. I believe we are in a desert place as long as our spirit is dry and without nourishment. We have always known that we have inner desires and dreams, but finding them can be elusive. It is no mystery that we are confused. There is a real force or power working to steal all of our spiritual gifts – and that force is evil, ruled by Satan and his empire of dark angels and spirits.

Yes, if you want to make this journey, you must understand what obstacles are going to get in your way. It won't be bandits holding you up with a gun – it will be demons whispering wrong thoughts and ideas, causing you to make wrong turns!

Jesus told us that He must go to the Father in order to send us the Holy Spirit who will instruct and guide us and indwell us. I believe the light is rekindled in our soul at the time of our baptism. It is the light that went out when Adam and Eve fell into sin. This light is rekindled in our spirit by the indwelling of the Holy Spirit. It begins like a small candle burning in a vast darkness. Now, we must nourish our spirit with the help of the Holy Spirit who guides us through this stage of our journey. The Holy Spirit is gentle and grants us the power to discern good from evil. The Holy Spirit works through our senses to impart wisdom for making right choices.

The Holy Spirit is that voice deep within that has

been called intuition or hunch, but it is a very real force that is within us. It is the light that can lead us across the wilderness. We struggle with our flesh as we learn how to live and survive in the spirit. This is where the opposition begins.

Be prepared to do battle with the enemy. These battles take place in the mind as we struggle for survival. On the journey we are beset with fear, the ultimate fear being death. The Israelites were beset with fears of death by the very basic needs of the flesh, to find water and food in the desert. Their survival depended wholly and completely on God as provider. So too does our successful journey depends on complete trust in God as our deliverer, provider and protector.

It is in the wilderness that we encounter confusion, and it is in this stage of the journey that we must learn the difference between the needs of the flesh and the needs of the spirit. We have been trained in the way of the world. The way of the spirit is in total opposition to the way of the world. This opposition is vitally important to understand.

Jesus taught us about the opposite way to deal with enemies – love them, don't curse them. He taught us how to give in order to receive. He taught that if we would seek we would find. These new insights on just how well the spiritual realm works to promote us is a very important step in making our journey as we learn about our very own individual destiny given us by God. Yes, I said *destiny*. Destiny is something very deep that we know, but we have such difficulty locating it. By strengthening our spirit, we become transformed and we find that special gift that God gave to us – our own individual destiny!

He calls blest the destiny of the just. Wisdom 2: 1

CHAPTER 2

OPPOSITES AND THE THEFT OF YOUR GIFT

Michelle and I together discovered the wonderful use of antonyms in revealing how the gifts given us by God are stolen by the devil. We have discovered that God imparts a special gift to each of His children. This gift is not easily discerned. To complicate the matter, we have discovered that Satan knows about our gift and comes to steal it while we are still very young.

Yes, I'm telling you that Satan, that most vile, evil and wicked spirit, even steals from children! I am reminded of the Last Supper when Judas took the morsel of bread, and as it is written, *Satan entered into him*. We see the thief comes immediately upon receiving to steal from us. Therefore, we must be on our guard and we must also be aware that our children need protection and special care to prevent the thief from stealing the gifts God has imparted to them.

Chapter II – Opposites and the Theft of Your Gift

As we continue our journey, we rejoice to know that God does have a plan for our life and we trust Him to fulfill the good work that He began in us. We know that we are heirs to the abundant life that Christ won for us by his victory over death. He made the sacrifice and we do not refuse Him who calls us to Himself.

We each have a God-given destiny. It is wonderful when the light shines into the darkness and exposes that something way down in our very soul that has been hidden too long. It is our special gift from God; our talent, our dream - our destiny.

Yes, we have read in the Bible that God has destined in us a future. He has given each of us gifts. And we are instructed not to bury these gifts in the ground, but trade with them, use them until he returns. Of course, that devil has had a hand in hiding our gift from us. He will do everything in his power to keep us from fulfilling the destiny that God has given us. He is the thief that comes to steal, kill and destroy. We have been warned about him, being trained to choose right from wrong, light over darkness, and not to lean unto our own understanding. This enemy is so cunning that he can appear as an angel of light - when he is full of darkness. It is no little wonder that we become confused, led astray and never seem to find the destiny that God created in each of us.

The devil attacks us in the gray wilderness portion of our journey. Since we can't seem to discern black from white, we just go with the flow. My favorite teacher tells that it is easy to take the wide path - there are lots of people on it. The narrow path - the right path is lonely and it is going in the opposite direction. Yes, we have to learn to swim upstream.

The devil pulls out all the stops to keep us from reaching our destinies. Over a lifetime I have come up against many of his negative attacks. It is when we discover negatives occurring in our lives that we need to stop and identify them.

Use a dictionary or thesaurus to look up the opposite of the negative that you are encountering and find out what that thief is stealing from you. If you are experiencing fear – he is taking your faith. If you have been shamed – he has stolen your glory. If you are shy – he has stolen your boldness.

We all have experienced negatives, but the point is to learn how to find the opposite. We must realize that the great opposition to God is Satan - and everything he does is opposite.

I am amazed and you will be too, as you grasp the magnitude of this concept in your very own life and discover what the devil has reversed in your life. This exercise will give you an insight into the things that God has destined for you. Look at the antonym for shame. The first word is glorify, other words are: exalt, honor, praise and worship. These are gifts from God for us to use for His glory! We are not destined to walk in shame.

The most overused tactic the devil uses to turn people around in the opposite direction of their destiny is to attack them with rejection. Rejection means reverse. I'm sure everyone has experienced rejection. The devil would make you think you were the only one who ever suffered this humiliation, when in actuality he uses this on everyone. This is an easy tool the devil uses to turn us away from our gifts.

I must interject some of my pastor's sermon recently on the very subject of rejection. He said that the ultimate rejection of self is suicide. This is a very serious attack.

Other tactics are disapproval, dishonor, shame, and guilt. These are the opposites of our gifts and cause the forfeiture or loss of our destiny. Just as it is written, *the thief comes to steal, kill and destroy* the future that God has instilled in us.

Chapter II – Opposites and the Theft of Your Gift

We all need to walk in the gifts of God, being filled with mercy, grace, honor and all those glorious, shiny things. I see God's glory as powdery gold dust - and I want to walk in it all of the time!

I believe God gave me the ability to write - to be His scribe and write books about His truths. This gift of the spirit was manifested in my flesh as I worked as a secretary. Yet, this job became a bondage to me. My spirit was yearning to do the work God had given me. As I grew in my spirit, I became most dissatisfied with my work of this world. I was writing everyone's words but God's, just like the Israelites were building pyramids for the Egyptians, instead of building a grand temple to the Lord! We must learn to walk in the spiritual realm in order to find our destiny.

It was an exciting discovery when Michelle and I realized the opposites that were in our lives. These opposites are hindrances to our journey and they keep us turned in the wrong direction. A sample list of opposites is presented at the end of this chapter to demonstrate the significance of the lies that hide our gifts and keep us turned in the wrong direction. By replacing the negatives with positives, we make use of a spiritual type compass to guide us through this journey of life.

We each desire to reach that perfect paradise where there are no more tears or suffering. We have been told that Jesus is the way. The way is the direction of our journey to God and all of His promises.

It is written that Jesus gave Himself for our sins, that He might deliver us from the wickedness of this present world, according to the will of God. It is God's will. Meditate on His promises.

> *Christ has redeemed us from the curse of poverty, sickness and spiritual death.*

The fact that we are each created uniquely by God means that we have different, yet similar, talents or gifts. The devil is aware of our special gift from the moment we enter the world, and he immediately goes after that gift to turn it around. He attacks us in our childhood, and uses rejection, fear, disapproval or similar tactics to provoke emotional reactions that stop our spiritual growth and conceal our gift.

Discover your gift by finding the negatives in your life. You know where your weakness lies. The devil directs your focus on your weaknesses as he camouflages your gifts. So, discern the problem because it is masking your gift. Once you determine where your weakness lies, you can more quickly discover the opposite which is your God-given gift and your most powerful asset! Finding out the truth can set you free! You can discover your strengths as you turn to Jesus and ask the Holy Spirit to guide you in the path that God planned for you.

The following narrative was written by Michelle about the spiritual journey and how to overcome the obstacles along the way. It is an inspired message.

CRUCIFY THAT FLESH

How do we cross the Jordan to get to the Promised Land? The Jordan represents our flesh. If we can crucify our flesh and get it into submission, we will find God's plan for our life.

How do we crucify the flesh? We do not give in to our feelings. Feelings are by-products of the flesh. Feelings will get you into trouble when you listen to them. Do you think we would have all God's blessings, if Jesus would have been led by his feelings rather than his spirit? What if every time Jesus was rejected, he went to his disciples and complained and cried, "It's not fair!" Or, what if He became indignant, "Can you believe they said I was the lord of the demons? That just hurts my feelings! I think I'm going to the wilderness and cry all by myself, because life isn't fair!" Jesus didn't act like that, but we do. Where did Jesus go when He felt unjustly ridiculed or treated unfairly? Did He run to his friends and complain or did he run to God for strength? He went to God and lifted those evil people up to Him and prayed for them. He asked God to give Him strength to endure the trials He was going through. Why? Because God promised Him glory. Not mediocrity - but, Glory! So, how do we crucify our flesh so we can enter into the Promised Land? Why did an 8-day trip turn into 40 years for the Israelites? It is because they feared and refused to believe, after they were freed from their bondage in Egypt. Egypt represents the place in our life where there is no light, that place where sin and lies keep us from reaching our potential.

So, once we are freed from the bondage of the world, where do we go? The Israelites went out of Egypt into the desert of 'Just Enough'. They had exactly what they needed - no more, and no less. So, when we accept Christ, we go into the land of 'Just Enough' and remain there thinking this is the great promise of God. Eventually, it gets old and we want more. God has promised us so much more. He promised the Israelites more and even showed it to them, and they still didn't know how to get there. They wandered 40 years not receiving the promise of God. All they had to do was cross the Jordan. How do we cross the Jordan in our life so we can receive the promise of God? Choose God's will, not your will.

Michelle

I woke up one morning, shortly after this particular study on opposites to a wonderful love song running through my mind. It was an explosive and emotional confirmation to me that the map and the study of opposites were correct. The song was *Turn Around – Look at Me*. Tears fell when I heard the verse *I've been waiting, but I'll wait forever – for you to come to me*. It was my kind and patient Lord conveying His message in beautiful melody to my soul. It is in these beautiful moments of awareness that we find the magnificent, loving and protective presence of Our Lord.

I resolved to find a copy of this beautiful song that woke me up this morning then turned around in my bed to look at my picture of Jesus on the wall.

Yes, it is you singing that song to me in my spirit. You really do love me so much, Jesus. All these years I have been searching for that deep love, that protective all encompassing love – and I cried because I was looking the wrong way. All the hurts and pains that I suffered – when all the time you were there waiting for me to turn around and take your hand. I'm so sorry, Jesus. Thank you for waiting and loving me forever. I turn around – I take your hand. I have found You and Your wonderful, almighty powerful, gentle and protective love. Thank you Jesus for your great love! Hold me tight and never let me get turned the wrong way again – forever – I take your hand everywhere I go. And, I let your love flow from me to all those in the world that you love and want to comfort and heal. Such great love, such very great love. Thank you for your great love.

Everyone strives to reach that perfect place that Jesus described in His word. He told us the kingdom of God is at hand. He said we could enter into His rest; that we could have life and have it more abundantly. So, how do we get to the Promised Land while we are still in this natural body living in the world? Jesus said we could have so many things because He suffered and died for us to have them. It seems blasphemous to live in a world of sickness, poverty and anxiety when Jesus put all that under His feet.

> *I have overcome the world! Abide in my word, and I will abide in you.*

We are all on a journey and it has been the same journey ever since the beginning of time. What happens to get us off track or delayed? It is lack of faith.

How do we determine between believing the truth and believing a lie? I found a very simple, yet profound and mountain moving truth: *Turn Around – Look at* Jesus.

OPPOSITES

THE LIES   *GOD'S GIFTS*

THE LIES	GOD'S GIFTS
ANGER	PEACE
REJECTION	ACCEPTANCE
HUMILIATION	DIGNITY
SHAME	HONOR
DISAPPROVAL	FAVOR
ENMITY	LOVE
CRUELTY	KINDNESS
CONDEMNATION	FORGIVENESS
POVERTY	PROSPERITY
GUILT	INNOCENCE
SORROW	JOY
ANXIETY	CALM
FEAR	COURAGE
DOUBT	CONFIDENCE
LOSS	RESTORATION
GRIEF	COMFORT

This list of opposites will help you identify some of the negatives that are disguising your gifts from God. Find the negative traits that are operating in your life and turn them around. It only takes a turn to put you in the right direction. When you are headed the right way, all things will work together for good.

TURN AROUND AND RECEIVE GOD'S GIFTS

Chapter II – Opposites and the Theft of Your Gift

Then the Lord said to Moses, "Why are you crying out to me? Tell the Israelites to go forward.

Exodus 15, 15

CHAPTER 3

SIGNIFICANCE OF TWO

I was drawn to study the significance of the words spoken by Paul to the Ephesians when describing Jesus:

... He it is who has who has made BOTH one, and has broken down the intervening wall of the enclosure, the enmity in his flesh... that of the TWO he might create in himself ONE NEW MAN, and make peace and reconcile BOTH IN ONE BODY to God by the cross, having slain the enmity in himself.

... I exhort you to walk in a manner worthy of the calling with which you were called ... ONE BODY AND ONE SPIRIT.

And coming he announced the good tidings of peace to you who were afar off ... and those who were near, because through him we BOTH have access in one Spirit to the Father. Therefore, you are now no longer strangers and foreigners, but you are citizens with the saints. In Him the whole structure is closely fitted together.

Paul describes Jesus making two one by destroying the enmity in his flesh, thus revealing that sin divided us in two. I believe the *two* that is being referred to in this passage are the spirit and soul that are contained in the flesh. These were separated by the darkness that entered through sin, and Jesus is the true light that came into the world.

At last the redemptive plan of God is seen being fulfilled in Jesus. He came in the flesh, the very container that held our body and soul, to win the victory over darkness. He destroyed the enmity in His flesh, thus bringing our soul and spirit back into the light of God, so that we enter in one spiritual body through His Holy Spirit.

The process of liberating our body and soul from the prison of darkness that separated us from the Father was accomplished in Jesus. Now, we have access through the Holy Spirit to the kingdom of God by believing and accepting Jesus and his sacrifice, and thus becoming one with Him.

Two becoming one is indeed a great mystery. And the more I study and ponder the *two* – the more *two's* I discover.

Our power to choose signifies there are *two*. The *two* are obviously in opposition since we must make a choice. One or the other – the *two* choices are life or death, darkness or light, good or evil. God gave us the free will to choose. The decision sets our course in the direction of the kingdom of light or the kingdom of darkness.

As we grow in spirit we learn how to make quality decisions by refusing the wrong feelings and choosing the right knowledge of the one and only true God. The right choices empower us to enter into the kingdom of life.

We can enter into the kingdom of God while still in the body of flesh if we are led by the Spirit, and our spirit is born into God's kingdom.

Awake, sleeper, and arise from among the dead, and Christ will enlighten thee.

Ephesians 5:14

Jesus taught that we must be born again. I would describe being born again as a spiritual awakening that takes place in our very own spirit.

Again, the distance we travel in our earthly journey is entirely up to us. We can stay in the gray area of the wilderness and wait until we depart this body to receive God's promises. We can choose the darkness or go toward the light. The destination of our soul after we depart this body is dependent upon the choices we make in this world, and the ultimate mercy and grace of God. In choosing our destination, we must know the only door to heaven will be Jesus. We can meet Him now or wait until our departure from this world. How foolish to depart and leave destination to chance.

It seems sad, as well, to choose Jesus now, but postpone His promises until we arrive in heaven. He said we could have them now!

We enter into the kingdom when we submit our free will to choose God's will. This submission immerses us into the victory of Jesus and makes the two one. Our spirit and soul become one in God – no longer two – just one. We are led in our spirit by the Holy Spirit. Living the high life is living a spirit filled and fully submitted life. We step into Jesus and we become one with Him.

There are many instances of two's in the Bible. For example, Jesus sent the disciples out two by two; Noah took animals into the ark two by two; and the most unique example of two becoming one is where it is written that man and woman become one flesh when they marry. From Noah and the pairs of animals to Revelations where we find two witnesses, there is something very significant about two. We live in a world located between two kingdoms; the kingdom of darkness and the kingdom of light.

An almost elusive example of the reference to two persons is found in the following scripture.

*Then he came and found him sleeping.
And he said to Peter, 'Simon, dost thou sleep?'*

St. Mark 14:37

I read this scripture many times without noticing that Jesus 'said to Peter' - "Simon". The two names are used interchangeably here as Jesus speaks to Simon the man, but addresses him as Peter, the name given him by the Lord.

But, Jesus, looking upon him said, "Thou art Simon, the son of John; thou shalt be called Cephas (which interpreted is Peter)."

St. John 1:42

The significance of the use of two names seems to be for the purpose of defining two beings, one spiritual and one physical. Now, when we read that Jesus addresses Peter, we understand that He is speaking to the spiritual man. He asks Peter's spiritual person if his physical man, Simon, is sleeping. I believe this is a perfect example of our flesh ruling our spirit, and Jesus pointing out the importance of having the spiritual man in charge, rather than succumbing to the dictates of the flesh.

Often as I read the scriptures of Matthew and Mark, I wondered why Matthew described two possessed men coming from the tombs of Gerasa while Mark only described one. I now believe that Matthew could discern the spiritual as well as the flesh man, and that is the reason for the discrepancy in the number.

There is an interesting scripture that talks about a new name. This book pleads with the reader to *hear* what the Spirit says. The difficulty in reading this book is that it speaks to the spiritual nature while we try to understand it with our natural mind.

> *He who has an ear, let him hear what the Spirit says to the churches: To him who overcomes, I will give the hidden manna, and I will give him a white pebble, and upon the pebble a new name written, which no one knows except him who receives it.*
>
> Apoc. 2:17

The Spirit is exhorting us to overcome the flesh, and put our spiritual man in the ascendancy. Take charge over the flesh and become, indeed, a new man with a new name. This is the place where the power, security, peace, glory and all of God's gifts are obtained.

To ignore this message and refuse to advance in spiritual growth and knowledge is to refuse the sacrifice that Jesus made for us. We turn our back on Him when we walk in the limited capacity of the flesh by using our natural eyes and ears. This is the wrong direction from which we must turn around.

When we allow our flesh to rule we remain enslaved to the ruler of darkness who stole Adam's authority in the earth. Satan operates in the earth, and he cunningly makes captives of God's children.

The tools of darkness are just that - darkness. As long as we continue in the path of darkness, we are oblivious to the wonderful things happening in the light!

We have the power to choose and the choice is between two worlds. The significance of two is the choice we make. Do we believe and journey to the light of God and His promises, or do we doubt and follow the path of darkness?

Our destiny is our future. Of course, no one wants to choose the dark prison that beckons, but until we strengthen our spirit man, that old devil will continue to lead people in the wrong direction, not knowing the destination is a prison.

We have the freedom to choose between life and death, and that is a significant choice between two extremes.

> *Whoever tries to save his life will lose it; and whoever loses it will preserve it.*
>
> St. Luke 18: 32

> *Amen, amen, I say to you, he who hears my word, and believes him who sent he, has life everlasting, and does not come to the judgment, but has passed from death to life.*
>
> St. John 5: 24

CHAPTER 4
JOURNEY TO THE LIGHT

DARKNESS AND SIN

The great angel who opposed God was plunged into the darkness, and in his rage and retaliation against God, Satan determined to destroy God's beloved Adam.

Adam disobeyed God when he ate of the apple from the forbidden tree. This sin brought darkness to his once bright nature, and that darkness separated the soul from the spirit. It would have resulted in death, or total separation from God had He not immediately intervened. In wisdom and magnificent power, God captured the separated soul and spirit within a body of flesh until He could redeem it.

Adam's disobedience to God cost him his citizenship in heaven. This act of disobedience gave Satan jurisdiction and dominion over man.

God's intervention prevented the complete fall of man while He put into place His redemption plan. I believe that at the very moment Adam fell, God enacted another week of creation wherein He lengthened the time on earth to a ratio of 1000 years to one day in heaven. At the same instant He created a body of flesh to contain our soul and spirit until He effected the victory that would bring us back into the light with Him. That is why it is written that Jesus is the light that came into the world, and it is further written that He made the two one!

While man was in this state of suspension between darkness and light, God gave him the Commandments known as the Law. This law was the pattern of knowledge and truth that attests to God's justice, and through it came the recognition of sin. A study of the Book of Romans will give the reader much insight on the subject of the Law.

The soul is a foreigner in this world of flesh. It is searching for its native home and the return to its citizenship in heaven. The devil would lead you into hell where you would be an alien in a dark and horrible place. It is dark and horrible because it is without God. Let me reiterate these important facts. We are aliens to darkness, foreigners in the world and our souls long and yearn to be returned to their home with God in heaven. We are natives and citizens of heaven, but we must make a choice and choose God. That is the only thing God cannot do for us. God created us with a free will and if we choose to trust Him, he has offered us half his kingdom. We only have to ask. Our journey is one that takes us *way beyond the river.*

GRAY AREA IN THE NATURAL WORLD

Spiritually speaking, the world where we live is a gray area. It is that place in between darkness and light, and between death and life. We are born into the world in a state of darkness and sin, without hope; lost souls in an alien or adverse place. The message of the Gospel is one of hope.

We who believe the Gospel that Jesus died for our sins receive eternal life. When we accept Jesus as our savior, the light is rekindled in our spirit.

Paul explains this mystery most excellently in chapter two of Ephesians, saying:

> *And in him you too, when you had heard the word of truth, the good news of your salvation, and believed in it, were sealed with the Holy Spirit of the promise, who is the pledge of our inheritance for a redemption of possession*

So, now we have the Holy Spirit of truth who will guide us through our journey. As we leave the place of darkness behind, we travel as foreigners in the world, looking toward the redemption of that possession of the Promised Land.

We are not born into the darkness, but rather into a dimly lit intermediate area that we know as earth and home. We are torn in two directions because our soul or mind is looking toward the world which is ruled by the spirit of darkness, while our spirit man or heart is facing the light looking for God. We are presented with two conflicting ways to choose, and we must remember that God gave us the free will to choose. Sometimes the right and wrong seem to elude us in this gray place. It is like looking into a dimly lit room. Objects seen can be misconstrued since they are not seen clearly.

Only the light can reveal the truth of the things that are seen. Thank God for His Holy Spirit of truth that guides us as we make this journey from the dark side of the world to the light side. We certainly do not want to go back into the darkness. The desire of our heart is to enter into the light and the fullness of day where truth and understanding yield joy and peace.

We must learn to recognize those things which are from below and those that are from above. Just as light

Chapter IV – Journey to the Light

and dark are totally opposite each other, so are Satan and God who reign over those respective places. Satan is completely opposite or opposed to everything of God.

We must learn to evaluate our feelings. Those from God give us peace and joy, comfort and happiness. It is our feelings that must be controlled and brought into captivity; otherwise the devil will run us on a course of destruction by presenting us with feelings of fear, anger, rejection and every negative feeling that can be named.

We have a guide book called the Commandments or the Law, and we are under the Law while we are in the natural world. It is by the Law that we recognize sin and avoid the enemy. Our journey is through a strange land indeed, for we find that we are bombarded with confusion.

In order to learn the truth and overcome the enemy, we must do one simple thing. Turn around! Look at Jesus who is above and beyond and in the Light. Take your eyes off the enemy and you will no longer be torn between light and dark, error and truth, sin and righteousness. We must crucify the flesh with its desires and lusts; the tools the devil uses to entice us back into the darkness.

Thanks be to God who came in the form of man in Christ Jesus to offer the ultimate sacrifice for sin. He shed His blood that redeemed us from the enemy's control.

Jesus crucified the flesh, and when we believe Him, we are given the Holy Spirit who helps us deny this flesh and its desires. We then progress toward the land of promises.

We read in Ephesians that we were sealed in the Holy Spirit for the redemption of the promise. Jesus is our redemption, so in order to get into the Land of Promise, we must get in Jesus. We should surround ourselves with Him as our protector and deliverer. In Him we attain to the promises and enter into the Promised Land. He is our redemption! This is accomplished by faith for it is written that the promise is the outcome of faith.

The law attests to God's justice and justice is received by grace through our faith in Jesus. Grace is the favor of God upon His children who believe. It is also written that the promises are made through justice not the Law. Those who are led by the Spirit are no longer under the law. You must read Paul's accounts of this matter in the books of *Romans, Galatians* and *Ephesians*. As you study these great works you will be able to grasp the understanding with the help of the Holy Spirit.

I listened to one of my favorite teachers discuss how we must renew our mind. We can be born in the spirit, but if we do not renew our mind, we will stay in this same place. He taught that we must change our pattern of thinking after we are born again in the spirit, casting down imaginations and by tearing down strongholds in our mind. This comes through a renewing of our mind and attitudes.

Do not be deceived. The devil uses the cleverest devices to keep us out of the Promised Land. One I have found that we must overcome is that of "compromise".

The closer you come to entering into the promises, the more enticing this compromise becomes. My own experience involved my personal belief that drinking is no more of a sin than eating.

Moderation and temperance were my guides to virtue, while considering drunkenness and gluttony to be the sins. Then, one day I was convicted to stop drinking wine. This would indeed be a sacrifice, as I loved to have a glass of wine with my dinner.

I wasn't hit with the full conviction without warning. There were small signs such as occasional headaches or the tired sluggish feeling after drinking wine. I would not have the energy to do much once I had finished dinner until bedtime. Then, with undeniable understanding came the conviction. All of a sudden one day when I had just purchased two bottles of my favorite brand and placed them on the counter, I was hit with the strongest conviction.

Look at all that! I almost fell down thinking, *Not now – I just bought two bottles!* Well, let me tell you – I needed a compromise.

I met with my daughter a day or two later and told her I was really compelled to study about the two becoming one. She and I sat down with our Bibles and pens, and we studied together and discussed ideas.

I began telling her about my wine conviction and how I believed you should maintain moderation in its consumption. As we talked, I told her that I had decided to only have one glass in the evening. Much to my dismay, Michelle determined this was a compromise and looked up the word in the dictionary where she read: a thing intermediate or in between, concession, and to endanger life or reputation – to discredit.

Michelle then promptly advised me that I could not have one foot in the world and the other in the kingdom. That settled it. I decided to forego the wine. It was not because I was convicted that drinking was a sin, rather I had to submit my will to God's will in this circumstance. This was a very hard decision, however, because I knew that drinking was not a sin. There is a time and season for things, however.

I believe this was a time for me to be obedient to the Holy Spirit that was teaching me how to follow my inner voice. This was also a time to learn discipline, obedience and understand that God knew what was best for me.

The same thing happens when you commit to a fast. Eating is not a sin, however, fasting and prayer is a way to deny the flesh and take control of it. It is a form of sacrifice that enables us to grow in our spirit. If we desire to live in the promises that are sealed in the spirit, we must be obedient to the leading of the Holy Spirit.

This stage of our journey brings us into the place of discipline. My first introduction to the discipline stage came to me in a dream. In this dream, I was in a classroom and the teacher was my co-pastor, Sharon. She and her husband co-pastor the church I attend with my husband. They both are very special to me. In my dream, she told us that she was going to teach on discipline. My first reaction to discipline was: O*h, I don't like this*! I sat down at a classroom desk that was facing a man I didn't know, and I commented that I didn't want to take this course. He told me that he was glad he was there because he needed this in his work to be successful. Later, as I pondered the meaning of the dream, I wondered, was that man symbolic of Jesus? Was it actually me that needed discipline for the success of my journey with Him? I believe so.

HEAVENLY KINGDOM

We enter into the kingdom by being led by the Holy Spirit. Here is where the Law is established and here we find our acceptance. The fulfillment of the Law is Love. God is Love and we are home. It is written that by faith we establish the law. Therefore, we complete our journey by faith and we receive the promises made through justice, not the law (Romans 4:13). There is one last and very important direction in this wonderful journey towards the kingdom; that being God's favor called *grace*.

- o We receive grace through Jesus;
- o Grace brings about our obedience to faith; and
- o We are justified by grace.

When we come under grace we are no longer under the Law. We have arrived in the kingdom. We are under the law while we are in the wilderness. The law will never be done away with until all is completed. As long as there is flesh there will be law.

We desire to live the high life, to enter into the kingdom. It is possible to have that abundant life now. We do not have to wait until this flesh dies in order to enter into the kingdom. We are born again in the spirit while still in this world. If we so choose to deny the flesh and be led by the Spirit, we can attain to the high life. It is our choice.

This choice seems to be at the root of our difficulties as we travel looking one way and then the other. I have found that the ultimate release from this world of gravity as we soar into the world of the spirit comes when we submit totally and completely to the spirit, denying the flesh, and thus being set free from all those confusing choices.

Not my will, but God's will. This is the place that completes my happiness and joy. This is what kingdom living is all about. Complete trust in God. Letting God complete the work he began in us. This is the ultimate of letting go and letting God be in control. God's control is not bondage, but freedom - another opposite.

Imagine plunging into water until you are completely surrounded by it. Then, imagine that the water is God's light and love as you are immersed in complete peace and protection.

This is the place where you become one with God, living the spirit life even while still in the flesh. This is your choice. Now, there are no longer rules of do's and don'ts because everything is right! How wonderful is our counselor, the Holy Spirit of God, who guides us on this journey of truth. Give in to the spirit and you will be amazed at the greatness of the feelings. Also, be aware that your flesh will rebel against this submission. You must choose – flesh rules or spirit rules.

The flesh urges us to over-eat and over-indulge in many areas. These over-indulgences make us sluggish, overweight and slow our progress. Some over-indulgences lead to great sin. How much better we feel when we deny our flesh for a while in fasting and prayer. You will be surprised how much healthier your flesh becomes when you take control over it and let the Spirit rule. You will have more quality time for God and be useful to Him as well. You will find your destiny in Him.

There is so much to gain by denying the dictates of this flesh and letting the Holy Spirit guide you. You will discover a healthier, more energetic life that is accomplishing those things that satisfy your soul. You will discover your destiny!

God instructed the Israelites to take possession of the Promised Land. This is what we must do, also. We can be born in the spirit and continue to live in the world or we can determine to possess the promises, stake our claim in our inheritance, enter in and take possession of them. Here, again I believe we accomplish this possession of the promises by completely submitting our will to God. I believe this is when the spirit and soul become one – in harmony – no longer two – pulling in different directions. Now, the two have become one, the flesh has been crucified, and the spirit has the ascendancy, control and rule over our life. One must submit to the other in order to become one. When we submit our will and emotions (the soul) to our spirit, we become one in God's Holy Spirit.

This is a great mystery, yet such a wonderful revelation. It takes obedience and trust to finally realize that all along we wanted to be completely in God's will and become citizens again in our heavenly home.

The place where our journey began is the same place it ends. We start the journey home from that place of darkness and alienation from God, and we travel as foreigners in this land searching for our home. In order to become a citizen of a country we must pledge allegiance to it. This submission of our free will is our allegiance to our God, trusting completely in His decisions for us and finding the comfort of being home with our Father who created us and the Mother who loves us. Yes, God Himself is two in one.

CHAPTER 5

WHAT IS DEATH?

I had a chat with my niece, Christy, one day and told her how I believed that Jesus was coming very soon. I asked if she read a chapter I had given to her mother about His return. Her answer distressed me when she said she didn't even want to think about end times because she wanted to see her children and grandchildren grow up.

This signaled an alarm in my spirit because the rationale was in complete conflict with the ultimate goal of Christianity. The belief and expectation of our Savior coming to earth to raise us up to our eternal heavenly home with God was being negated by a real fear and dread of death and departure.

Not only is she afraid to leave – she is even unwilling to go. This meant she was actually afraid of the eternal life that we as Christians are seeking. Her sentiments were logical, but the end result was what signaled my alarm. She was certainly not alone in her feelings, because we all feel that way.

How do we put our natural feelings into perspective with our Christian beliefs? The two are in complete contradiction. The entire Christian goal is to return to our heavenly home, but the fact is we really don't want to leave. We have an instinctive and basic fear of death.

This is nothing new. Remember, the fear of death is what prevented the Israelites from entering the Promised Land for 40 years. They were confronted with fears of starvation, thirst and terrifying giants. They suffered these fears even when they had witnessed God's miracles over and over during their journey.

There is a great confusion about life and death. I prayed for understanding. I desired the wisdom that would prove there is nothing, absolutely nothing, to fear in the death of this physical body. I went to Him searching for the meaning of death.

I had to find a way to explain the truth without sounding like the bearer of gloom who says dying to Christ is not really dying! Of course we all want to live. So, now, how do we understand that dying is living? This is so difficult to understand when we exist in natural physical bodies. I began by recalling what I had learned from the scriptures as I searched for the answer.

Adam was dead to sin - but only in the spirit. His soul was alive. Being born again is to receive the Holy Spirit of God. His spirit gives light to our spirit. It is also written that if we grieve the Holy Spirit of God, the Holy Spirit can depart from us. This is a much more serious situation than dying in the flesh. For without the Holy Spirit to kindle the light of God in our soul, we would become as darkness and that is the only real death! When the bible speaks of life and death, it refers to spiritual life. We know that the physical life ends. but if the spirit leaves, we are spiritually dead, even while our bodies are yet alive!

Our body dies, yet we know that somehow our soul continues. So, what is the soul? Is there any such thing as a soul dying? The soul is the emotional realm; the part that identifies us as who we are. Just what is this soul? We learn in the bible of physical and spiritual death, yet the soul is never spoken of as dead or alive! It seems to just always be. It is our very existence, but not our life or death.

Thus, it seems that the soul never dies! From the time of Adam until the time of Jesus, souls were captured in hell. Jesus died on the cross and set the captives free. We learn from the Book of Revelations that those who remain on earth after Christ's second coming all die at the end time, and then are judged out of their works. They were left because they did not believe and were, therefore, unable to enter into the Rest with Jesus for a thousand years. It is by believing in Jesus that we receive life through His gift of the Holy Spirit.

The Holy Spirit brings our very own spirit to life. The spirit lives with the soul, taking up its image and its individuality which was made in the image of God. Our flesh covers this spirit body which looks just like us. It is our very nature that is covered by the skin so we look the same in the spirit as we do in the flesh.

> *Then the Lord God formed man out of the dust of the ground and breathed into his nostrils the breath of life, and man became a living being.*
>
> Gen. 2:7

> *Both the man and his wife were naked, but they felt no shame.*
>
> Gen. 2:25

This living being is the soul - the existence of man. However, in the beginning man existed in a spiritual body. He was not a sensual and feeling being because he was not in a physical body. He existed in the spirit and that is why he *felt* no shame.

Even when Adam was spiritually *dead* to sin, his soul still existed. Immediately upon falling into sin his darkened soul was clothed with a physical body. Adam and Eve were transferred into physical bodies and their perspectives changed as we read further.

> *She took of its fruit and ate it, and also gave some to her husband and he ate. Then the eyes of both were OPENED, and they realized that they were NAKED.*
>
> *When they HEARD the sound of the Lord God walking in the garden in the COOL of the day, the man and his wife hid themselves from the Lord God among the trees of the garden. . . .*
>
> *And he said, "I HEARD you in the garden, and I was AFRAID because I was NAKED.*
>
> Gen. 3:7-10

This scripture shows how the spirit is no longer dominant. They *see* their nakedness or their bodies; they *hear* God walking, but they can no longer see Him because they are veiled in flesh and no longer see in the spiritual realm. They can *feel* the cool of the day and they *hid* among trees. They immediately were taken out of the spiritual realm and placed in an animal type covering or skin that veiled God from their view. They were no longer spiritual but rather physical beings, and they hid their bodies behind trees!

As I read about Adam and Eve in Genesis, my thoughts ran to the ancient and rare story of *The First Book of Adam and Eve* which I stumbled onto during my own spiritual journey. This ancient story elaborated on the lives of Adam and Eve as they came out of the garden and the hardships they faced in their new physical environment. It shed new light on the transition we will make when we return to the spiritual life.

I marveled as I read the story of Adam discovering his new physical body. He was horrified by the flesh covering him, and wept bitterly over his altered condition. He previously had been a bright nature and had been able to see the angels in heaven. I realized that he and Eve looked the same; however they were in a different state, physical rather than spiritual. I learned that they were terribly frightened by the hard ground and rocky place they entered when they came into the world. They were no longer in the beautiful garden. Their greatest loss was no longer being able to see their Father.

They feared this strange and hard land. This place that we know as home is not really our home! It is not a good place, but a hard place to live. It seems the more we realize who we are and where we belong, the better we can understand the transition that we are going to make when we are changed into our spiritual bodies. We will look the same; however, we will be bright natures who are no longer limited, inhibited and stymied by the body of flesh.

Instead of the notion of life and death, we gain an understanding of our very own existence. We do not live or die, but rather we exist. Our soul is our very existence and it never dies! We are on a journey in a strange land until that time that we may re-enter our real home.

God communicated for awhile with Adam and Eve. They did not know how to eat or take care of their bodies. They didn't know they had to drink water. Their new home was a cave, and when the first night came, they were terrified by the darkness. God loved them very much, and told Adam that He would come in 5 ½ days and bring him back to live with Him. He further explained that these 5 ½ days would be equal to 5500 years on the earth. The New Testament also gives testimony that a thousand days on earth is as one day in heaven.

Not until Jesus the Word of God came were we able to receive our spiritual life again. He died on the cross for the redemption of our spiritual life! Jesus stressed the importance of our spiritual life when he said it is better to cut off our physical hand if it offends us rather than risk losing our spiritual life. The physical body was not made to live forever!

When Adam and Eve lived in the garden they had a spiritual nature. They were created as bright spiritual beings and could see the angels and God. When sin entered in, so did the darkness. Their souls were immediately covered with flesh because they lost their bright nature to sin and death. They still looked like Adam and Eve, but they were changed. This physical body is subject to physical senses of hot, cold, noise, pain, hunger, and thirst. We are subject to sensual circumstances and cannot prevent the ultimate death of this body of flesh. If we could prevent our bodily death, we might never lay it down to enter into that spiritual life at home with God.

When Adam and Eve were in their bright spiritual natures, they were free from both the pains and the pleasures of the flesh. The physical body is subject to all the elements and does not go on forever. On the other hand, the spirit is free of pain, sin and death. The spirit lives forever.

We were created in the image of God, having a physical body, a spirit and a soul. We are three in one.

The flesh covers this three in one creation. The heavenly body is described as a glorified body. That body is bright because of the light in our spirit. The soul and spirit are contained within the body.

The soul exists forever. We determine or choose whether to live in the spirit or be dead in sin. This has nothing to do with the body. We must learn to see the body as the covering for our soul, and our soul is the image of our person that exists forever. We must not look to the flesh for our life as it is just a shell. The soul is what we must save from eternal death. This death would be the eternal existence of our souls away from God and home. Receiving the Holy Spirit by believing in Jesus Christ is the only way to life.

The First Book of Adam and Eve describes Adam passing by the tree on his way out of the garden. Its appearance had been changed and it was withered. This example of the apple tree being changed into another form that was withered seems to describe our soul being changed into another form; the bodily form rather than the spiritual form. Our physical bodies also wither! The life that we should be seeking is spiritual life.

We strive to save our physical life because we don't understand our spiritual life. Through prayer and God's Word, the Holy Spirit is enabled to impart to us this knowledge and understanding and we can actually overcome the fear of physical death.

Adam and Eve wept when they came into their natural bodies! Here we are trying to save something that was actually abhorrent to our father and mother. Not only are we striving to save the physical body, we are even trying to remain in this physical world! This is the same place that terrified Adam and Eve when they came out of the garden. They described this place as their prison and place of punishment. How ironic; we believe this is our home and we never want to leave! We just don't have a clue how much better life is with God! Adam and Eve found this world a place of gloom and darkness, unlike the bright place where they had been with God. Instead of a cave for a roof over their head, they had been used to the mercy of God overshadowing them. They wanted to die rather than go on in this world in their physical bodies. They mourned because their eyes no longer beheld the angels.

Let's understand that we are not in paradise. This world is a gloomy place in comparison. Thank God for our salvation through Jesus. We find peace and joy in our spirit when we are born again! This place doesn't seem so bad when we find joy, comfort and the peace of God that surpasses understanding. But, let's not lose sight of the source of our joy. It comes from within our spirit.

We, being born again in the spirit, have newfound hope, peace, and joy! Do not confuse these good feelings with bodily pleasures. The things that bring true happiness cannot be described in physical terms but, rather spiritual terms. It is in our soul or our mind that we enjoy the fruits of the spirit. The joy, love, peace, happiness, and life itself are from within!

I find it difficult to describe the fleshly pleasures. Therefore, I know that I want to be with God in heaven in the spirit! Fleshly enjoyments consist of eating, drinking, being clothed and sheltered. As you think about the fleshly things that bring pleasure, you will discover they are usually those things that our bodies require to survive. This body is not so great when you really think about it. It gets hot, cold, hungry, hurt, and diseased! Why do we want to save it? Our soul is what we should be concerned with saving, since it is the part of us that does go on forever. We all look alive in our bodies, though some of us are dead in sin while others are alive by the gift of the indwelling of the Holy Spirit. Just as trees in winter all look the same, you can tell which ones are alive in the springtime. So, too, will our souls be revealed in God's time.

Adam did not want to enter into the overhanging rock but obeyed God's command. Don't we also find it difficult to go to the rock of our salvation? But because of obedience to God we do that. That rock is Jesus and we must be obedient! We, too, must enter in so we will not again be transgressors.

It is written in the scriptures that *Christ redeemed me from spiritual death*. He died to save our souls from spiritual death, not to preserve our physical life. We must get beyond what we see in the natural with our physical eye. There is so much more to see and perceive in the spirit!

Spiritual life with God is to behold all things with love, peace and joy. Spiritual death or darkness is to live in dread, fear and confusion.

When we accept Jesus, we receive the promises that are written: *We are delivered from the powers of darkness and translated into the Kingdom of His dear Son . . . where no evil shall befall . . .*

Death should not be understood as no longer eating or breathing in this physical body. Our bodies have nothing to do with life and death! What a great expectation to know that when we lay these tired old worn out bodies down, we will awaken in our new, regenerated spiritual body. The glorified body that is bright, free and no longer subject to the dictates of the flesh!

In the Book of Ephesians, Paul prays: *we know the love of Christ which passes knowledge*. To know Christ's love is to experience it in the spiritual, because it goes beyond our physical ability to know. I believe the life and death in the physical body is a semblance of our life and death in the spirit.

We struggle to keep our physical life, yet, the most important and overwhelming truth is that we must strive to live in the spirit where we do go on forever. Life and death, however, are different in the spirit than in the body. We lay these bodies down, we don't just quit existing. Our souls enter into *life* with our Father in heaven. There is light, peace, joy unspeakable and full of glory and above all, love. Or, we lay down this body and enter into darkness, away from the face of God. This is a place of evil, where we would exist in an eternity of sorrow rather than joy, hostility rather than peace, evil rather than good, hatred rather than love!

Knowing the truth sets one free, indeed. Life and death would be a simple matter if we just ceased to exist. Our body has absolutely nothing to do with our life and death. It is merely a cover for it to be able to exist in this place. And, we should learn this from that. If we so desire our bodies to live, how much more should we desire our soul to live in the Holy Spirit and that life that Jesus made again available to us - - after Satan deceived and stole it from our father Adam.

The First Book of Adam and Eve describes God explaining to Adam how the great angel Satan sinned against Him, and that He cast Satan and his angels out of heaven into darkness. God further explained that when Adam fell into sin, He caught him up in this body of flesh to preserve him until he could come and redeem him. Then God told Adam that had He cast him into the darkness it would have been the same as if he had killed him. There it is! Death is as darkness!

I looked up some other words to describe death, and found the words: departure and passing. We do not die as in ceasing to exist. We depart. We pass from here to heaven; or to hell! We have the right to choose life or death, blessing or cursing. We must choose life!

The soul exists forever, so determine to keep it alive eternally in the light of our Father and in love. No longer should we fear the death of the flesh that covers our soul. We are who we are and we do not change - not in looks or in emotions. We make the decision to choose life or death. We choose to live in the Light!

This makes so much sense to me now, and I pray that you, too, will find understanding in these words. Ask the Lord for the perfect understanding that He imparts through His Holy Spirit. Jesus warns us that He will come as a thief and we must WATCH. If we do not wish to go - how can we be ready and watching? Let us watch in anticipation not dread, knowing full well that He comes to give us life, abundant and full of glory. Glory is described as magnificence, grandeur, eminence, and distinction. So, rejoice in the Lord and endeavor to enter into His glory, no longer fearing the unknown, but understanding that we are truly going home. We are no longer strangers and foreigners on a journey in a strange land.

This is where I originally ended this chapter on life and death. However, since that time, our family has suffered the death of close loved ones.

First, we lost my sister. Yes, the mother of Christy, for whom I wrote this chapter. Then, my grandson lost his father in a tragic accident. I pray this chapter would be a comfort to those who have lost precious loved ones.

It seems that nothing can stop the pain of losing someone very near and precious to you. I have written another chapter on how God dealt with me on this issue and what He said to me about His comfort. I would encourage those who have lost loved ones to please read the next chapter as it deals with the anger and hurt that we suffer.

I feel compelled to warn those who are hurting to be aware of the spirit of grief! This is not a spirit from God. It is straight from hell. True, a person must grieve for a time, but beware of the spirit of grief for it is a device of Satan to bring persons into bondage. He convinces them they will never be happy again. Forbid this demon to run continued thoughts of your loss like an old movie being played over and over in your mind. This tactic is a tool from hell that the devil uses to cause you to plunge into a dungeon of depression, where he can shackle you in iron and keep you in misery for as long as you allow it to continue.

Yes, you must fight this spirit of grief, and recognize the enemy when he provokes you. Be keenly aware that the only way out of this situation is to make a decision to turn to God, and look away from what the devil is continually showing you in your mind. Realize what the devil is doing.

You must make a decision to resist this evil. It will not go away until you determine to resist it.

I had not planned to write so much about death, but it seems that just as I discovered the power of opposites in other areas, that same principle works in this instance. The devil uses the death of one person to rob another one of life.

We must grasp the understanding that we are all going to be re-united in the spiritual realm of heaven. Of course, our focus should be on getting there, not on staying here!

Our loved ones that departed have just arrived sooner. They are the better off for it, too. Weep not for them, and stop crying over yourself. God has a plan for you, too. Reach out for what God has, and stop taking what the devil is giving you. You know that he is a liar.

Grief is a natural process that we use to deal with the passing of a loved one. Of course we miss them! Sometimes life can seem unbearable without the presence of the person we love.

This grief should make us aware of the bigger picture that it represents. It is a loss. It is the loss of sharing our love with a special person. Grasp the significance that grief represents. You see, the greatest love that exists is the love of God! He is love, and it is by sharing this emotion in the natural realm that we are made aware of the wonder and magnificent feelings that love radiates.

As we ponder the loss of a loved one, we should take into consideration the greatest love of all, and that is the love of God for His children. We have been separated from Him by this body of flesh, but there is always a shadow of the spiritual truth in this world, if we can perceive it.

As I thought about the emptiness and sadness that follows the loss of a loved one, I better understood the gravity of the judgment.

A nun once taught me that hell is being away from the presence of God's face and His love.

We are taught that we will all come into the presence of God, but not all will be able to stay, depending upon the choices we made in this world. In that instant when we see, feel and experience the presence of God, we will immediately understand true, all-encompassing powerful love. That emotion or feeling that we understood in the flesh and seem to never quite attain, will, at last, be manifested in our soul as we come home to the great love of our Father! To experience the fullness of love, and then not be able to remain in it - that to me would be the true meaning of GRIEF!

Oh, how important it is to understand true life. Our soul lives forever in our spiritual body, and we choose our own destiny. Take it seriously!

CHAPTER 6

THE PRESENCE OF GOD

February 22, 1997 at 4:30 a.m. is a time I will remember always for at that very hour I came into the presence of God. The feelings are so very difficult to explain - no adjectives seem great enough to describe the most awesome experience of hearing God talk to you. I say God, not Jesus, not the Holy Spirit - but God, Himself, talked to me directly and revealed mysteries and wonders by His very presence!

Now, I must start at the beginning to unfold the events that led up to this extraordinary moment. My husband and I were out of town at a toy show (his hobby). We had set up the toys upon our arrival in preparation for the toy show that would begin the next day. We met another couple attending the show and we had a nice visit with them before retiring to our room for some sleep. I awoke at 2 a.m. and tried for the next two hours to get back to sleep. At 4:30 a.m., I began replaying the conversation I had shared with the wife, while our husbands discussed toys. I was appalled when I realized that my entire discussion had been about people who had made me angry lately.

Chapter VI – The Presence of God

As I reviewed the three specific episodes of persons who were rude to me, I traced these episodes back to one point in time; the recent death of my sister. I had already begun to pray and ask forgiveness for my anger, as I knew this was not my nature. I love people, and I couldn't figure out why I had all this pent-up anger, until I perceived the time that it had begun. As I prayed, I thought that I had dealt well with my sister's death, and had been comforted by the Lord. I didn't know that I was angry about her death. I had accepted that the Lord had, indeed, delivered her from a long-suffering battle. I was glad that she no longer suffered, and knew beyond any doubt that God had reached down and taken her in her sleep. I had even dreamed about her, seeing her so beautiful and smiling from ear to ear. So, I wondered about the anger some more, and I found it.

I was angry because her daughter had been robbed of a wonderful mother-daughter relationship such as I have with my daughter. I was angry, too, because Marcia had suffered so many years and had literally been robbed of life!

Yes, God, I am angry for it was just NOT right! How could I possibly feel any other way?

Oh, praise God He showed me! He showed me so much in a short time; and He even spoke to me. By the time He finished I no longer had any anger. I was cleansed and I felt so happy.

When I presented to him my anger over Christy's great loss; He said, *"YOU DON'T KNOW HOW I CAN COMFORT HER"!*

After He spoke this to me, I knew beyond any doubt that He could and He would - and that He cared and could certainly do things beyond anything I could hope to do. It also relieved me of the responsibility of trying to do the things for her that her mother would do.

Even though I knew I could never take her mother's place, I felt so compelled to do something to fill the gap. And thus my anger was because I knew that I couldn't take the place of her Mom. No one could do that! My helplessness in this situation caused my anger.

But, that all subsided after He said, *"YOU DON'T KNOW, HOW I CAN COMFORT HER!"*

He continued with the most loving and profound statement: *"I AM THE FATHER WHO CREATED YOU AND THE MOTHER WHO LOVES YOU!"*

Oh, what a wash and flood of rejoicing, relief, and astonishment I felt as these words touched me in the very depths of my soul! Of course, He can comfort her like no other because He is also her mother! What a revelation!

And then, in my own mother's voice, I heard God say, *"WHY ANNE, I HAVE ALWAYS BEEN THERE FOR YOU."*

It was a witness from Him to me that He can comfort like no other, because He is also a mother to us.

All during this time in the presence of God, I could - - *oh, how to explain the feelings?* I could actually *sense* the understanding of God's plan, God's power. It was as though everything inside of me *knew* the whole plan, the whole story - and there were no more questions.

Verses from the Bible came to mind and seemed so profoundly easy to understand.

And the Word was made flesh and dwelt among us, is one verse I remember.

I also remember telling God, that I had difficulty discerning the Holy Trinity. I knew Jesus as a bridegroom and romantic lover as written in the Canticle of Canticles, and as the Son of God. I recognized the Holy Spirit as that quiet voice inside me that sounds like my own voice, and witnesses to my spirit and sheds light on the truth in so many areas of life, especially while reading the scriptures.

"But," I said, "God, I just can't comprehend you - or how to put you into the picture of my mind. I know Jesus is your Son. Your Holy Spirit is upon Him; so, then where are you? Jesus is on the cross; the anointing is on Him; I can't place you God and I am so sorry."

"I AM THE <u>POWER</u>, THE LIGHT AND THE GLORY IN HEAVEN! MY WORD BECAME FLESH AND JESUS IS MY WORD. I AM IN JESUS. MY UNDERSTANDING AND WISDOM ARE IN MY SPIRIT WHICH GOES FORTH TO THOSE WHO LOOK FOR ME. AND, AT ALL TIMES, I AM ALL IN ALL."

As far as understanding the reason for us being here, I knew that when we read in the Bible that Adam and Eve *knew* sin after eating the apple - that it was not the knowledge of sin in their mind as we understand it; but it was more like a leprous disease that contaminated them. They were no longer perfect as God had created them to be in His perfect kingdom. So, God had no choice but to put them out - quickly. He had to stop the infection so as not to let it spread into His perfect kingdom. He was *purging the evil from the midst.* This line just jumped out to me in understanding. And, we will be returned to His kingdom perfectly purged from all evil. He found the way through the mysterious blood; that blood that keeps us alive in the temporal world until we are washed with His blood and brought back into the eternal perfect kingdom. We must all remember to purge the evil from our midst, just like I had to purge the anger from my heart.

The devil is indeed a cunning deceiver. Here I had been obediently reading scripture and praying every day - never missing a day, and I was all tangled up in anger!

But, my God is so good, He freed me from this snare, washed me and put me back on track. Oh what a joy! What a renewed and new confidence I have in Him. To experience the presence of God is to know beyond any doubt how big our God is and how nothing is impossible to Him. I always want to be in His presence and His love. Then, I can confidently say, *I can do all things through Him!*

The hour approached for our wake up call at 6 A.M. I wiped some hot tears from my face - not a lot - just a few that slipped down while I was being cleansed. When my husband awoke I explained that I had not slept again this night, but that I had thought about some things and felt much better. He asked me what, and I was somewhat at a loss as to how much I could tell him without causing alarm. So, I explained that I had traced my anger back to Marcia's death, but I had dealt with it and felt much better. After my husband dressed and brought me coffee, he headed over to the show. I, of course, had the leisure to enjoy the room until check out time. As I had my coffee I began my daily prayers and scripture reading as I do every morning.

I continued to dwell on the wonderful experience that I just had, and prayed. While in this meditative state I was thinking about my beautiful niece, Christy, when the Lord said to me, *"TELL HER TO EXPECT GREAT THINGS!"*

The way He handles his words leaves no doubt as to his ability to bring it to pass, or its meaning. The way he emphasized GREAT THINGS was awesome. I gathered my coffee and phone card and proceeded to place a call to my niece.

"Oh, Christy how I wish I was there, because I have something to tell you and I don't know where to begin."

So, I just blurted out to her that God told me to tell her to *EXPECT GREAT THINGS* - and re-emphasized GREAT THINGS.

She let out a mixed sigh and laugh of relief. I told her I had been talking to God - not Jesus, not the Holy Spirit; but God. I asked if she had done that, too. She told me how she also had discovered anger in herself and had prayed, not knowing what to pray. So, she had decided that night to pray for the whole world!

She said, "I doubt that anyone prays for it."

She talked to me about how her doctor had been rude when she took her daughter to have a cast removed from her arm. She finally realized that it was not the doctor, but his reaction to her. She reminded me of how usually people smile at us, and we understood that people were drawn to us when we were full of the light and spirit of the Lord. But, since we had let anger slip in, people were, indeed, being rude to us. It was not their fault.
When you are bound up in sin or anger, you give the devil place to cause these things to happen. That is why it

is so important to keep the evil purged from your midst. Ask God in prayer to guide you so anger and other sin cannot slip up on you unawares. The devil especially uses unforgiveness to trip people.

Of course, you want to be justified when someone is mean or rude to you. But the fact is that had you not been in a state of sin or unforgiveness, there would have been no opportunity for the injustice. You must stop blaming everyone else - and look inside to see what is the matter with you!

God is quick to show you the snares, if you have the good sense to realize when things go wrong that something is more than likely wrong in you!

Strive to free yourself from sin. Become aware of your circumstances. That old devil cunningly plots to get you into situations that deprive you of God's help. He knows all the tricks, and you should get wise and stop the pattern that keeps you turned in the wrong direction.

It is the focus of your attention that determines your outcome. If the devil can direct your attention to self-pity, anger, resentment, jealousy and the list can go on and on; then you are missing the gifts God has provided for you. Joy, peace, health, beauty, prosperity and everything good that can be named is right here, you just have to receive it.

As you determine to become aware of your emotions, you should also determine to change your circumstances. That seems very difficult when you are right in the middle of a crisis, but that is why you must make a break! Change your direction! As long as you allow the spirit of darkness to hold your attention, you are missing every good thing that God has provided for you in the light.

It isn't easy to change old habits, but it is certainly worth it. Forgiveness is one of the hardest things you may have to do in life, but once it has been fully attained, your soul will thank you! You will find yourself joyful and happy, and oh how much better you will feel when you can rejoice from the inside out, instead of grieving or hating from the outside in! It is simple, if you will do it! You get over it!

> *And Mary said, "My soul magnifies the Lord, and my spirit rejoices in God my Savior; Because he has regarded the lowliness of his handmaid; for, behold, henceforth all generations shall call me blessed; Because he who is mighty has done GREAT THINGS for me, and holy is his name; And his mercy is from generation to generation on those who fear him.*
>
> St. Luke 1: 46-49

CHAPTER 7

TRAGEDY

After the tragic death of a loved one, I searched for a way to deal with the pain. Not just for myself, but for the widow, the children, the parents and the loved ones who were hurting so much and being tormented by emotions of sadness, anger, despair, loneliness and on and on. I knew all these feelings were not from God just by their very feel and description. Yet, how are we to overcome this great loss – this assault on our emotions? Here is how I began.

First, I tried to understand what we were dealing with, so I looked up the words in the dictionary. You will be amazed at what came from this quick search.

Tragedy – this is what I looked up first as it seemed to describe what event took place in our lives through the horrible, sudden death of our loved one. This led me to other words: disaster, calamity, catastrophe, and cataclysm. Here are some of the definitions:

Disaster – an unforeseen mischance bringing destruction of life or property.

Calamity – grievous misfortune.

Catastrophe – A disastrous conclusion, an event or situation that EFFECTS COMPLETE REVERSAL!

Here is the truth of the matter. Tragedy is a device the devil uses against those who are suffering the loss of a loved one, and it can ultimately cause complete reversal!

Why am I not surprised? The devil is hell-bent on keeping souls turned away from the healing light and love of God. Of course, the devil unscrupulously uses tragedy and grief to snare more victims. He directs their attention to the loss, enticing their emotions with grief, anger and resentment. These victims are left in the dark, wondering why and torturing themselves with constant remembrance of the loss.

I also found that tragedy excites our emotions of pity and terror. So, we should learn to recognize these emotions and understand their impact. We must grieve, but not so long as to let the spirit of grief overtake us. There is a time, indeed, to grieve and cry in order to cleanse the wound and allow it to heal. However, there comes a time when we must stop scratching the wound or it will never heal!

The emotion of pity causes great suffering and as I thought about what it was to suffer, I wondered what would be the opposite of suffering. I have found it is important to look at the other side of negative things in order to find the positive side. Suffer; I found, was to permit and endure. The opposite of this was to resist and oppose. No wonder I couldn't pinpoint the opposite of suffer. That old devil camouflages it with so much self-pity and emotion that we can't see past it to understand there is another side to it. We can resist self-pity and the emotional turmoil and we can oppose it. We don't have to suffer it!

We must get control of our negative emotions – those feelings ruled by the ruler of darkness. For if it is not checked, see what we just learned. The effect can be complete reversal!

We know better than that. We don't want to walk in the direction of darkness – but in the light of God!

How do we begin? We look for the opposite of the negatives. I was amazed and joyful to find the opposite of catastrophe is blessing!

That is the direction we want to take; to go toward the blessing and receive it.

I prayed immediately:

We claim a blessing for the catastrophe that has befallen all of us who are hurting and missing our departed loved one. The thief can't have our blessing. You, oh God, can turn a desert into a wetland; and can certainly turn our catastrophe into a blessing. Take your hands off our blessing, Satan, in the name of Jesus! As great the disaster – so much greater the blessing! We expect great things indeed, Father, in Jesus name. Amen.

As I wondered what happened to this handsome, strong and loving father, I thought about the gifts that the devil stole from him and the lies that he used to reverse his gifts. He was one of the strongest young men that I had known; so very handsome, intelligent, smiling and caring.

In the end the thief had turned his strength against him and made it his weakness His health was changed to sickness and his rosy cheeks turned to an ashen gray.

Chapter VII – Tragedy

Oh, if only someone had given him this book and showed him what a liar that devil is. I pray that this book will help set people free from the debilitating chains of self-destruction which are brought on by believing the horrible lies of the devil who enslaves so many to misery and death.

I do not believe that he died in vain. I know that he is now free in heaven, a great angel with Our Lord who watches from heaven above and guards his children.

I believe, too, that his children will receive the inheritance that the devil thought he stole from their father. They will get 'double for their trouble' as my favorite teacher says.

Yes, to them belong great things from God. The strength, beauty and success that the devil thought he stole from their father must be given to them in abundance. He is not dead – he lives with Jesus in freedom and joy. His beauty and strength have been restored, and now he soars as on eagles' wings to watch over and protect His children.

CHAPTER 8

EXPECT A BLESSING

I began searching for that miracle working God in 1980. I spent the next six years failing miserably, because I was down in the valley when I started to search for him. I was seized by fear in every direction. In my health, finances, security, home - - everything was under attack. You cannot receive from God unless you believe, and fear is unbelief.

I would encourage those who are having smooth sailing to get into the Word of God, so that you can stay on the smooth road. If bumps occur, you will know how to deal with them. Don't wait until it takes a miracle, because it is next to impossible to build your faith while sliding down a mountain!

My life began a turn around when I learned the act of forgiveness. My first reaction to the advice I received from a young counselor was skeptical when he handed me a note that read, *I forgive him as an act of faith in Jesus' name.* How could he expect me to forgive the monster I had married who brought me to the depths of depression and loss? Didn't he understand that I was trapped in a hopeless situation with a bona fide sociopath?

I was in a desperate, hopeless and dangerous situation and I was willing to try anything. My survival depended on it. So, very reluctantly, I began reciting that mantra every time the fear, resentment and anger came to mind. I didn't truly forgive him, but I kept repeating those words.

I continued this act until sometime unbeknownst to me those words sunk deep into my soul and took root. Eventually a change came and at long last I was free from the situation that had brought me so low.

I know beyond any doubt that I would never have come out of this situation without the act of forgiveness. Yes, it began as an act, but those words took effect and turned my life around. Finally, I was free and happiness filled my soul instead of grief.

My faith grew and my devotion to God increased. I learned to tithe, giving to God the tenth while standing on His Word as it is written:

> *Bring the whole tithe into the storehouse, that there may be food in my house, and try me in this, says the Lord of hosts: shall I not open for you the floodgates of heaven, to pour down blessing upon you without measure?*
>
> *For your sake I will forbid the locust to destroy your crops, and the vine in the field will not be barren, says the Lord of hosts.*
>
> *Then all nations will call you blessed, for you will be a delightful land, says the Lord of hosts*

Malachi 3:10-11

As the years passed I became lax in my devotion. I was busy with work and my new life. I stopped attending church and was neglecting God, although not completely. After a couple of years, I searched for a new church and found a marvelous one that was filled with music and a minister who gave the most profound Holy Ghost sermons. I was happy in this church. People should be happy in the church of their choice!

My life continued to be happy. I met the man of my dreams in 1990 and we married in 1992. He lived in a small town about 90 miles away from the city. I moved to the country and enjoyed watching my husband working on his farms where he planted wheat and took care of his cattle and horses. I enjoyed planning Thanksgiving and Christmas family dinners and get-togethers held at my daughter's home in the city.

After the summer and fall turned to winter, the realization that I was no longer working set in! I had always worked and my last few years were spent at very busy jobs in law offices and then statewide campaigns. Now, I was in the country and things went so slow! What was I going to do with myself?

I was not much of a reader because I never took the time to sit still. But that seemed the logical answer for this slow time. One mystery writer that I liked had a new release and I went to the small town library to get a copy. It was on a long waiting list so I made a new decision. I decided to make better use of my time. I decided to read the Bible!

One of my favorite evangelists always said that you would receive a blessing, if you read the New Testament and Acts in 30 days. So, that was where I started. I finished it in less than two weeks and became really excited and expectant!

I was expecting a really big blessing for this. I almost couldn't get to sleep the first night. Then, three days later my favorite boss who had moved to Washington D.C. called me! She wanted me to come to D.C. for 2 weeks and help her organize her office! Two weeks paid to D.C. I was ecstatic! And, I was convinced that I would continue in God's Word.

I would encourage you to read from your Bible every day! Since I began reading, my life has become an adventure. My husband decided to go back to work as a catastrophe insurance adjuster and we have spent the past years traveling from coast to coast and lots of places in between, from the LA earthquake to blizzards on the East Coast, to hurricanes and hailstorms. I am able to help him in his work and I get to meet so many wonderful people all over the country. It is a ministry in a way to visit with people and help them after they have suffered loss from catastrophic weather conditions. I believe that God ministers His love through me and these people are a blessing in return. Life has been so good to me since I started believing God and expecting blessings.

And the king said to her: What wilt though, Queen Esther? What is thy request? If thou shouldst even ask one half of the kingdom, it shall be given to thee.

Esther 5:3

CHAPTER 9

THE REVELATION OF ABEL

I began a wonderful adventure the day I picked up my Bible and decided to read it. This is when I began my homeward bound journey. The day I made a decision to read God's word, was the day my life took a turn. It seems the more I read, the hungrier I grew for the knowledge of God and His plan for man. A fire was kindled deep in my soul that could not be quenched. I had to know more and more about my wonderful Creator, My Lord and my God. And, just as it is written and promised in His word, God granted me the desire of my heart.

As I read and meditated upon His word, I discovered the wonderful phenomenon of revelation knowledge. How do you explain knowing something that you haven't learned, or understanding something you haven't been taught? That is the wonder of revelation knowledge. It's what the evangelists speak of when they say, you know that you know. You are reading along and all of a sudden, Pow! You get a revelation that just wasn't there the last time you read this. How could you have missed it? It literally jumps out and shouts: "Look – look!"

Chapter IX – The Revelation of Abel

As I read through the Bible, I kept getting this feeling about Jesus that I couldn't quite put my finger on. There was more to Him than just the story I was reading. And, then it all started coming together. I must share this remarkable revelation that I had about Jesus. It came over a long period of study, and as I began to unravel the mystery, I discovered that Jesus had been here before. Yes, I believe that Jesus was and is Abel, the son of Adam. I don't believe this has ever been taught anywhere, and I may be the only one in the whole world who thinks this, but this understanding (which I believe is revelation knowledge) gives me an insight into the mystery of the cleansing blood. The idea of Jesus being Abel gives me a clearer insight and understanding of God's love and plan of redemption. The whole mystery of God is made so much clearer with this new understanding of Jesus.

Let me first interject that I do not wish to state a new religious truth, nor is this personal belief to be taken as a doctrine. This is my story about my personal relationship with Jesus. Whether Jesus was or is Abel would not change His work or His power. The ultimate sacredness of Jesus is that He was God's Word made flesh. My presumption that Jesus had been in the flesh once before would not in any way alter nor diminish the power of Jesus, who is the Word of God made flesh. Neither do I purport to hold up any theories on reincarnation, however, I certainly believe in God's resurrection power. Even the Bible intimates that John the Baptist was Elias the prophet who was to come before the Christ. This is similar to my belief that Jesus is Abel.

Let me take you on my journey and relate how I came to this understanding of Jesus. It begins at the very beginning in Genesis where we read the story of Adam and Eve. This story tells how Satan disguised as a serpent deceived Eve and caused her and Adam to eat of the tree of knowledge. After they ate of the apple, they became aware of good and evil. This knowledge of evil made them afraid and ashamed. God was angry that they had believed Satan. Their disobedience to God was the downfall of mankind. They fell under the power of Satan and out of God's grace through their act of disobedience. God then spoke the following words to that serpent, Satan:

> *"I will put enmity between you and the woman, between your seed and her seed; he shall crush your head and you shall lie in wait for his heel."*

Genesis 3:15

This verse confused me as I read it over and over trying to understand it. I was drawn powerfully to this verse, so I prayed that God, by His Holy Spirit, would explain what this meant.

As I broke the sentence down, I understood this:

I will put enmity (hatred) between you (Satan) and the woman (Eve), between your (Satan's) seed (Cain) and her (Eve's) seed (Abel).

This was the understanding that I perceived from the first part of the quote. God was speaking to Satan and God was speaking about the seed of Satan and the seed of Eve. Therefore, I understood that Satan's seed was obviously Cain, the child who became a murderer; and Eve's seed was Abel, because he pleased God.

The second half of that quote was much more difficult for me to determine who "he" and "your" was referring to. Then, like a bolt of lightening it struck me, and I will never forget what a surge of wonder and excitement rushed through me as I finally understood the second half of that verse. The persons are named in place of the pronouns:

God spoke this:

CAIN shall crush ABEL's head and ABEL shall lie in wait for his CAIN's heel."

He and *his* refer to Cain; while *you* and *your* refer to Abel.

God spoke of the persons as shown above, but Satan understood them exactly the opposite. Satan understood it backwards.

Satan heard:

"I will put enmity between Satan *and Eve, between Cain and Abel;*

And he missed the meaning and got this part backwards:

Abel shall crush Satan's head and Satan shall lie in wait for Abel's heel."

God purposely and intentionally tricked Satan with His words. When God showed me how the sentence changed in midstream, it made complete sense to me. It is much easier to understand than it is to explain. This is what was shown to me.

God started the verse speaking to Satan. He was speaking directly to Satan, and so it made complete sense to Satan, the serpent, to understand that God was telling him that he was going to get his head crushed. Satan believed that he would lie in wait for the heel of Eve's seed to crush his head. It seems like a logical conclusion to draw from the words God was speaking to him.

But, here is what God showed me in that very sentence that made it so completely different from what Satan heard and understood.

If you look at the sentence, you will note the first portion is set off with a semicolon. The second portion seems to be the conclusion of God's statement, but it is actually where God CHANGES the person to whom He is speaking.

Listen carefully and pay close attention and you will understand. God started out speaking to Satan, but in the second verse He switched persons and addressed His words to another.

God concluded the sentence this way:

Satan *will crush* Abel's *head, and* Abel *will lie in wait for Cain's heel!"*

Satan missed the all important meaning of God's words and God intended for him to misunderstand. For God devised a plan at the very moment that His children were deceived to redeem them. And, God's plan far outweighed and overshadowed anything this fallen angel of evil could devise or understand.

And the Word was made flesh and dwelt among us.

St. John 1, 14

As God spoke the second half of that sentence, He immediately implemented His incredible plan! Beyond our imagination and the understanding of Satan, God created and planted His seed! That seed was His Word. And His

Chapter IX – The Revelation of Abel

Word became flesh and dwelt among us in the body of Abel the Just.

Yes, His son was named Abel – and appropriately so for He was *able* indeed to save all of mankind!

God also placed the "enmity" between the seeds of Cain and Abel.

How does God do anything? WITH HIS WORDS!!! Immediately after speaking the words that He would *put enmity* between them, He accomplished that by His spoken word. Now, in the very next breath in that fragmented conclusion of the sentence God immediately speaks His word of *enmity* to His seed, Abel. Then, when God continued with "*he* shall crush *your* head and *you* shall lie in wait for *his* heel" - Satan heard it backwards! He believed God to say that His seed (Abel) was going to crush his head. And why not, since God was speaking to him? God said *your* head and *you* shall lie in wait.

God planned for Satan to misunderstand to his own defeat! Here is what really happened between the beginning and the end of this sentence. First God spoke to the serpent. Then, God spoke to His seed. Thus, the fragmented sentence was directed and spoken to God's seed, Abel!

The fact that God spoke the words: *you* and *your*, when He first began speaking to the serpent, and, again in the second fragmented sentence, would lead one to think that He was still talking to the serpent!

However, God, as soon as He spoke the words that He would *put enmity* between Satan and Eve's seeds, by his very word being spoken, planted and created Eve's seed. And that seed planted by the Word of God was Abel.

Thus in the concluding fragment of the sentence when God makes use of the words *you* and *your*, He is now speaking to Abel, the seed of God. He is not speaking to Satan.

What an explosion of revelation! Not only did the Lord confirm that His revelation of Himself to me as Abel and Jesus was true; He showed me where the seed was planted at the beginning by God's word. That word was Abel.

The devil was deceived because he misunderstood the words that God spoke! No wonder Satan planned from the beginning to kill Abel, the seed of God. Satan's opposite misunderstanding was that Abel was going to kill him! As usual, and true to form, the devil had everything BACKWARDS! Satan thus unwittingly fulfilled God's word when he caused Cain to crush Abel's head. Then, as foretold by God, Abel returned to earth as Jesus and did lie in wait for the heel of Satan's seed!

He who eats bread with me has lifted up his heel against me.

John 13:19

That is why the victory of Jesus is so significant. Satan was deceived – just like it all began. Only this time the deception was reversed and so was the outcome. The children of God were redeemed to return to heaven and their home. The deception of God's children caused the fall from heaven, and the deception and defeat of Satan brought them back in glory!

Christ, having slain the enmity in himself

Ephesians 3:14

The scriptures describe Jesus as the one who *lies in wait for his heel*. Now, we can identify the persons depicted by the pronouns in the last part of God's sentence. The first set of pronouns referred to Cain and Abel, while the second set of pronouns still described the seed of Satan in the body Judas, and the seed of Eve in the body Jesus

Chapter IX – The Revelation of Abel

Christ. Abel and Jesus are one and the same seed and Son of God, while Cain and Judas are the seeds and sons of the devil. What an amazing story! I get just as excited after many years since my revelation, as I did when I first discovered it.

I jumped ahead from the beginning of the Old Testament to the New Testament, from Abel to Jesus. Now, let me get back to where I began this journey in the Old Testament. It is written that Adam called his wife Eve, because she was the mother of all the living. Eve and her seed of God were alive. Adam, however, by his action of treason against God was considered dead in his spirit, yet alive in the flesh. The cause of spiritual death is disobedience to God.

The *Forgotten Books of Eden* described Adam's soul being darkened after he ate the forbidden fruit. Eve was distraught over causing Adam's fall from God's grace, but she had not committed treason. It was before she had been created that God explained to Adam that he must not eat form the tree of knowledge or he must die.

> *And the Lord God commanded the man thus, "From every tree of the garden you may eat; but from the tree of the knowledge of good and evil you must not eat; for the day you eat of it, you must die."*
> *Then the Lord God said, "It is not good that the man is alone; I will make him a helper like himself."*
>
> Genesis 2, 16-18

The first few pages of Genesis reveal a mystery about the blood, for God tells us that it speaks! I selected some Psalms that I read and understood to be spoken about Jesus and Abel and their wondrous blood. My journey through the Bible aroused my curiosity about Jesus being here before, and these verses and the knowledge that I gained about Jesus are a treasure to me.

The voice of your brother's blood cries to me from the ground.
Genesis 4:10:

For the avenger of blood has remembered; he has not forgotten the cry of the afflicted.
Psalms 9:13

The Lord said to me, "You are my son; this day I have begotten you. Ask of me and I will give you the nations for an inheritance and the ends of the earth for your possession. You shall rule them with an iron rod; you shall shatter them like an earthen dish."
Psalms 2:8

What is man that you should be mindful of him, or son of man that you should care for him? . . . You have given him rule over the works of your hands. . .
Psalms 8:5

He rescued me from my mighty enemy . . . they attacked me, but the Lord came to my support. He set me free in the open and rescued me, because he loves me.
Psalms 18

Behold I come; in the written scroll it is prescribed for me, to do your will.
Psalms 40:8

Other scriptures seemed to leap from the pages as I continued my reading through the New Testament. One scripture verse that always grabbed my attention was where Jesus said, "*I will rise again*". And so many more times it was written the he *rose again from the dead*. So, when did He first rise? Was he Abel who God raised from the dead? I certainly believe He is.

God has raised him from the dead . . .
Romans 10:9

Christ died and rose <u>again</u> that he might be Lord both of the dead and of the living.
Romans 14:9

For since by a man came death, by a man also comes resurrection of the dead.
Romans 15:20

As I read this scripture of death coming by a man, I recall that Abel was the first man to die on earth. And the next scripture of the natural and spiritual body reveals to me that Abel was born of the flesh, whereas Jesus was born of the spirit – being conceived by the Holy Spirit! Thus, if Abel and Jesus are, indeed, one and the same, then each birth is significant; first, in a natural body and, again, in a spiritual body. Abel was raised from his physical body of death into the spiritual body of Jesus!! This makes sense to me! However, it could more than likely be nonsense to you. That is entirely up to you. The point I would like to make is not whether Abel was Jesus, but that God's Word is exciting! You should read it - all of it - for yourself.

What is sown a natural body rises a spiritual body.
Romans 15:44

Abel, being the natural body sown, rose as Jesus in the spiritual body who became our savior!

Death is swallowed up in victory! Jesus swallowed up death in victory!
Romans 15: 55

Christ who has made both one, and has broken the intervening wall of the enclosure, the enmity, in his flesh . . . having slain the enmity in himself.
Ephes 3:14

This is that word that God first spoke to Satan, enmity (hatred). The scripture says that Jesus has slain the enmity in Himself. The enmity was first placed between the seeds of Eve . . . *between her seed and Satan's seed*! This Jesus must have been Abel. How else could He destroy the enmity in Himself?

By faith Abel offered to God a sacrifice more excellent than did Cain, through which he obtained a testimony that he was just, God giving testimony to his gifts, and through his faith, though he is dead, he yet speaks.
Hebrews 11:4

This scripture tells us that Abel still speaks. Jesus is the Word of God in the flesh that spoke to us. Again, this seems to be one and the same, Jesus and Abel.

Jesus - the author and finisher of faith . . . resisted unto blood the struggle with sin. . .
Hebrews 12:2

Chapter IX – The Revelation of Abel

Here we see Jesus resisting unto blood the struggle with sin. Abel also resisted unto blood the struggle with sin; that of his brother's sin of murder. It makes sense that Abel is the author and Jesus the finisher of faith.

> *Christ, died once for sins, the Just for the unjust . . . Put to death indeed in the flesh, he was brought to life in the spirit.*
>
> 1 Peter 3:18

Christ is being described in this scripture as the Just like Abel the Just, who was put to death in the flesh. I believe God brought Abel back to life in the spirit, as Jesus.

> *Whoever is not just is not of God, nor is he just who does not love his brother . . . like Cain who killed his brother who was just.*
>
> 1 John 3:10

As I read about the sign in the sky in Apocalypse (Revelations), I thought about Abel again being described in this sign.

> *She brought forth a male child who is to rule all nations with a rod of iron; and her child was caught up to God and to his throne.*
>
> Apocalypse 12:5

Couldn't this verse be describing Eve giving birth to Abel, and the devil desiring to have her children? The one born to her was to rule all nations with a rod of iron; thus the savior. And her child was caught up to God and to His throne. I think that when God heard the cry of Abel as he was being murdered caught him up to his throne. I found Psalms 18 to be the most vivid scriptural description of, not only the death of Jesus, but even more so, the death of Abel. As you read this Psalm, think about Abel giving this account:

> *I love you, O Lord, my strength, O Lord, my rock, my fortress, my deliverer. My God, my rock of refuge, my shield, the horn of my salvation, my stronghold! Praised be the Lord, I exclaim, and I am safe from my enemies.*
>
> *The breakers of death surged round about me, the destroying floods overwhelmed me; the cords of the nether world enmeshed me, the snares of death overtook me. In my distress I called upon the Lord and cried out to my God; from his temple he heard my voice, and my cry to him reached his ears.*
>
> *The earth swayed and quaked; the foundations of the mountains trembled and shook when his wrath flared up. Smoke rose from his nostrils, and a devouring fire from his mouth that kindled coals into flame. And he inclined the heavens and came down, with dark clouds under his feet. He mounted a cherub and flew, borne on the wings of the wind. And he made darkness the cloak about him; dark, misty rain clouds his wrap. From the brightness of his presence coals were kindled to flame. And the Lord thundered from heaven, the Most High gave forth his voice; he sent forth his arrows to put them to flight, with frequent lightnings he routed them. Then the bed of the sea appeared, and the foundations of the world were laid bare, at the rebuke of the Lord, at the blast of the wind of his wrath. He reached out from on high and grasped me; he drew me out of the deep waters. He rescued me from my mighty enemy and from my foes, who were too powerful for me. They attacked me in the day of my calamity, but the Lord came to my support. He set me free in the open, and rescued me, because he loves me.*

The Lord rewarded me according to my justice; according to the cleanness of my hands he requited me; for I kept the ways of the Lord and was not disloyal to my God, for his ordinances were all present to me, and his statutes I put not from me, but I was wholehearted toward him; and I was on my guard against guilt. And the Lord requited me according to my justice, according to the cleanness of my hands in his sight. Toward the faithful you are faithful, toward the wholehearted you are wholehearted, toward the sincere you are sincere, but toward the crooked you are astute; for lowly people you save, but haughty eyes you bring low; you indeed, O Lord, give light to my lamp; O my God, you brighten the darkness about me; for with your aid I run against an armed band, and by the help of my God I leap over a wall. God's way is unerring, the promise of the Lord is fire-tried; he is a shield to all who take refuge in him.

For who is God except the Lord? Who is a rock, save our God? The God who girded me with strength and kept my way unerring; who made my feet swift as those of hinds and set me on the heights; who trained my hands for war and my arms to bend a bow of brass.

You have given me your saving shield; your right hand has upheld me, and you have stooped to make me great. You made room for my steps; unwavering was my stride. I pursued my enemies and overtook them, nor did I turn again till I made an end of them. I smote them and they could not rise; they fell beneath my feet.

And you girded me with strength for war; you subdued my adversaries beneath me. My enemies you put to flight before me, and those who hated me you destroyed. They cried for help - but no one saved them; to the Lord- but he answered them not. I ground them fine as the dust before the wind; like the mud in the streets I trampled them down.

> *You rescued me from the strife of the people; you made me head over nations; a people I had not known became my slaves; as soon as they heard me they obeyed. The foreigners fawned and cringed before me; they staggered forth from their fortresses.*
>
> *The Lord liveth! And blessed by my Rock! Extolled be God my savior. O God, who granted me vengeance, who made peoples subject to me, and preserved me from my enemies, truly above my adversaries you exalt me and from the violent man you have rescued me. Therefore will I proclaim you, O Lord, among the nations, and I will sing praise to your name, you who gave great victories to your king and showed kindness to your anointed, to David and his posterity forever.*
>
> Psalm 18

This Psalm speaks to me of the plight of Abel at the time of his murder, and tells how God rescued him from the enemy. I believe God raised Abel up, trained him for battle, and then sent him back to earth as Jesus. Jesus and Abel, being one and the same, would be the only seed of God that was born of flesh and spirit, being free from sin because they were the seed of God.

> *The Lamb who was slain from the foundation of the world.*
>
> Apocalypse 13:9

CHAPTER 10
MYSTERY OF INIQUITY

I believe the Holy Spirit is moving me to a new level of understanding. So, now, after stopping work on my book so long ago, I woke up around 5:30 am and knew - it was time to study again.

I opened the Bible and wondered where to begin. I had read the book through twenty times in eight years, before I got more than a revelation that I was doing something wrong!

Pastor Paul of Prescott stood at the front of the church and during his sermon, held up the Bible and said "Don't make this your idol!"

Did I get a revelation! Then, my favorite bible teacher followed up with her discussions on legality and getting bound up in laws and ritual, rather than the spirit of the thing. Yes, I had lost all revelation in my reading and it was only a monotonous ritual that I had been performing the last few years.

Chapter X – Mystery of Iniquity

I remembered how exciting it was when I first began to read. I was hit with explosions and tidal waves of revelation knowledge about Jesus and Abel. But, now! Oh, my. Now! I am right back where I stopped.

My last unanswered question is just where my Bible opened this morning! I was very excited. You see, the last place I had a real question was in the Second Book of Thessalonians. Who is the son of perdition and what is the mystery of iniquity? I know the journey into this realm of study will be more explosive than the revelation about Jesus that I found on my first journey. The scripture that captured my curiosity was full of pronouns and I couldn't understand who God was referring to as *"the man of sin"*, *"the son of perdition"* and the pronouns *"he"*, *"him"*, *"what"* and *"it"*.

This is the scripture that caught my attention and brought me into a new study about the mystery of iniquity:

> *Let no one deceive you in any way, for the day of the Lord will not come unless the apostasy comes first, and* THE MAN OF SIN *is revealed,* THE SON OF PERDITION, WHO *opposes and is exalted above all that is called God, or that is worshipped, so that* HE *sits in the temple of God and gives himself out as if* HE *were God. Do you not remember that when I was still with you, I used to tell you these things? And now you know* WHAT *restrains* HIM, *that* HE *may be revealed in* HIS *proper time. For the mystery of iniquity is already at work; provided only that* HE WHO IS *at present restraining* IT, *does still restrain, until* HE *is gotten out of the way.*
>
> 2 Thess. 2: 3:

This was a lot to sort through and only by the help of the Holy Spirit was I able to discern the answers that I searched for.

My first revelation was that of "he who is". Grammatically there are three persons: First person: I; second person: you; and third person: he. Therefore, I determined that Jesus, being the third person of the Holy Trinity is the HE WHO IS, being the third person of the great first person: "I AM WHO AM".

Next I found other scripture that used the pronouns I was seeking to identify:

And the beast was seized, and with IT the false prophet WHO did signs before IT . . . and were cast alive into the pool of fire . . . and the rest were killed with the sword of him who sits upon the horse, the sword that goes forth out of his mouth . . .

Apocalypse/Revelations 19:20

The Beast is called: *IT* and the false prophet is called: *WHO*. These are the verses that revealed to me the identity of the *IT* and WHO.

As I studied this same scripture, I realized that just as I had learned about Jesus being Abel, I now also understood that Judas was Cain. Remember Cain killed Abel, and Jesus was then deceived by Judas who lifted his heel against Jesus.

He who eats bread with me has lifted up his heel against me.

John 13:19

Where the verse refers to the *SON OF PERDITION*, we find Jesus identifying Judas as that man while praying this verse about his disciples:

> . . . *and not one of them perished except THE SON OF PERDITION*, in order that the Scripture might be fulfilled.
>
> St. John 17:12

Now we can identify *WHO* as the false prophet; also called *THE SON OF PERDITION* as Judas; and I concluded that *THE MAN OF SIN* would be Cain, the first man who could not overcome sin.

First we had the seed of the devil and the seed of God being Cain and Abel. These were the first men of the world and they were fleshly beings. Then, as I believed that Abel was taken up to heaven and returned again as Jesus, I realized that Cain came back at the same time again with Jesus, only this time he was in the person of Judas. The battle was not just of the flesh, the battle was twofold in that it also had to be won in the spirit.

I believe Jesus made the flesh person and the spirit person one because he overcame the first death in the flesh as Abel, and then overcame the second death in the spirit as Jesus. Jesus returned resurrected in his glorious body and He is rightly called the King of Glory.

The goal of our journey is to become a glorified body in Jesus. This is the ultimate union of the soul and spirit of a man with God. When we choose discipline and obedience to God's will, we bring the two into harmony with God's Holy Spirit by the grace of God. Grace is God's unmerited favor. I believe we can actually walk in that glory here on earth when we are in God's favor.

The glory is the anointing and the power of God alive in us who are pleasing to Him. I know we can have this life, for Jesus told us that He died so that we could have life and have it more abundantly.

As we become one with God through Jesus, who is in Him and in us, we walk in the anointing of the Holy Spirit. This anointed state can bring into manifestation those things that are from the spiritual realm of God. We can walk in faith as the disciples did with signs and wonders following them. The realm of the glory or spiritual world is where God creates all things and they can be manifested into this realm when we get to the faith of believing and "calling those things that are not as though they were." We can get answers to our prayers in the spiritual realm, but it takes our faith to bring the answers into the physical realm.

Christy asked God many times why her mother wasn't healed after so much prayer. Some time after her mother's death, she had a dream that her mother was in a dance leotard that was pink with red stripes. Christy and her mother had operated a dance studio together, so this outfit was not so much out of the ordinary, until she realized the true significance of the dream. Those red stripes on her mother's leotard were symbolic of the scripture, that "by His stripes she was healed!" What a revelation this was. Her mother had received her healing in the spiritual realm, but it was never manifested in the physical realm.

We must get the importance of this revelation. God's word never fails; we only fail to receive it!

MORE ABOUT THE SIGNIFICANT TWO'S

As I became more and more aware of the significance of two's in the Bible, I found another interesting analogy of the two sons of Adam and Eve. They were the first two born into the world. Cain and Abel have always represented the opposites of right and wrong, good and bad, obedient and disobedient.

Since I had been led to believe that Abel and Jesus are one and the same person of God, I later began to understand that Cain and Judas were also one in the same. These persons of God and Satan came at the same times for purposes of fulfilling and completing the mysteries of God and the mysteries of iniquity which brought me into this phase of study.

So, from the scriptures we learn that Jesus made the two one. What two did He make one? It was the soul, contained by the flesh, and the spirit. The first conflict was in the flesh when Cain murdered Abel. The second conflict was in the spirit. It is written that Satan entered Judas when he dipped the bread and he went out to betray Jesus. This was a betrayal and spiritual assault. When the final battle comes, Jesus returns as the Lord of Lords and King of Glory, to defeat the beast and false prophet.

I realized that just as God is defined in Three Persons of the Holy Trinity: the Father, Son and Holy Spirit; that it goes to follow that Satan, who is in complete opposition to God, has manifested his own three persons of darkness as Satan, the false prophet and the beast. In every area that God existed in light and right, Satan existed in opposition and darkness. Satan had a three-part existence.

THE HOLY AND UNHOLY TRINITY

God	Satan
Son	False Prophet
Holy Spirit	Beast

THE SEEDS OF GOD AND SATAN

Abel	Cain
Jesus	Judas

Then the wicked one will be revealed whom the Lord Jesus will slay with the breath of his mouth and will destroy with the brightness of his coming.
And his coming is according to the working of Satan with all power and signs and lying wonders, and with wicked deception to those who are perishing.

2 Thess. 3: 8-9

    This whole scripture sums up the battles the Lord has won for us in both the physical and spiritual realm. The final battle is when Satan is finally revealed and destroyed by God. The battles are past, present and future. The mystery revealed is God's marvelous redemption plan which was put into play at the very beginning. He captured us in the flesh to keep us for the completion of His plan so He could bring us home. He reigns forever and ever in heaven, where the counting of time ends and the complete reversal of the fall of mankind is completed.
    I can now better understanding the victories that God attained over Satan through His Son, Jesus. I also

recognize the persons in that confusing scripture from Thessalonians.

The only mystery left is: WHAT RESTRAINS HIM?

And now you know WHAT restrains HIM, that HE may be revealed in HIS proper time. For the mystery of iniquity is already at work; provided only that HE WHO IS at present restraining IT, does still restrain, until HE is gotten out of the way.

2 Thess. 2: 3

He who restrains it refers to Jesus restraining the beast. The WHAT that restrains the beast eluded me for only awhile.

And I saw heaven standing open; and behold, a white horse, and he who sat upon it is called Faithful and True, and with justice he judges and wages war. And his eyes are as a flame of fire, and on his head are many diadems; he has a name written which no man knows except himself. And he is clothed in a garment sprinkled with blood, and his name is called The Word of God. And the armies of heaven, clothed in fine linen, white and pure, were following him on white horses.

And from his mouth goes forth a sharp sword with which to smite the nations. And he will rule them with a rod of iron . . . And he has on his garment and on his thigh a name written, "King of kings and Lord of lords."

And I saw the BEAST, and the kings of the earth and their armies gathered together to wage war against him who was sitting upon the horse and against his army. And the BEAST was seized, and with it the FALSE PROPHET who did signs before it wherewith he deceived those who accepted the mark of the BEAST and who worshipped its image. These two were cast alive into the pool of fire . . .

And I saw an angel coming down from heaven, having the key of the abyss and a great chain in his hand. And he laid hold on the dragon, the ancient serpent, who is the devil and Satan, and bound him for a THOUSAND YEARS. And he cast him into the abyss, and closed and sealed it over him, that he should deceive the nations no more, until the thousand years should be finished.

Apocalypse 19:11- 20:3

It was in these scriptures that I recognized and understood what was holding the beast. It was TIME! Just as Satan will be bound for a thousand years until he is completely destroyed by God, I understood that time was the restraint that Paul referred to in his message to the Thessalonians.

I recalled from *The Forgotten Books of Eden* God telling Adam that he would return in 5 ½ days and explained that a day in heaven was equal to a thousand day on earth.

There is a significant importance about time that I will address in another chapter.

At last I finally understood the scripture about the mystery of iniquity. The scripture is re-written below with the pronouns listed with the names:

Let no one deceive you in any way, for the day of the Lord will not come unless the apostasy comes first, and THE MAN OF SIN (CAIN) is revealed, THE SON OF PERDITION (JUDAS), WHO (FALSE PROPHET) opposes and is exalted above all that is called God, or that is worshipped, so that he sits in the temple of God and gives himself out as if he were God. Do you not remember that when I was still with you, I used to tell you these things? And now you know WHAT (TIME) *restrains* HIM (the BEAST), *that* HE (the BEAST) *may be revealed in* HIS (the BEAST's) *proper time. For the mystery of iniquity is already at work; provided only that* HE WHO IS (Jesus) *at present restraining* IT (the BEAST), *does still restrain, until* HE (the BEAST) *is gotten out of the way.*

2 Thess. 3:3

CHAPTER 11

UNDERSTANDING THE TIME

Jesus spoke about the importance of understanding the times when He was on earth. For had they known the time of the Savior or Messiah's visitation, they would have believed He was the Messiah. It is through our belief that Jesus died for our sins that we receive the salvation that he purchased for each of us by His sacrifice on the cross. He also advised us of the importance of watching for his return and gave us some examples of those times. The final battle is about to play out and we who are still on earth will reign with Him, if we are ready and watching for Him. Therefore, we should understand the times.

As the Holy Spirit leads me on my wondrous journey, I have uncovered many truths about the signs of the time. As I studied the word, I was led to look more closely at the significance of the number three. There is the Holy Trinity made up of the three persons of God; the third day when Jesus rose from the dead; and Jonah being in the belly of the whale is how Jesus relates the three days from his death to his resurrection.

Chapter XI – Understanding the Time

I found a remarkable verse while reading the prophet Osee (Hosea), in the Old Testament. This is the scripture that took me on a journey of revelation about the importance of the number 3:

> *He will revive us after 2 days - on the third day he will raise us up, to live in His presence.*
>
> Osee (Hosea) 6: 2

Let's first look at the significance of Jesus and Jonah's third day experiences. What happened on each of the three days?

On the first day Jesus died on the cross and Jonah was thrown into the ocean.

On the second day Jesus went into the depths of the earth - into hell, and Jonah went into the depths of the ocean.

The third day is significant of resurrection or return. Both Jesus and Jonah returned to the earth alive. Both overcame death and the pit. And, as spoken by the prophet, 'He will revive us after 2 days - on the third day he will raise us up, to live in His presence'. The third day is significant of life.

God's plan and timing to bring us back home is extraordinarily wonderful. There are three periods of time that God put into place to complete His plan of salvation. These times represent to us the past, present and future.

To better understand the times, we look at God's calculations. From the scriptures we learn that a day on earth is equal to a thousand days in heaven. Then, I found in the *Forgotten Books of Eden* that God told Adam He would return in 5 ½ days or 5500 years. God created all things and He created the times. He gave us to know time on earth in periods of days and weeks, and He has shown us from the scriptures how to better understand the times of the past, present and future.

The prophecy that he would revive us after two days and on the third day raise us up is significant of the three days from Jesus' death to His resurrection. It is also significant of the past, present and future.

The word "day" is described in the dictionary as 'a specified time or period'. I have defined the periods by days in the following chart.

PERIODS OF TIME

PAST 1ST DAY	PRESENT 2ND DAY	FUTURE 3RD DAY
CREATION	SALVATION	RESURRECTION
SPIRITUAL LIFE IN HEAVEN	PHYSICAL LIFE IN THE EARTH	RESTORATION
SPIRITUAL DEATH	SPIRITUAL REBIRTH	SPIRITUAL LIFE IN HEAVEN

THE PAST

The story of creation tells how God worked for 6 days and rested on the 7th day. We immediately see God dividing the time of creation into the period of one week. The past is representative of the first week, and I have described this period of time as the first day. This is when God created man in his image, as a spiritual being. It was also during this period of time that we were separated from God because of sin. I also read in the *Forgotten Books of Eden* that Adam fell into the power of Satan and was put out of heaven on the 6th day and at the 6th hour. How excited I was to read in the New Testament that Jesus died on the cross at precisely the 6th hour of the 6th day! We can see that God is completely aware of the times, and that His plan is being effected perfectly to turn around the events that caused us to be separated from Him.

Man was created in the image of God in light, but sin brought darkness and separated us from God. I believe this also caused the schism or separation of our soul and spirit. Adam who was created in God's image as a spiritual bright nature was then caught up in the flesh, as part of God's plan of salvation. This fleshly covering was placed over the once bright spiritual nature to keep the spirit and soul from plunging into eternal darkness or death. God prevented death by preserving the soul and spirit in a body of flesh until His plan for redemption was completed. It is impossible for one to live in heaven without that bright spiritual nature. But God immediately put a plan into effect to restore all of us to our bright nature so we could live again with Him in heaven. He appointed a time for our return. God had a plan from the beginning of time.

THE PRESENT

Since the past was placed into the time period of one week, I believe that this period of time in which we are now living can also be described as a week. In the *Forgotten Books of Eden* God tells Adam He will return and bring him back to heaven after 5 ½ days. God further explained to Adam that each day in heaven was as a thousand days on earth and, therefore, it would be 5500 years before God would come back for Adam to redeem him.

It is during this week or present time, that God redeems his children through the blood of Jesus. We are living right now in this second period of time. If we are given to understand that Jesus came on the 5th day of the week or after 5000 or 5500 years; then it would follow that there are only 2 days left of the week after Christ's death and resurrection. These days being counted as 2000 years on earth would bring us very close to the current time. We just celebrated 2000 years AD, Anno Domini, the year of our Lord, which began its count at His incarnation. There is no completely accurate count of time, and Jesus told us that the days had been shortened. So, as the Lord warned us to watch, for we know not when He will return, we can be certain that we should understand the times!

THE FUTURE

Jesus promised us when He rose from the dead that He would come again. This is the future described in scripture. The time when the heavens and earth will pass away and we will all live forever in heaven. This is when the counting of time ends and eternity begins. The scripture tells of a thousand-year reign of the saints with Christ – I believe this is the first day of the future. However, this will be the only day that is counted in this time, in that it will start with a day – but will never end.

SIGNIFICANT DAYS

I have described the past, present and future times in terms of weeks and days. Now, I would like to discuss the significance of the days. The Bible makes note of certain days. There is the third day when Jesus was raised from the dead. There is the Sabbath day or 7th day on which God rested.

In the battle of Jericho, the Israelites marched around Jericho for 6 days, and on the 7th day they sounded the trumpets, shouted and the walls fell down. I believe this story is representative of the present time or week. After 7 days the Lord will come.

> *For the Lord himself with cry of command, with voice of archangel, and with trumpet of God will descend from heaven; and the dead in Christ will rise up first. Then we who live, who survive, shall be caught up together with them in clouds to meet the Lord in the air, and so we shall ever be with the Lord.*
>
> Thessalonians 4: 16-18

The walls that will come down at this time are the barriers between the heavens and earth as we who were watching and waiting ascend with the Lord. This is the 7th day, the Sabbath day of rest for the believers who will reign with Christ for 1000 years – or 1 day!

I found another extraordinary and important day in the Bible, that being the 8th day. The Old Testament signified in Leviticus 12:3, the 8th day as the day for circumcision.

> *On the **eighth** day Moses ordered Aaron and his sons to prepare offerings saying that **today** the Lord will reveal himself to you.*
>
> Leviticus 9

> *The glory of the Lord was revealed to all the people, fire came forth from the Lord's presence and consumed the holocaust.*
>
> Leviticus 9:24

In the 14th and 15th chapters of Leviticus we read about atonement being made on the eighth day.

The Lord spoke to Moses about the significance of the eighth day.

> *When an ox or lamb or a goat is born, it shall remain with its mother for seven days; only from the **eighth** day onward will it be acceptable.*
>
> Lev.22: 27

> *For seven days the firstling may stay with its mother, but on the **eighth** day you must give it to me.*
>
> Exodus 22:29

Continuing in Leviticus 23 we see that a sacred assembly is to be held on the *eighth* day and the **first** and the **eighth** days shall be days of complete rest.

Now, let's look at the days when the Lord was crucified. Friday is the 6th day of the week and the 1st day of the Lord's death; Saturday is the 7th day of the week and the 2nd day after his death; and Sunday is the 8th or new day that starts the week over, as well as the 3rd day on which he arose.

SIGNIFICANT DAYS AND TIMES

Friday	*Saturday*	*Sunday*
6th day	*7th day*	*8th or 1st day*
1st Day	2nd Day	3rd Day
Jesus is Crucified	Jesus in the Tomb	Jesus Rises
Past and Death	Present & Salvation	Future and Eternity

Just as the weeks signified the cycles of times past and present, I believe there are days that are very significant of the times past, present and future. Look at the chart which depicts the past being designated by the first day and the present by the 2nd day. Then, Jesus is raised up on the 3rd day.

You will note that I listed the 3rd day also as the 8th day. And, as I showed in the Old Testament scriptures that the eighth day is a significant day when the Lord says you must give them back to me, I have found the relevance of this in the New Testament.

> *And indeed his works were completed at the foundation of the world. For somewhere he spoke of the seventh day thus, "And God rested the seventh day from all his works"; and in this place again, "They shall not enter into my Rest." Since then it follows that some are to enter into it and they to whom it was first declared did not enter in because of unbelief,* He AGAIN FIXES ANOTHER DAY TO BE TODAY.
>
> Hebrews 4: 3-7

Look again at the day God called *today*. In Chapter 9 of Leviticus: *On the EIGHTH day Moses ordered Aaron and his sons to prepare offerings saying that TODAY the Lord will reveal himself to you.*

Here is the significant **eighth** day that God spoke of in the Old Testament as Paul describes it in the New Testament, saying that God fixes another day to be TODAY.

It is the **eighth** day, the day after the 7th or Sabbath rest day for those who did not believe and were unable to enter in. Now, they too can enter into the rest of God.

I believe this is the day that begins eternity as I described in the future event. This is why I believe there is only 1 day in this future period of counting.

You see, there was the 1,000-year reign of Christ with

His saints which is significant of the 7th day rest. Then God fixes another day – and this falls on the day after the rest or 7th day, therefore it is the 8th day.

This is the last day to enter in because time stops after this day. This is the beginning of eternity.

> *He will revive us after 2 days - on the third day he will raise us up, to live in His presence.*
>
> Osee (Hosea) 6: 2

How wonderful this prophecy comes together. You will notice that the 1st day, 3rd day and 8th day all land in the same place. That is because the circle is completed. The beginning and the end come together here on the ***eighth*** day of the previous week or the 1st day of the new week. They are one and the same. Just as the Lord says I am the beginning and the end. The new heaven and new earth - old things are passed away. What also passes away here is the counting of time. It is finished, and there is no longer a counting of time for we have been caught up to God.

If you study your Bible, I believe these prophesies will become more and more clear to you and the Words of the Lord will impart to your soul a deeper understanding. What a wonderful adventure the Bible is - a mystery so wonderful that only God could know the outcome.

The information provided in this chapter was gleaned early in my studies. The days and times have intrigued me ever since discovering the 5 ½ days as prophesied in the Lost Books. I have tried unsuccessfully for years to figure out when that ***eighth*** day would begin but the answer always evaded me. Remarkably, as I neared the end of the third manuscript and was planning to publish this trilogy, I was dumbfounded when out of the blue I was shown to use the 3 ½ days discussed in the Apocalypse and the numbers added up.

Chapter XI – Understanding the Time

The following scripture takes place after the Two Witnesses finish their testimony of prophecy. And the beast comes up after the 1000 years in the abyss to wage war against them and kills them.

> . . . *And after the three days and a half day, the breath of life from God entered them. And they stood up on their feet, and a great fear fell upon those who saw them. And they heard a great voice from heaven saying to them, "Come up hither." And they went up to heaven in a cloud, and their enemies saw them. And at that hour there was a great earthquake and the tenth part of the city fell; and there were killed in the earthquake seven thousand persons; and the rest were affrighted and gave glory to the God of heaven.*
>
> Apocalypse/Revelations 11:11

COUNTING THE DAYS OF ROPHESY

Event	Days BEFORE Christ 5 ½ (5500)	Days AFTER Christ 3 ½ (3500)	TOTAL DAYS
Flood	2212		
Abraham	912		
Moses	430		
David	510		
Captivity	500		
Christ	400		
	4964	*3500*	*8464*

4964 represents the date of Christ's incarnation and it is short of the prophesied 5500 years by 536 days. Hence we see a shortening of the days in this instance.

THE DAYS THAT WERE SHORTENED

BEFORE CHRIST	**AFTER CHIRST**	**DAYS SHORTENED**
5500	8464	
-4964	-8000	
536	*464*	*1000*

8464 was the total number of days shown in the first chart, so I subtracted 8,000 from that figure to find the number that would have to be shortened to keep with the counting of 8 days. Thus, I arrived at 464 for the days that would be shortened after Christ.

3500	3 ½ Days Prophesied After Christ
-464	Days to be shortened to make 8 days
3036	The New Day Begins - the **E*ighth* Day** when the counting of time ends in the earth.

The year 3036 represents the *eighth* day. Hence the rapture would occur approximately in the year 2036 when the saints will reign with Christ for 1000 years or 1 day in heaven as it is written. On the *eighth* day it is written that God casts Satan into the pool of fire, heaven and earth pass away, judgment is pronounced and there will be no more counting of time.

It is written that no one will know the day or the hour, and obviously the estimated times vary just as the methods for counting time over the centuries has varied. Jesus did, however, warn us to know the times.

> *When it is evening you say, 'The weather will be fair, for the sky is red.' And in the morning you say, 'It will be stormy toady, for the sky is red and lowering.' You know then how to read the face of the sky, but cannot read the signs of the times!*
>
> St. Matthew 16: 2-4

CHAPTER 12

DESTINY

As we discover who we are and where we are, we realize that we are "we", indeed. There are two of us in this body of flesh: The soul man who is led by the spirit of darkness of this world, and the spirit man who is led by the Holy Spirit of God and the Father of Light.

We must make a choice when we accept the sacrifice that Jesus made to redeem us from our wickedness and sin. Our natural man doesn't know any better than to believe all the lies that are presented to him in this world by the father of lies - Satan. The world teaches us that we will believe it when we see it! So, as we try to believe in Jesus, whom we obviously can't see with our natural eye, we become confused.

The devil uses the tool of confusion so cleverly to keep us from making our journey home to the Father. We know from scripture that Jesus died so that we could have life and have it more abundantly. Then, the world shows us a life of debt and poverty, or just managing to get by and we wonder how in the world we can find that abundant life, that healthy life and all those promises that we believe God made, but we just can't see! The world shows us poverty, hunger, pain and sickness. Jesus said He came and destroyed these things, so why do we still see it?

The fact of the matter is this. Jesus won the battle in the spirit! The abundant life comes from the inside out. We have eyes that see, but don't perceive. We have ears that hear, but do not understand. How do we achieve perception and understanding of spiritual things? It takes a journey to get there, and before you can make a journey, you must make a decision to go. The hard part of making a journey to a new place is being able to leave the old place behind. We are comfortable in surroundings that we know, and to venture into a new area takes a brave soul and a trusting and believing soul. To fully realize a new place, we must completely let go of the former place. This is the key to making a successful journey.

If you believe you are healed, you have received it in your spirit. Don't let the liar keep you from having the manifestation of your healing in the flesh. Yes, what is done in the spiritual realm can only be manifested in the natural or physical realm as we are able to believe it. It is by turning away from the liar and focusing on our Heavenly Father, and by looking to Jesus and believing and building ourselves up with the help of His Holy Spirit that we receive our blessings.

As you make your own individual journey, God will lead you and teach you as you go. You will meet all three persons of the Godhead that complete you. You will learn to know God as your father who created you and protects you. You will also know him as your mother who loves you. He is your maker. Then, you will learn to know Jesus as your brother or your bridegroom. Jesus is the person of God that we can relate to as a physical person, since He came to earth in the flesh. In Jesus we can see the person of God. The Holy Spirit is the voice of God that speaks to us and shows us the way we should go. His voice sounds like our own voice as the Holy Spirit witnesses to our very own spirit, and our spirit then witnesses to our soul or mind. We can be guided by this divine witness within us, if we so choose. The Holy Spirit will never force anything on us, but we must learn to follow the gentle urging and prompting that the Holy Spirit gives to each of us. The Holy Spirit unites us to God like an electrical cord. By the power provided by the Holy Spirit, we can walk in the manifested power of God in our physical bodies.

This journey is not one that happens immediately. Connecting to the power of God can only happen after the flesh has been completely submitted to Him. Each of us has a different road to travel. Only as we let go of the things we learned in the world, and turn to go in the direction that God shows us, while letting go of those things that are behind and reaching toward the things that are ahead, shall we find ourselves walking in miracles, and knowing that God is in control. We are safe in His arms.

Knowing that you are going through a battle and recognizing the enemy and his tactics will make it possible for you to win. In fact, Jesus already won the battle - that is why it is written, "The battle belongs to the Lord".

Those who overcome get new names. Abel overcame death of his body, and was given the new name of Jesus. Jesus then gave up His spirit and picked it up again - overcoming this death. He has the keys of death and hell. He overcame in both areas - saving the soul and the spirit and making them both one. He will come again to take us home.

The fact is that we have been redeemed from death and hell. We can't do it by our works, for that would be impossible and is not a part of God's saving plan. We are saved because we have believed that Jesus died for our sins. Jesus won our victory. We only have to choose life instead of death - believing the victory of Jesus.

This sounds simple; however, it is truly a struggle between good and evil. Satan, who has ruled the air and bombarded us with fears from the beginning of time, teaching everyone in the world the wrong ways, the upside down - backwards truth, is the king of liars.

Remember, we have a soul which is dictated by the fleshly feelings and emotions, and then we have a spirit which is led by the heart and the urging and gentle prompting of the Holy Spirit. Imagine if you were a Siamese twin. Who would lead? Obviously, the strongest one would lead.

Well, the soul is well trained in the way of the world and leads us in the direction of the world or the natural order of things. Our spirit must be strengthened also. The study of God's word is, therefore, essential for us to learn God's ways and to gain understanding of revelation in our spirit. God's word causes our spiritual growth as we learn the truth and discover the error. We make a wise decision when we choose to move forward in the spirit on our journey toward life. We overcome that enmity which was placed in the flesh.

The conflict is real and it is between two persons, our spirit person and our soul person. The good part of us can actually watch the bad part of us misbehave! That is why it is so important to strengthen our spirit with God's Holy Spirit who teaches and guides us. We struggle because we are strong in the ways of the world and weak in the ways of God!

The ways of God are foreign to us. In fact, they go completely in opposition to what we have learned in the world! It is good to have a choice, but oh how difficult to die to self - the pride, the me, me, me's. Yet, how wonderful it is to rise up strong and completely renewed - no longer doomed to the destructive forces of the evil nature. Complete bliss, joy, peace, and every good thing that can be named are now ours to enjoy forever! It is worth the trip.

It is so important to know that we have the kingdom of God at hand. It is within us. Life on earth can be one long struggle or we can get wise and find the kingdom of God while we are still here.

Satan tries to keep all of God's children in bondage. The bondage is established by fear, defeat, rejection, worry, anger and on and on. Even worse, Satan uses religion to steal our freedom through condemnation and guilt. These are terrible, terrible burdens to bear. Find the Lord, Jesus, who has forgiven all these things, believe Him and ask Him for help. Let go and Let God - is a truth. Break out of the prison that has held you captive. The saddest part is realizing that we put ourselves into these prisons! Satan can only deceive us; we make the choice to believe him!

Michelle told me a story that she had heard from a preacher on television or somewhere. She asked if I knew why elephants, as big and strong as they are, can be held by a simple rope around one foot? She explained that when elephants are young, a heavy chain is placed around that foot and they struggle against it in vain until they give up. Later, when the elephant is very big and strong, he doesn't even try to break the rope around that foot. He is bound and doesn't even realize he could set free so easily.

This is a good example of what Satan does to us. Find your chains, ask the Holy Spirit to show them to you. Set free from the lies of the devil and soar with the truth of God.

Satan is described in the scriptures as the thief that comes to steal, kill and destroy. He is indeed a fiend and a cowardly one. He has no qualms about attacking us in our childhood. That is why our journey sometimes is a very long one, as we uncover the seeds of destruction that were planted while we were still young and helpless and completely unaware that they were planted. I have found that the devil uses the tools of physical, mental and verbal abuse to plant seeds when we are young. He destroys marriages so children have no role model for learning the basics of trust and dependence.

How can we know God as a father and protector, unless we had a good father who provided the security we needed as children? How can we know Jesus as a husband, unless we grew up in a family where there was a husband who provided for his wife and children?

The devil stirs negative emotions that can result in divorce, or worse, if a loved one passes on, he will exaggerate the grief to stop your growth. He has a bag full of tricks, but no power to enforce them. It is our choice to believe him or reject him. These are all tools the devil uses to confuse us and keep us from the knowledge of the love of our heavenly Father.

As we each make our own spiritual journey home, the Holy Spirit shines a light into our heart and shows us the bondage that has held us captive to the ways of the world and prevented us from going higher in our spiritual growth. This bondage melts away in the light of God.

As we put the Word of God into our spirit and grow stronger, we learn how to listen to the Holy Spirit of God. Here is where we learn discipline and obedience, and in doing this we gain freedom and abundant life.

As we study God's word, He builds us up in His strength. So, when the bondage is broken, we are strong in the Lord. We do not collapse when the old yoke is broken, for now we are built up together with Him in strength of spirit. God does work all things out for our good.

No matter how rotten or unfair we think our life has been - God can turn it completely around to the good! It is indeed wonderful and joyful as we get turned right side out! When this happens, we get completely connected to God, and look out devil for the power of God is awesome, and demons will flee!

As we discover the tricks that Satan uses to sow the seeds of destruction when we are very young, we understand what a vile wicked demon Jesus defeated! When we are grown, it is with great difficulty that we find the root of our problems, since the seed has been growing unnoticed for so very long. Only through the wisdom and light of the Holy Spirit can we be set free. Jesus is the champion who overcame the world! We have an advocate with the Father who intercedes for us. Ask and you shall receive: wisdom, understanding, cleansing, knowledge and unspeakable joy as you are set free from the bondage of the lies of the wicked one.

BREAK THROUGH

I made a major break through recently. I believe it might help some who are running up against some walls to understand how cleverly the evil one hides blockades within us. We can be running the race, fighting the good fight of faith, overcoming many obstacles, yet failing miserably in some areas, all at the same time. How can this be? I wanted to know, and by prayer, fasting, meditation and determination, I found the source of a problem that had hindered me for over twenty years.

I kept coming up against a wall in my life, and I couldn't understand why! My barrier was that I could not work for a woman. I am a good, hard, conscientious, loyal, competent worker and I have always been promoted in any job that I tackled, unless the boss was a woman. Whenever I worked for a woman, I suffered verbal and mental abuse, harassment, unfair treatment, and eventually quit or, if I tried to tough it out – I got fired! What was going on? I am a top-notch employee that has always soared to the top of my field. This was an intermittent problem that lasted over twenty years! The best way to keep it at bay was to not take a job for a woman.

The past ten years since I married my husband, I have worked temporary jobs between traveling with him in his work. This has given me an opportunity to work for many people, from all walks of life. I like meeting people and I am a people person, so this has been an exciting adventure. It has also thrown many women in my path.

Recently, I took an assignment working for another woman. It was only a matter of a couple of weeks, when I became so flustered because I knew that I couldn't work for her. That old barrier showed up again, and I knew that I either had to deal with this and find an answer, or give notice that I would not be working there much longer. I came home on a Friday evening and determined that something had to happen before Monday rolled around. I was in a state of high anxiety, and I was pretty sure that my decision on Monday would be to give my notice to leave.

I really meditated and prayed asking God to show me what was wrong. As I made a list of all the women over the past twenty years that I had worked for and couldn't get along with, I wondered – am I the common denominator? At the same time, my favorite boss had also been a woman, and this contradiction gave me much to puzzle over. What was the difference between her and the others? She was smarter, harder working, more energetic and, mainly, she was never intimidated by me. She admired my qualities and was happy to have me working for her. The others seemed to dull in comparison to her. Then, again, this last woman I was working for was super-sharp. She reminded me a lot of my favorite boss, yet she had driven me into a state of anxiety and I wanted to get away from her. What was the problem?

I determined to fast and pray all weekend, because I had a decision to make on Monday. It was more than changing temporary jobs, which wasn't a big deal. It was about finding out what wall was getting in my way as I pursued God's will in my life. This was very serious stuff!

Praise be to God! I got the answer! I got a breakthrough and deliverance from a bondage that had hindered my growth in certain areas of my life for the past twenty years! It was so simple, yet so elusive. I *was* the common denominator.

God showed me exactly what trick the devil pulled on me. You see, twenty years ago I married a sociopath. This man was abusive, destructive and brought me down to the lowest point of my life. I even sought counseling for the deep depression that I plunged into during this horrible time of my life. A wonderful young man with a degree in psychology and theology told me I needed to forgive this man. That's a story in itself, but the fact is, after a long time, the forgiveness as an act of faith grew and I succeeded in forgiving him. I also was delivered out of this horrible mess, and he went away.

It was during this marriage that I came up against my first woman boss and quit a government job because of her after fourteen years of civil service. It was one of the hardest things I ever did, to walk in and turn in my badge, giving up the only career that I had ever known, with all the benefits and retirement. The count of women began here. And, now twenty years later, I have pinpointed the beginning of this cycle of conflict with women bosses. I even discovered from listing them, that my favorite boss was the only one that was married on the list. As I thought about all of the conflicts being with single women, it finally came to me. They represented me, the foolish single girl who chose to marry a sociopath, as well as the single girl who came out of that marriage at the lowest point of her life. I had come through hell, but I had survived. I was going to church, tithing and believing in God to provide for me as I began my career all over again. It was wonderful to be free, and I was taken on a wondrous journey and adventure with wonderful bosses and great jobs. But, down the road, the cycle of conflict with women supervisors returned after a nice long stretch with my favorite woman boss.

Well, I was about to tell you what God revealed to me about myself. I had forgiven my ex-husband, I had even forgiven all the women on my list as I went along with my life, being always obedient to God and forgiving those who hurt me. Finally, the revelation came! I hadn't forgiven me! How did I miss that? I had spent years working on forgiving anyone who ever hurt me.

How could I not realize that I needed to forgive me? I had forgiven the man who had brought me into great shame and disgrace. But I hadn't forgiven *me* for marrying him, against my Mom's right advice. I hadn't forgiven *me* for being put in such a place of shame, disgrace and humiliation. I came out of that marriage with all that shame and unworthiness, and I had carried this baggage for twenty years!

God showed me how I thought I was okay, but I actually had been rejecting those bad feelings and, instead, projecting them (completely unknowingly) upon those women I worked for. Therefore, without even knowing it, I had no respect for them. They represented *me* when I was in that place of shame. I couldn't bear it, so I had buried it. I discovered I was projecting it on the women supervisors, and even though I thought I was working just as hard for them as I did for a man, I realized that my inner feelings or vibes were actually showing them disrespect – though not openly or physically. This is something that was happening so deep, that I doubt they even knew why they reacted to me the way they did. It is something that takes place in the spirit realm and is not perceived by the physical senses. What a revelation this was!

My breakthrough was immediate. I read my prayer book on receiving my own forgiveness. I forgave myself after all those years. The yoke of bondage was broken. I went back to work on Monday, and I actually found that I loved working for this woman! God is wonderful! God is Great, indeed.

If you have blockades in certain areas of your life, determine to break them with the help of God! The devil uses the same old tricks over and over, and you might find you are not receiving God's best, because you don't believe you are worthy of Him and His blessings, somewhere deep down, not in your consciousness.

One of the most important revelations in this book is turning to Jesus. Yes, literally turning the other way.

Another turn that I read about in the Bible just after this experience was when Jesus said "turn and become like a little child". That is how we should come to Jesus, as an innocent child, before the devil fills us up with junk. We must become that beautiful, innocent child that God created, when He smiled and said, "It is Good!"

I lost my father when I was four years old, and just recently I went to the home of my grandparents as it was being emptied of ninety years of memories to be sold. I brought back pictures of my dad, and a favorite is one of me at about age three with my dad. I am a pretty little girl with lots of curls smiling with my tiny hand on my dad's shoulder; he is smiling back at me. I framed this picture and put it in my dressing room. I see it every day, and every day it reminds me of how God sees me as his child, smiling at me, loving me, and I am worthy of his love – as that innocent child.

Turn, and become as a child – and enter into the kingdom of God, the place where your dreams are fulfilled and you find your destiny.

CONCLUSION

    This concludes my writing for this book. I am very excited about the great things God has shown me in my journey. I also know my journey is ongoing, and I am expecting great things from God.
    Begin your own journey in the Bible and enter into your own conversations with God. He has places for you to go, people to see, things to do - and a destiny that you never dared to dream before.
    As I began my journey, I always pleaded with God to do something that I could see, say something that I could hear, show me something that I could grasp with my physical senses. As I progressed in my journey, I repented of my selfishness of wanting to reduce my great and all-powerful God to a physical state of comprehension. I rejoice now that God is so big, so great that I can know He is always with me, while at the same time His eyes see everything that is going on in the world around me.
    I thank Him now that He is so vast and great and I ask His forgiveness of my selfishness and ignorance in trying to reduce God to something I could understand in my small mind. I am so glad that the Lord never changes. We would not want a God that could be manipulated by our desires, and I rejoice that He has perfect wisdom and

judgment. I rejoice that my God will not be brought down, but instead raises me up to Him. I rejoice that He never changes, so that my trust in Him is forever firm. I can always count on Him to be there and to know what is in my best interest.

I have certainly learned that I don't always choose the right way or understand a circumstance correctly. That is why I thank God that He has given me His Holy Spirit to guide me in the right direction, and His Son, Jesus, who washes me in His cleansing blood when I slip, and raises me up with Him in heavenly places. Home is where the heart is, and our home is with our heavenly Father in the heavenly places – higher than we can see or imagine.

As I concluded this book, my pastor gave a sermon on the question that Pontius Pilate asked Jesus. What is truth? I have presented some new ideas in this book about Jesus, and I was wonderfully reassured that this book was pleasing to Him when I asked Jesus that same question that day: 'What is truth?" He answered immediately, "Knowing Me."

The perfect ending for this book is a Word from the Lord. This Word was given to Michelle and I reprint it here with her permission.

IT BREAKS MY HEART TO SEE MY CHILDREN HURTING AND SUFFERING. IF THEY WOULD ONLY RECEIVE WHAT I HAVE TO GIVE. I ALLOWED MY SON TO LIVE AND DIE AMONG YOU, YET YOU WILL NOT ACCEPT THE GIFTS I HAVE OFFERED FOR YOUR LIFE AND YOUR HAPPINESS. I AM CAPABLE OF REMOVING ALL YOUR HURTS, TEARS, SADNESS AND SORROWS. IF ONLY YOU WOULD RECEIVE MY SON, AND RECEIVE MY HEALING I HAVE TO GIVE TO YOU. MY LOVE FOR MY CHILDREN IS GREATER THAN YOU CAN COMPREHEND. WHEN MY EYES SCAN OVER THE EARTH THEY ARE FILLED WITH TEARS BECAUSE YOU REFUSE MY SON. I HAVE SO MUCH I WANT TO GIVE YOU, TO FILL YOUR HEARTS AND LIVES WITH GREATNESS AND SUCCESS. WHEN I COME BACK TO GATHER MY CHILDREN, ALL OF MY SADNESS AND ALL OF YOUR HURTS WILL BE NO LONGER. THE WORLD WILL BE RESTORED TO HOW I FIRST CREATED IT. I CREATED THE WORLD WITH PERFECTION AND I WILL RESTORE IT BACK TO MY FIRST CREATION. AND THEN EVERY KNEE WILL BOW AND EVERY TONGUE CONFESS, AND ALL OF THE WORLD WILL BE TOSSED AWAY – AND WE WILL REJOICE TOGETHER IN MY PERFECT WORLD.

BOOK II

DEDICATION

I would like to dedicate this book to some of my Irish friends and relatives who brighten my life with their love, wit, charm, laughter, wisdom and understanding. To Brigid who inspires me to excellence, Modean who encourages me, Phylis who loves me the way I am, Gay who taught me how to dream, Christy who dances for me, Mom, the FBI (full blood Irish), who shared some of her genius with me, and to my strawberry blonde daughter, Michelle, who gives me strength, and her son, my grandson, Casey, the baseball star, who makes me so proud.

I remember when I was a very little girl how Lillian would rock me and sing the song "Casey Would Waltz with a Strawberry Blonde". It is not so surprising that my daughter is a strawberry blonde, since her mother is, but who would have guessed that she would have a son and name him Casey? It is amazing how a dream can get planted, take root and grow. Someday I'm sure the song Lilly sang to me so long ago will come true when my grandson learns to dance, and I watch Casey waltz with my strawberry blonde as the band plays on.

Anne Urne

THE

WALLS

CAME

TUMBLING

DOWN

THE WALLS CAME TUMBLING DOWN

CONTENTS

Chapter One	141
The Walls of the Enclosure	
Chapter 2	149
Constructing The Walls	
Chapter 3	161
The Temptation	
Chapter 4	167
Discipline	
Chapter 5	173
The Spirits of God and The Spirits of Error	
Chapter 6	187
Why A Tent?	
Chapter 7	193
The Wall Between The Holy and The Profane	
Chapter 8	203
The Two Witnesses	
Chapter 9	215
Significance of The Third Day	
Chapter 10	221
The Story of Eve	
Chapter 11	235
How To Dream	
Conclusion	241

FOREWORD

The Bible is the most widely read and published book in the world. Christians truly believe it is the inspired Word of God. They also believe that God's Word was manifested in the flesh in the person of Jesus, His Son, who was sent to redeem mankind from their fallen state of grace, and bring them back home to His kingdom. As we see Jesus as the Word of God, I am reminded of the following scripture.

> *Behold, this is the third time that I am coming to you:*
> *"On the word of two or three witnesses every word shall be confirmed."*
>
> 2 Corinthians 13: 1

This scripture is an important reference to keep in mind as you read this book. I will be referring back to it as I talk about some interesting witnesses I have discovered in God's Word, as well as the importance of the "third time". There are mysteries in God's Word, and finding answers are an extraordinary experience.

The Bible never grows old or boring, because God's Word lives and inspires every reader. The best part of this wonderful book is that God's word is directed personally to the reader who seeks His truth. The excitement of reading the Bible is having your spiritual eyes and ears awakened to perceive and understand God's wisdom. A wonderful relationship with God is waiting inside the pages of His Holy Bible.

My studies have included apocryphal works which are scriptures that were eliminated by various councils and persons who compiled and selected the works to be included in the standard Bible.

The term apocryphal was applied to the works that were not included in the Holy Bible. These books were considered, but for various reasons they were not selected. Some of the authors were unable to be authenticated and some works were excluded because of personal and doctrinal reasons. Whatever the determining factor in leaving these books out of the Holy Bible, the fact still remains that many of these books were obviously well known to the prophets of old, as well as the apostles of the New Testament, and they are useful as historical evidence.

I make many references in this book to information that I discovered in the apocryphal scriptures, however, I have been careful to identify that information as such; and where I have found a cross-reference in the Bible, I have documented1 that, as well. It is interesting to see how the prophets and apostles knew the information contained in these books.

My intent is certainly not to introduce my theories as new doctrine; but rather to share my own personal enlightened revelations as I journey through God's wonderful Word. I hope my personal adventure will inspire you to take your own personal journey to search for the treasures God has to share.

Personal revelation is what makes reading the Bible so exciting and adventuresome. There are so many mysteries that God will bring to light if you earnestly pursue His truth. Expect to find great things along the way as you make your own personal journey.

After finishing this book I gave a copy to my mother. She pointed out the walls indeed had come tumbling down this year in the 911 terror attack. This book was started early in 2001 and on September 11, 2001 the walls of the Twin Towers in New York City came down to our horror. The title of this book came to me in February, just months before *The Walls Came Tumbling Down*!

CHAPTER 1

THE WALLS OF THE ENCLOSURE

One day I disappointed a friend, though not on purpose, and as a result I felt just awful and helpless to please. I asked God what was wrong. I trust in Him because He never disappoints me. He always turns my wrongs into rights and my misfortunes into good fortune when I let go and give them to Him.

"Why isn't it working now?" I asked Him.

From deep inside I heard a voice say, "How would you like to feel like this ALL of the time?"

Then, I understood. God was revealing to me, through my own disappointment, the pain that another person was suffering on a continual basis. My feeling of disappointment was just a temporary condition, but He showed me that my friend was trapped in this circumstance.

It was only a few days later when the gentle urging of the Holy Spirit was letting me know that I should start writing another book. I complained to God that I didn't have a title. I told Him that the last time I had written a book He had given me a title before I began writing. I complained, hoping to put off a task I just didn't feel capable of doing.

"The Walls Came Tumbling Down," my inner voice echoed into my consciousness.

"Oh, I guess I could use that for now, until you give me the real title!"

How, can I be so dense, sometimes! Thanks be to God and His mercy. He knows my heart and forgives my stupidity. I began writing that morning.
While I was writing, my daughter popped in for a few minutes. She had taken my grandson to baseball practice. During her short, impromptu visit I showed her that I was writing again. When I told her the title, she told me there was an old song by that name and she liked it.
I decided this was a witness to the book title and that made me feel good. I continued writing after she left. When the mail came later, I was surprised and thrilled to find a thank you card from my pastor for giving him a copy of my last book. In his note he blessed me and my writing in the future!
What a witness! Wow – a blessing on my new book from my pastor, on the very day it began. No, doubt God had this all under control. I just needed to sit back, be obedient and write! I love this!
I went to bed that night thanking God for the encouragement and witnesses to the title of my book. Before I went to sleep, He reminded me that my last book was *Way Beyond the River*, and showed me the significance of the title, *The Walls Came Tumbling Down*.

It was in perfect biblical sequence. I was reminded that right after the Israelites crossed the river they immediately marched around Jericho until the walls came tumbling down!

"OK, God – I get it!" I prayed. "This is, indeed, the title to the new book that you are giving me to write. Thank you for your patience, your encouragement, your mercy, and your love. I may not think I am worthy of your attention, but you continue to show me your great love. And, I know this book will touch the hearts of prisoners who feel unworthy of your love, and set them free to bask in your light, while enjoying the pleasure and the freedom of your wonderful love. Love is the key that unlocks the prison door, brings down the walls, and sets the captives free!"

I have to admit that my work on this book has been a slow go, and it seemed that I would write a little and make notes of some of my thoughts, and then put off writing for some lengths of time. During these times when I felt I didn't know what to write, I would get encouragement from the Holy Spirit.

A significant day that I will remember was that of February 11, 2001. This was the day of my husband's toy show in Carthage, Missouri. It was my favorite show, because I knew I would be staying at my very favorite motel. Having traveled all over the country with my husband in his work as a catastrophe adjuster and staying in motels for months on end, I learned to appreciate a really nice room.

The best of the best is at this motel. Upon entering the beautiful lobby filled with flower arrangements and art with quiet sounds of symphonic praise music wafting through the air, you feel you have stepped into a new and peaceful world.

Chapter I – The Walls of the Enclosure

The centerpiece of the lobby is a huge circular staircase that circles right up to an enormous crystal chandelier. This was just the beginning, because I knew my room would welcome and pamper me. I loved the soft water that made my skin so silky soft and sparkled my wedding ring so it looked like new. Then, there was the wonderful bedding and plush pillows. I would ask for an extra pillow so I could float on a bed of luxury and comfort. There was candy on the night stand, wonderful sweet aromas, and lovely pictures on the walls. I loved to come here because I was treated like a queen! This was living in the lap of luxury! Each time I left this motel, I wanted to take the whole room home with me! This was my haven, my get away, and my place to dream.

What a wonderful place for God to grant me another desire of my heart. This desire that had been hidden for so long, I didn't realize I had such a desire. Now, here is what happened to me in the adventure of finding my spirituality. Oh, yes it is an adventure, entering into a place where we have never tread before. It seems familiar, yet it is so foreign at the same time.

When I felt drawn to write another book, I simply and blatantly told God that I just couldn't write a book without Him giving me a title for it. That is how it happened the first time, and that would be how I knew that He was directing the writing, and not my imaginings. So, he indulged me.

My daughter, Michelle, told me she had a dream the night before I went to Carthage, and the name Carthage kept repeating in her dream. Then, she saw us trying to gently open a large egg, like a duck egg, and being extremely careful not to damage the yolk. She even described the lobby, so we wondered with anticipation what was going to happen there. We knew God was going

145 The Walls Came Tumbling Down

to show us something, and I promised to talk to her as soon as I returned home.

I was alone in the room and I turned on the television while I ran my bath and happened to see the implosion of the Three Rivers Stadium in Pittsburgh. I didn't think much about it, but they ran the implosion two or more times from different angles. Later that day, I mentioned it to my husband, and he told me that I just loved to see things get torn up! He was kidding, of course. He thinks I rattle the dishes too loudly in the morning when he is trying to read his paper. He always asks me what I'm breaking or tearing up.

We returned home that night and I was somewhat disappointed that nothing had happened that I knew of while in Carthage. I had expected something to happen, and now I was home, tired and disappointed. I had spent several hours alone in the room, trying to relax, meditate and pray. I had truly expected to hear from God – but nothing. Yes, I was disappointed, and now I was feeling unloved.

My husband was in the living room, and my thoughts ran to rejection from God to rejection by my husband. On the way home I had heard a sad country tune about loneliness and how the sun never shined in apartment number nine. I was beginning to feel that loneliness, and then anger. What in the world was happening to me? I tried to repent of the anger, because now I was so upset, I wanted to hit my husband! And, he hadn't done a thing! Was this a hormonal rush?? Help me God! I'm out of control here. I tried to get comfortable in my bed, but it wasn't as plush as the motel bed had been. My down pillow feathers were prickling my skin – "I NEED NEW PILLOWS!" These were awful!

My feet hit the floor and I headed into the living room like a bear to gripe at my husband for not turning off the TV and coming to bed. It must be his fault that I couldn't sleep! I fixed some toast and milk, while he went on to bed. I began to cry and feel so unloved.

What in the world had come over me? I'm not like this – really, I'm not! I'm a happy person who loves life and I adore my husband, but tonight I was feeling awful. I put three pillowcases over the sticky pillow, vowing to get new ones by the weekend, and tried to go to sleep. I must have finally dosed off, because I awoke abruptly at 2:00 a.m., seeing a replay in my mind of the implosion of the Three Rivers Stadium.

It was the walls tumbling down, crumbling down to destruction in a cloud of dust! Oh, my gosh! That's what's wrong with me – it's the walls coming down! Something did happen in Carthage, just as my daughter dreamed. My walls had come down – and my soul was seeing what it had missed for so long. Michelle's dream where we were carefully opening an egg to protect the yolk was significant of the walls coming down that had imprisoned my soul.

There was a realization beyond what my mind could conceive. It was a knowing deep down that I was indeed the daughter of a king, and deserving of the luxury that I felt while in my favorite room. I didn't have to live in this world of drudgery – I was a queen, a princess, and a daughter of the most high God. This was the rage that had welled up inside. It was the realization that I had been locked away in a prison and the devil had convinced me to build the walls of it! But, these walls are down now – and oh what expectation of great things I now have.

The anger has turned to joy and rejoicing! I'm coming home, Father! There is no place like home! I love my home and my Father. Home with Him is the place of peace, comfort, love, joy and abundance. No more deprivation, I am worthy. The devil lied and told me I wasn't – and I believed that lie! Not any more! You are finished; under the feet of Jesus: "Do not touch my anointed!" says the Lord!

There comes a knowing and a righteous anger, indeed, when we realize we have been duped into living in the curse instead of the blessings. Stooped over, enslaved to unfulfilling hard work, living in debt and poverty or just getting by and doing without, without, without!

Our Father is the King of all things! How could we believe we have to do without! We are worthy of our Father's love, created in His image and destined to live a life of freedom, success and abundance, fulfilled with joy and love and peace.

From the moment we come into the world, Satan, the ruler of darkness and that cunning old deceiver teaches us the ways of the world. That thief delights in stealing our identity as children of God. We are indoctrinated into the ways of this world by the devil who employs every spiritual deception to bring upon us feelings of rejection, abuse, shame or any other lie he can use to cause us to believe that we are unworthy of God's blessings. It is time to confront the lies of that devil and discover the walls he has caused us to build to defend against his attacks.

The walls in our lives are not hard to tear down; they are just hard to discover. Most of the walls go unnoticed since we have grown up with them, and learned how to put them up with hardly a thought to their construction. Most of us have no clue that we even have walls. When we finally learn about the promises and the blessing that God has for us, and we can't understand why we aren't receiving them, then it is time to look inside and find the blockade. If we just ask God to shine His light by His Holy Spirit into our inner life, we will find those hidden walls. Prayer and a desire to be set free are all that is necessary to discover and tear them down. The walls actually vanish once we become aware of them. It may have taken years and years to build the walls in your life,

Chapter I – The Walls of the Enclosure 148

but once enlightened you can find them. Discovering the walls is essential to obtaining our freedom and release.

CHAPTER 2
CONSTRUCTING THE WALLS

Have you ever dropped an egg and caught it by pushing your body against the dishwasher, smashing it and watching it ooze all over your clothes and drip into your shoe? What an awful mess! It is so ridiculous that it can only be funny! Stuff does happen and we must learn how to deal with it.

It seems that the egg keeps coming to mind as I write this book. So, let's see what it's about. The egg is made up of a shell that contains a yolk surrounded by egg white. This compares to our makeup in that we have a body that resembles the shell, a soul at our center like the yolk, and our spirit is symbolic of the egg white. Taking that thought a little further, we can see that if the egg is fertilized, it will grow into a live chick that pecks the shell away to enter the world. Similar to fertilization is the individual who plants the Word of God into his spirit.

The Word changes our inner makeup and causes us to grow into a mature spiritual man in possession of his soul. This leads us into a spiritual birth into God's kingdom.

The born again spiritual man must tear down the walls, much like the chick tears away the shell, to enter into life. It is a bit of a struggle, but certainly worth it.

Now, I return to my original dilemma of the mess of the broken egg. How do you react when presented with life's surprises? Most of us react in kind, right? Someone hurts our feelings, so we try to retaliate and hurt back. People are mean to us, so we resent them. The flesh reacts to stimulus, usually in kind. Anger reacts with anger.

React means to act in turn or return, to exert a return, reciprocal or counteracting influence; or to show a reaction or REVERSE trend. It means to turn BACK to a prior condition. This definition amazes me as I read it, because in my last book there was great attention given to being turned the right way. We must turn the right direction in order to get into the kingdom of God. This reaction is another obvious trick of the devil to get us turned in the wrong direction.

Respond means to answer. An answer is a correct reply or the solution to a problem. Answer is defined as: to give that which is necessary in return. This action would get us headed in the right direction. When responding we can move in a positive direction and expect good results. When we react, however, we can start a chain reaction of negative events. This is definitely an area in which we should strive to discipline ourselves to think before we speak or act. Counting to ten could prevent a lot of problems.

Understanding that we are spirit and flesh, we should realize that it is the flesh that reacts, and the spirit that responds. The spirit analyzes the situation and does not fuel the fire or fan the flame with a quick knee-jerk reaction. The spirit uses insight, perception and understanding to respond.

The difference between reacting and responding is the choice of using physical eyes and ears, or choosing to use the senses of sight and hearing which are spirits of God imparted to us. These senses allow us to perceive and understand a situation, so we can respond appropriately.

When a person is screaming angrily at us, the natural reaction is to reciprocate with anger. The spirit, on the other hand, hears beyond the shout and understands the pain of the person crying out, and gives that which is necessary in return. Compassion and love can heal the pain that is causing the anger in the person who screamed.

The way we relate to others is not only important for the health and uplifting of others, but it is essential for our spiritual growth in living that overcoming powerful spiritual life where we enjoy God's abundance now.

When I am trying to figure out a solution to a problem, I find the best way for me to get a clear picture of the situation is to make a chart and study the various contributing factors. It is similar to working out an algebra problem. You can only find the answer when the opposites are moved to the other side of the equation, taking the negative to the positive to work out the answer. Our life is so similar to an algebra equation. We have the dark side ruled by the world which I would put on the negative side of the equation, and then we have the light side ruled by God on the positive side of the equation. Successful living is as simple as moving all that is on the negative side to the positive side. It is going from physical to spiritual and being sure that our spirit is guided by the Holy Spirit of God.

There is, of course, a spiritual side that is in darkness and the ruler of darkness in Satan. That is another reason for the necessity of our spirit to be reborn into the light.

Everything that was born into the world after Adam's disobedience was born into darkness. Now, that Jesus has won our victory, we have His power through believing in Him to be born into that light.

I prepared a Cause and Effect Chart to depict some of the factors that go into building the walls in our life. I believe it is helpful to discover how the walls are constructed by observing some of the factors or conditions which result in the construction of walls.

A study of the causes and effects may assist us in determining a pattern of conditioned response that has developed in our life from childhood. If, indeed, we discover such a pattern, we can more easily pinpoint how to change our reactions to responses. Then, instead of building a wall of so-called protection which in reality is an isolation device, we can begin tearing down the inner prisons that have kept us from receiving all the great things that God has provided for us.

I have found that God's promises are certainly true, and if we have difficulty receiving them it is NEVER His fault! If we aren't living in God's promises – we are the only ones who are stopping them. The devil does not have authority over God's children! Jesus overcame the world and set the captives free! Those who don't know this fact have been duped into believing that the way of the world is the only way. The devil rules the darkness, and until we come into the light and step out of our self-made prisons, you can bet your bottom dollar the devil will let you stay in that cubicle of darkness and defeat.

Review the Causes in the center of the chart and identify the direction you choose. Is it positive or negative?

CAUSE AND EFFECT

NEGATIVE FFECT   ← CAUSE →   POSITIVE EFFECT
—   +

Walls	Reaction	CAUSE	Response	Freedom
Separation	Fear		Forgiveness	Inclusion
Suspicion	Anger	Physical Abuse	Compassion	Trust
Shame	Hate	Verbal Abuse	Love	Confidence
Unworthiness	Hopelessness	Sexual Abuse	Hope	Worthiness
Sickness	Gluttony		Moderation	Health
Destruction	Addiction	Lust	Temperance	Fitness
Isolation	Sorrow	Grief	Joy	Comfort
Intolerance	Worry	Loss	Generosity	Prosperity
Poverty	Strife	Theft	Compassion	Restoration
Indifference	Dishonor	Infidelity	Courage	Honor
Guilt	Condemnation	Rejection	Mercy	Success
Defeat	Resentment	Disapproval	Kindness	Glory
Hopelessness	Doubt	Oppression	Faith	Confidence
	Indulgence		Humility	
Death	Self-Pity	Pride	Patience	Life

This chart should be useful in visualizing the construction that is going on in your individual life. My spiritual journey has taken me into a deeper understanding and discernment of the walls people have erected that cannot be penetrated. Through deceptive tactics that encourages us to react negatively, the devil succeeds in isolating us from God as we foolishly construct the very walls of our own isolation!

Just as the chart depicts, we are the center of our own being. Our direction is determined by the choice we make.

Reaction takes us into the negative realm where Satan rules. Walls of protection and isolation are built to prevent the hurts that we reacted to initially.

Response, on the other hand, takes us into the positive realm where God reigns. There are no walls in this place for our protection is love.

I have written previously about making wrong turns and discovering whether we are receiving our gifts from God or letting the devil steal them through negative patterns. As we learn to discern the source of our thoughts and feelings, we can choose to accept or deny them. We should make the wise choice to accept the positive thoughts that result in our receiving God's gifts, and discipline ourselves to reject the negative thoughts that steal God's gifts. For when we react by choosing the negative, we enclose ourselves with walls of obstruction that prevent us from receiving our gifts from God. We make the ultimate choice to receive or to reject God's gifts.

The list of Opposites was presented in my previous book, and it is a useful tool to demonstrate the lies that the devil uses to steal our God-given gifts or talents.

Michelle and I discovered the amazing tool of using antonyms to uncover what the devil was stealing from us. We did a study in opposites, and traced it back to its beginning when Satan opposed God.

This very opposition is what cost Satan his high position in heaven. Being an expert in the field of opposition, Satan uses this force against God's children to tempt them into living forever in the fallen state with him.

OPPOSITES

THE LIES	*GOD'S GIFTS*
ANGER	PEACE
REJECTION	ACCEPTANCE
HUMILIATION	DIGNITY
SHAME	HONOR
DISAPPROVAL	FAVOR
ENMITY	LOVE
CRUELTY	KINDNESS
CONDEMNATION	FORGIVENESS
POVERTY	PROSPERITY
GUILT	INNOCENCE
SORROW	JOY
ANXIETY	CALM
FEAR	COURAGE
DOUBT	CONFIDENCE
LOSS	RESTORATION
GRIEF	COMFORT

This list of opposites will help you identify some of the negatives that are disguising your gifts from God.

TURN AROUND AND RECEIVE GOD'S GIFTS

The devil uses the things of the world to turn us the wrong way because we are familiar with worldly things. The state that we exist in seems familiar, but we are not of this world. We must choose by exerting a definite force to reject the negative thoughts and feelings that come from the dark side and choose the positive gifts that God has provided for us.

Make a decision to stay aware of the choices you have available to you when you are attacked with negative feelings and emotions.

Jesus overcame this world and paid the price for us to enjoy God's gifts. How can we deny what Jesus did for us? We are deceived into believing that we are unworthy, yet Jesus died so we would be worthy and acceptable children of God.

As we awaken in our spirit to know God's love for us, we begin to understand how much He loves and cherishes us. God does not see the sin, because Jesus washed it away with His blood. Satan deceives us into rejecting Jesus and all that He won for us.

Our reaction to circumstances is the beginning of the construction of walls in our lives on a subconscious level. Hopefully, you will become more conscious and aware of some of the subtle ways in which we fabricate our walls of isolation to form our individual prison.

I like that word 'fabricate'. Its very definition has a dual meaning. It both describes the construction of the walls, as well as their materials, which are lies!

I have become keenly aware of walls that people have built as barricades of protection, when in reality they are barricades to God's blessings.

The devil excels in cunning and deception. How in the world do we cut through all the confusion? Simple! Ask God, by His Holy Spirit to shine His light on the truth, because nothing concocted in darkness can remain in the light of God. It just cannot stand, because it is a lie, a fabrication and distortion of the truth. The truth does set captives free.

Surely, you have met a person who maintains a space or barrier that cannot be penetrated. Don't let people with walls catch you off guard. They may seem unapproachable by displaying personality traits such as gruffness, anger, or even shyness. Instead of being put off by such behavior, realize that walls have been built to protect the hurting person from further pain. Prayer, compassion and understanding could go a long way in responding to these persons, rather than shunning or avoiding them. Let the spirit lead you, and don't react in the physical and logical sense. Be aware of your spiritual senses.

Let the love of God flow through you as you develop your spirituality. Then, God can use you to minister to his hurting people. Just as God showed me one person's pain, He also led me to pray for that person's healing.

As you become more spiritually sensitive to peoples' needs, God can use you to pray and intercede for their deliverance and healing. Prayer is a powerful tool of God, and His children should be seeking His guidance in prayer for others, as well as themselves.

How do we build a wall in our life? Look at the materials in the chart. We build a wall as we react to negative circumstances, believing that if we ignore the pain it will go away. Unfortunately, we end up storing the pain behind a wall, and we no longer know it is there.

When we suffer an outright enemy attack, we should learn how to confront the attacker rather than hide behind a wall. We are children who are worthy of God, and the devil pulls out all the stops to convince us we are unworthy. Rejection is a potent tool the devil wields to inflict pain. Reacting negatively to rejection with anger and unforgiveness lays the foundation for the construction of a wall. Learning to respond positively to a negative attack is essential for our physical, emotional and spiritual health.

Once walls are subconsciously constructed by our negative reaction, they isolate us and keep us out of God's will. We can be praying to God, while at the same time keeping Him and the answers at bay. Walls block our connection with God. Once we discover the walls, we must begin to dismantle them. The eradication of the walls will uncover the hidden pain, and healing begins only with forgiveness.

The thief comes to kill, steal and destroy. Do not be surprised by the attacks, we have been forewarned. "Do not be ignorant of his devices", Paul warned us in the scriptures. Arm yourself against the enemy. Read the Epistle of St. Paul to the Ephesians and learn how to put on the whole armor of God, for we do not struggle with flesh and blood, but with principalities, powers and rulers of darkness.

Therefore take up the armor of God that you may be able to resist in the evil day, and stand in all things perfect. Stand, therefore, having girded your loins with truth, and having put on the breastplate of justice, and having your feet shod with the readiness of the gospel of peace, in all things taking up the shield of faith, with which you may be able to quench all the fiery darts of the most wicked one. And take unto you the helmet of salvation and the sword of the spirit, that is, the word of God.

Ephesians Ch. 6: 13-17

We are definitely engaged in a spiritual battle. The only way to win is to find Jesus, because He has already won the battle. Until you find your Savior, the old devil will continue to roar like a lion. When you come to Jesus, you will step out of the dark prison and into the light. The light reveals that devil as a defeated, cowardly, helpless and ugly liar. Choose Jesus because His success and victory are yours.

Chapter II – Constructing the Walls

And to Josue the Lord said, "I have delivered Jericho and its king into your power. Have all the soldiers circle the city, marching once around it. Do this for six days, with seven priests carrying rams' horns ahead of the Ark. On the seventh day march around the city seven times, and have the priests blow the horns. When they give a long blast on the ram's horn and you hear that signal, all the people shall shout aloud. The wall of the city will collapse, and they will be able to make a frontal attack.

Josue 6: 2: 5

CHAPTER 3

THE TEMPTATION

After Jesus was baptized the Spirit drove Him into the desert where Satan tempted Him with three temptations. As I studied the temptations, I realized that Jesus was tempted in his body, soul and spirit. We, too, are tempted in these areas, so it is important to recognize the temptations, and remember how Jesus responded. He never reacted. To respond is to provide an answer whereas to react is to turn around! We don't want to turn the wrong way. Let's look at the temptations.

The first temptation was that of the body, in the form of hunger. Jesus had been fasting, so Satan asked him to turn the rocks into bread.

Jesus responded: "Not by bread alone shall man live, but by every word of God."

We are all tempted by food, drink and even drugs. The body is tempted to overindulge for in this way the devil keeps us from experiencing our real spiritual nature. Food, wine or drugs when used in excess make us sluggish and unable to connect with our spirit. Moderation with occasional fasting of foods, along with prayer and meditation bring our bodies into submission to God. This is how we learn to choose the right things and discard the wrong things or ideas. Our spirit being is real, but we must nourish it with the word of God. As we learn to move into this realm of discipline and self-control, our spirit will come to the forefront and we will realize the gifts of kingdom living. The joy will begin to bubble up from within and spread out to our bodies. We will be leaner, more energetic, look and feel more beautiful. Beauty does come from within, and it certainly shows when we bring it forth from within.

The second temptation of Jesus was that of the soul. Satan showed him all the kingdoms of the world and said, " . . . to thee I will give all this power and their glory, for to me they have been delivered. Therefore, if thou will worship before me, the whole shall be thine."

Jesus answered, "The Lord thy God shalt thou worship, and him only shalt thou serve."

This temptation was for the capture of the soul of Jesus. Satan tempted Jesus with wealth and riches and *worldly* honor and glory.

Once we get into kingdom living, the wealth and success will come to us. We should learn how to handle this rightly. If we look to the riches and the power of the world for our strength and security or happiness, we will be bowing our knee to those false idols. That is why Jesus taught us to give. Yes, if we can give things or money away, then we are safe from worshipping the gold and silver as false gods. Once we take our eye off God and put it on the worldly riches, the devil has succeeded in turning us in the wrong direction.

He can then keep us in bondage by the worry over maintaining and keeping these worldly riches, and this worry is a lie of the devil to cause us to turn our attention from God to the material things. I don't believe a diamond ring, fur coat or flashy car will be much consolation to a spirit that has left the body behind and finds its eternal home in the darkness, away from the face of God. That is the final outcome, you see. That is the place without love, and who could bear eternity without love? God is love and that is why our soul desires to be loved.

We are the image of God and His love is greater than any love we can experience in our bodies. Do not be confused. Love is not fulfilled by the lust of the flesh; it comes from within and from God. Worship God – not the false idols.

The third temptation of Jesus was that of the spirit. In this temptation, Satan took Jesus and set him on the pinnacle of the temple and said to him, "If thou art the Son of God, throw thyself down from here; for it is written, 'He will give his angels charge concerning thee, to preserve thee'; and, 'Upon their hands they shall bear thee up, lest thou dash thy foot against a stone'."

And Jesus answered and said to him, "It is written further, 'Thou shalt not tempt the Lord thy God'."

Here, the devil is trying to get Jesus to use God's power to show off, or to use it on a whim or temptation. Jesus says, "Do not tempt the Lord thy God!"

We must understand that God has made us in His image, and given us spiritual gifts and power. The power is not to be used at our discretion, but only as we are led by the Spirit of God. I believe that most of us do not walk in the power of the spirit, for we do not understand God's will in our life, and we are not led by the Spirit.

God never gives us more than we can handle, and I remember Jesus saying that blasphemy of the Holy Spirit will not be forgiven. I believe Jesus was referring to the abuse of God's power when he taught about this blasphemy.

The scripture continues right after the temptation, that Jesus returned in the *power* of the Spirit into Galilee, and the fame of him went out through the whole country. We have the power within us, but I believe that God has given us a protection that prevents us from abusing this power. When we learn to submit to God in every area of body, soul and spirit, I believe that we, too, can walk in the power of the Spirit, setting the captives free and healing the sick, and even raising the dead.

Why do we go through trials? The trials are caused by a war that goes on within us, between our flesh and our spirit. Our soul, made up of our mind and emotions, is caught between the two worlds. Looking toward the spirit man, our soul enjoys the success of kingdom living with health, abundance, peace, joy and life. On the other hand, if the soul is looking to the world ruled by Satan, it suffers lack, sickness, failure and death. This is a huge controversy and it takes time to grow spiritually through discipline and self-control, so that our flesh no longer rules. The trials are not sent from God. The trials are a real battle between our very own flesh and spirit for the capture of our soul. The answer is submission to God. We must make a choice, and the Holy Spirit of discipline is our helper in bringing us into the submission of the perfect will of God.

If our soul never finds the new birth that is available into the spirit, it will exist in the limitations of this body of flesh. We can have life in the kingdom now through a spiritual rebirth.

We must make a determination to find our way back home. Jesus is known as the word of God, and by His word our spirits are awakened to the truth that sets us free from the dominion of the world. Our flesh only knows the worldly ways, but we do not go on forever in the flesh. Our flesh is a temporary container for our soul, and our soul does not die.

There are two worlds that our soul may enter: one is light the other is darkness. The choice seems very simple, but unless we bring the desires of the flesh under the control and guidance of the Holy Spirit, how will we enter in? It is true that our flesh rules from our beginning in this world, but God has given us His Spirit to teach and guide us so that we can find our way back home.

After Jesus overcame the temptations of the hunger of the flesh and the lust of the soul for worldly riches and glory, the devil came to tempt Him in his Spirit, asking Him to jump off a cliff to prove that God would not let Him get hurt. This proves that after we take control of our flesh, we will become aware of the very power of God that is within us. We must be careful, for we see the devil doesn't leave just because we aren't letting our flesh rule.

Now, the devil must really put on the pressure. Obviously, that old devil doesn't want us walking around in the spiritual power of God, setting captives free and healing the sick, or raising the dead. So, he tries to tempt us to abuse God's power. Of course he is an expert in this area. He permitted his pride in the spiritual power available to him as a great angel of God to be puffed up into believing that he could exalt himself above God!

It is written that his pride caused his downfall and that is why God cast him down from heaven.

Yes, he gave himself the glory and honor and thought he could take over the kingdom. The power of God is in us for we are created in His image. The activator of the power of God that is within is the Holy Spirit. The Holy

Spirit is very sensitive to our motives and will guide us into wise and prudent use of God's power. When we get to the spiritual place where we can walk in the power of God, we must be very careful stewards in this area. We are warned not to grieve the Holy Spirit of God or He will depart from us. It is also written that once a person has tasted the power of God and then turned back, it is next to impossible for him to be saved again.

I believe God is very patient with us, so that we will succeed when we step into this new level of our spiritual walk. Here is where we must learn humility. To God be the glory – for it is not what we can do, but what God can do in us. We must seek God's will and not that of our sinful nature. Never confuse the two.

The three temptations of Jesus in the desert were temptation of body, soul and spirit. He overcame in every area. He won our victory. In Him, we overcome, because he has overcome the world.

CHAPTER 4
DISCIPLINE

A recent published national survey ranked my home state very high in the number of overweight people, smokers, drinkers, and young people growing up in poverty. This was given as reasons for large corporations not choosing to locate in this state. Just before hearing about this survey, I was talking to Mom about the unruly behavior of children in the schools. It all seemed to boil down to one factor; we have no discipline! Now that everyone can do whatever he pleases, the world seems to have gone completely mad! We can have it all and we want it all – all that the world has to offer, so we think.

Discipline is defined as order, training which perfects, and control gained by enforcing obedience. Some antonyms are disorder, clutter and confusion.

Now, this is enlightening. Discipline is described in the scriptures as coming from the Holy Spirit of God. It seems so simple.

We are obedient to God's leading, and we gain the control of our soul; that control comes from our spiritual man. Otherwise, we can live in confusion and disorder being led obviously by that king of confusion, the ruler of this world.

Discipline is that guidance we get from above, that voice that speaks to our inner man to keep us out of harm's way. However, while we have been enjoying every freedom, the discipline of the Holy Spirit has been falling on deaf ears.

Our flesh rules and the spirit submits to that rule as long as we indulge our every desire. If we are fat, we probably overeat. If we drink too much, it is because we refuse to set a limit. If we smoke or take drugs, it is because our flesh screams for it and we say here take all you want! And in the end, after giving in to the whims of the flesh, we are miserable! Too fat, too tired, too broke, and too incapable of succeeding in anything. Why? Because we indulged ourselves until we landed in a state of obesity, poverty or addiction. Now we suffer depression because everything seems to be failing in our lives. We find ourselves in a spiraling decline into the depths of darkness, sickness, depression and hopelessness. Why did this happen to us? We pitifully wonder why God would let this misery overtake us.

Wait a minute! God was there all the time! We just weren't listening. We thought we were being good, but we never listened to Him. We followed the desires of our flesh and found ourselves in failed marriages, failed health and prisons of defeat with no seemingly understandable way out. Too many good people fall victim to overwhelming circumstances, and lose all control over their lives. And they can't understand why they have become victims of abuse, sickness, debt and every negative circumstance.

Athletes practice discipline. They set goals, and through discipline achieve them. These are usually physical goals, and somewhere, some place, sometime we discover that nothing satisfies this flesh we live in.

Over-indulgence is not any better than self-denial, since it all takes place in the flesh. If the flesh is in control, it will use either direction to lead us into failure. Be it obesity or anorexia, carefree or a nervous wreck, rich or poor. If it is the state of your physical being, the inner man will not be fulfilled by either circumstance. If we think reaching the top of the ladder, making the most money or winning the contest will satisfy our souls, we will find a huge disappointment when we "arrive". This flesh will never gratify us.

We can make rules to not touch, taste, or do this and that. Rules work somewhat, but they are limited and not suited to every individual. We must realize that we are individually made in the image of God, and the greatness of God cannot be captured in one personality, size or shape. He is so big and so diverse, that it is impossible to comprehend His greatness. Just look around at the differences in people and realize that everyone is created in His image. How could one rule work for all? It doesn't.

There are, however, spiritual rules that are discerned in our spirit. We must go within and listen to the inner voice of the Holy Spirit. The leading of the inner voice will direct you in right choices in any circumstance. The Holy Spirit leads us in love, which is kind, patient, gentle and temperate. God is love, and so we use the spiritual rule of love to keep us in God's protection. Love is a spiritual action, not a physical one.

Therein lies the secret to who is in control. The spirit rules in love, the flesh rules in selfishness and indulgence.

We are born into this physical world that is in the control of the ruler of darkness, and until we are spiritually born into the light, we are held captive to the dictates of the flesh, being led about by our emotions that are enticed by the ruler of darkness.

As a physical person, we must abide by worldly laws and regulations. We think discipline is hard and we shun it. But, after being awakened into the spirit we begin to hear the gentle urging of the voice inside. The Spirit of God will set us free from the bondage of worldly rule.

Discipline frees us to fly and soar as an eagle. No longer bogged down by the flesh, we learn to eat properly, put down harmful things and limit dangerous things. There is no rule for all; there is individual guidance for each. We are special in the sight of God, and we have special, individual needs.

When we learn to listen and become obedient to the leading of the Holy Spirit, we will find ourselves succeeding where before we were failing. We will be happy instead of sad or worried. We will be healthy instead of sick. We will have more energy to devote to good deeds, aiming at charity and finding fulfillment and success in all that we put our hands to.

Discipline is not easy at first, because our flesh screams at us to ignore it. You see the flesh hears the voice of the world that is ruled by the ruler of darkness. The devil seeks to destroy us, but our inner man when awakened hears the voice of the Holy Spirit who leads us through the minefields in this world while safely keeping us out of the dangers of failure and hurt.

I grew up with the religious philosophy of moderation in all things. This works for me, as long as I listen to my inner voice to understand true moderation – not what the world lets me get by with. There is a difference. The world will take you down a primrose path to hell, and just like Pinocchio when he got off track and followed the bad boys, we can sometimes find ourselves deluded into thinking like the world that all is well, and find ourselves in a wrong situation.

We must learn to analyze our situations and determine what is from God and what is not. As we learn by trial and error, we discover the truth in following the spirit and denying the flesh. Be assured it takes time to uncover our spiritual gifts of understanding, perception, discernment and right speaking, because they are just a mirror image of the fleshly hearing, seeing and smelling.

As you learn to walk in the Spirit of truth, you will do well to understand the spirits of error. The devil will try to throw you into a state of confusion by his lying, cunning and deceitfulness.

One tactic that we should learn to recognize immediately is that of condemnation and unworthiness. We are incapable of becoming good on our own and we must understand that our righteousness is a gift. Jesus died so we could be reconciled with God who accepts us, not because we are worthy on our own. Jesus made us worthy. We must receive, accept and believe that we are worthy because He made us worthy. It is His grace that brings us out of darkness into the light. There is nothing that we can do to earn it.

The world would have you believe that you have to earn God's love or respect, because that is how the world works. God does not grade us on our own merit. He made us worthy. He is our Father, and He loves us in spite of the errors we have committed in this world.

This is so important for us to comprehend. The world will do everything in its power to prevent the children of God from receiving their inheritance. It is easy too, because the devil accuses us of being unworthy. He attacks us with rejection, so that we believe we are unacceptable to God. Condemnation is a lie that would make us believe we are unworthy to receive God's gifts of health, prosperity and abundant life.

We are the righteousness of God! No one can take that away from us, because Jesus overcame the world! He overcame death and He defeated Satan and all the demons in hell that held souls captive up until that time. We have been set free. Jesus opened the door, and no one can shut what He opened. If we are not living the life Jesus died for us to have, it is because we have stayed in the prison, the cell of failure, not having the courage to walk out the door that Jesus opened for us.

Step out into the light. Take a chance, dare to dream, believe that it is yours – because it is. Jesus died for you to have God's promises. Refuse failure and step into success. Refuse the pain and resentment of rejection, and accept God's love. Refuse condemnation for you are holy just as He is Holy. Come out of that dark room, and step into the sunshine of God's love, protection and generosity. He did give us health, wealth and abundant life. We have just refused the gifts.

Pray, "Oh Jesus, I want you and everything you won for me by your sacrifice on that cross."

CHAPTER 5

THE SPIRITS OF GOD AND THE SPIRITS OF ERROR

After discussing the importance of the guidance of the Holy Spirit, it would be a good time to discuss the spirits that are in us. Since we have a spirit man that is contained within the flesh, it is important to understand how to operate in that spiritual place. We are fully aware of our five physical senses of sight, touch, taste, smell and hearing, but did you know that you also had spiritual gifts? God is described as having seven spirits with Him, and I believe God has imparted His spirits into us. As a spiritual being, I believe we should better understand spiritual actions.

Maybe you have seen the movie, *Ghost*. This movie portrayed a man who died suddenly and was caught in the spiritual realm, but was still on earth. I found it very interesting that he had to learn to walk through walls, and how much difficulty he had trying to pick up a quarter. He had to learn to do things differently when he was a operating as a ghost. This story was just fiction, but there is a significance to be understood here. We also must learn to develop our spiritual senses, as they operate differently than our physical senses.

I found the most interesting information about our spirits while reading from *The Testament of Reuben* in the *Forgotten Books of Eden*. These books along with *The Lost Books of the Bible* contain a collection of works which are considered apocrypha which means they were never authenticated to be included among the biblical works. However, before I present the list of the Spirits of Error and the Spirits of God, let me just explain that I have found mention of the *spirits of error* in the Bible, and it is also written that God has seven spirits. The elaboration of the spirits from the Lost Books gives us tremendous insight into our spiritual makeup.

I never cease to be amazed at the things that have been hidden or lost, that would help clarify the confusion that surrounds us as we attempt to discover our spiritual nature. First I would like to present the spirits we have received from God. It is so helpful to become familiar with the tools that God gave us so that we can use them.

Before I list the spirits as I found them in the testimony of Reuben, I would like to present some scriptures from the Bible that refer to these spirits:

> *We are of God. He who knows God listens to us; he who is not of God does not listen to us. By this we know the* **spirit of truth and the spirit of error.**
>
> 1 John 4:6

> *. . . and there are seven lamps burning before the throne which are the* **seven spirits of God.**
>
> Revelation/Apocalypse 4:5-6

THE SPIRITS OF GOD

1. Sense of Smell
2. Sense of Sight
3. Sense of Hearing
4. Sense of Taste
5. Power of Speech
6. Life
7. Procreation and Sexual Intercourse

The Testament of Reuben Ch. 1

There are four senses listed above. We receive from God the senses of smell, taste, sight and hearing, but not *touch*. It makes sense when you think about it, because touching or feeling is a physical attribute, and God is spirit and his gifts to us are spiritual.

See where the power is on the list of spirits. The power is in our speech! No wonder we are attacked by Satan in our feelings! This is where we can be easily enticed to react by SPEAKING those negative feelings into words; and those words have power! We are being duped into bringing negative results into our lives by reacting to the negative "feeling". This is the area that the devil specializes in. He is the ruler of this world; the temporary world of the flesh.

This is an adventure into the spiritual power that is within us. We must bring down the walls that separate us from God's love, so that we can enter into the kingdom. We cannot exist in heaven in the flesh! The battle is for our soul, and our soul resides between the flesh that is ruled by Satan, and the spirit which is led and taught by the Holy Spirit. As long as we insist on following our sense of touch (our feelings) we are completely out of tune with our spirit.

Become acquainted with the Spirits of God that are in of you. Understand that Satan attacks us in our emotions that are governed by our mind. Our mind is the place where we must choose to react or respond.

If we respond to physical stimuli, the feelings, we will end up building a wall that prevents us from reaching the very spirits imparted to us by our Father who created us in His image. Paul wrote that as long as the outer tabernacle was still standing, the priest could not enter into the true holy of holies.

The tabernacle is our flesh. Since Jesus crucified the enmity in His flesh, we have become partakers in His victory and can now enter into the holy of holies which is in the spiritual realm and the kingdom of God.

We are spirits and we have a soul. The flesh is just a temporary wrapper, and the devil spends all of his time and energy trying to excite our flesh into succumbing to his beliefs. That way we will miss our eternal life, the very spiritual life that God has placed in each of us. So, familiarize yourself with the Spirits God gave you and learn to use them.

THE SPIRITS OF GOD

THE SENSE OF SMELL is for discernment. It is an insight or perception that reveals the truth. With discernment we are able to recognize and distinguish between good from evil. We can separate ourselves from evil. We must not judge a person for that is a sin, but we can separate ourselves from those who partake of evil. It is a wise man who remains under the umbrella of God's protection by avoiding evil. We are still supposed to pray for our enemies, but we don't have to mingle with them! If we separate ourselves from those who live in darkness, they cannot hurt us.

THE SENSE OF SIGHT is for perception. This sense gives us insight into all situations. Pray that you can see as God sees. Then, the next time you are mistreated by someone, you might try to perceive that person's pain and pray for him instead of reacting with a physical emotion of anger or revenge. This could be a great step in preventing the construction of a wall of unforgiveness that would separate you from God.

THE SENSE OF HEARING is for understanding. The ability to understand gives us comprehension of a situation. Pray that you may hear as God hears, so that you will understand what exactly is being said. When you hear angry words, pray for God's understanding and restrain from reacting in a negative physical emotional way. Anger begets anger. Don't go there! Hear as God hears and understand the situation. Jesus said to turn the other cheek. The pain of the flesh will not prevent you from entering the kingdom, the reaction of the flesh to strike back and act out of anger will. Pray for those who persecute you. You will find that the power of God in your inner spirit will bring that shouting person to repentance or better yet, to healing. Usually one hollers because he is hurt. Hear their pain – don't let the devil deceive you into a sinful reaction!

THE SENSE OF TASTE eluded me for sometime. Then, I read in the Bible about those who taste the power of God and then shrink back. And there it was – the sense of taste is for tasting the power of God! And, no wonder the devil tempts us with food and drink that will make us sluggish in the flesh. He certainly doesn't want us tapping into the power of God, because after we taste the power, where does it come out but in our speech! This is incredibly important and the significance is life changing!

THE POWER OF SPEECH. God created with His word, and He has imparted to us the spiritual power of speech. This is not a sense, but a POWER! Become aware of what is coming out of your mouth. Do you want the things to manifest in your life that you are speaking? Listen to your words, and train your mouth to speak good things and truthful things.

LIFE. God gave us the spirit of life and this is the spirit that must be reborn into the light and victory of Jesus. Just as we were born in the flesh into the world of darkness, our spirit must be reborn into the light and life that God gave us.

PROCREATION AND SEXUAL INTERCOURSE.
I believe it is important to understand that reproduction goes beyond the physical all the way into the spiritual realm and it is a gift of God.

As we learn about the spirits of God that are in us, I believe we can better understand how to develop that spiritual power of God in us.

As I continued reading the testimony of Reuben, he told his children that intermingled in each of us are 7 spirits of error. It is no wonder we get confused!

I would encourage you to memorize both lists of the Spirits of God and the Spirits of Error so that you can quickly identify the spirit that is presenting to you in life's situations. Then, strive to walk in the spirits of God that have been given to you, and quickly identify and depart from the spirits of error. Each person has the freedom of choice. We can make a more deliberate and conscientious decision when we are able to recognize the spirits.

THE SPIRITS OF ERROR

1. Insatiableness
2. Fighting
3. Obsequiousness/Chicanery
4. Pride
5. Lying
6. Injustice
7. Fornication

Although these spirits of error are not listed in the Bible as such, I have found a pretty good reference to them in Proverbs 6: 16, where it tells of the 6 things the Lord hates and 7 that are an abomination. They are very similar to the spirits of error as you can see below.

ABOMINATIONS	SPIRITS OF ERROR
The false witness who utters lies	Obsequiousness/Chicanery
Feet that run swiftly to evil	Insatiableness
He who sows discord among brothers	Fighting
A heart that plots wicked schemes	Fornication
Haughty eyes	Pride
Lying tongue	Lying
Hands that shed innocent blood	Injustice

In Chapter 11 of St. Luke is the story about a dumb spirit that Jesus cast out of a man, and then the man could speak. Jesus continued that when a spirit is cast out, it wanders in search of a new place to abide. When it can't find a new place, it goes back to its old home, and finding it swept and clean, it brings back 7 other spirits worse than itself and the state of that man is worse than it was before.

Although scripture fails to list the spirits of error, it did not fail to warn us about them. So, let's study the spirits of error, since these are working in our flesh in order to quickly recognize these wrong spirits.

THE SPIRITS OF ERROR

INSATIABLENESS: Greedy, unfulfilled, unquenchable, and unappeasable.

FIGHTING: Combative and warring. To attempt to harm or gain power over an adversary by blows or with weapons.

OBSEQUIOUSNESS/CHICANERY: These two words are used together to alert us to trickery that is presented in a most flattering, fawning or attentive way, while pulling a deception.

OBSEQUIOUSNESS: An ingratiating flatterer; fawning, to court favor by a cringing demeanor.

CHICANERY: Trickery and deception.

PRIDE: Conceit. Inordinate self-esteem, arrogance.

LYING: Dishonesty, deception.

FORNICATION: Illicit, unlawful, wrongful sexual intercourse of an unmarried person, adultery, infidelity; in scripture, figuratively, idolatry. Idolatry, in turns, means excessive love or veneration for anything.

INJUSTICE: Violation of another's rights. An unjust act or wrong.

The spirits of God and the spirits of error are located within our spirit, and we must be more in tune to our spirits to discern them. We are accustomed to believing what we see, hear and feel. Jesus taught us to have faith by believing those things that aren't seen. We cannot see God, but we believe and know there is a God. This knowing comes from our spiritual senses. The world and ruler of the world works on our physical abilities and that is why we should avoid following our feelings and learn to operate in the spiritual realm using the senses God gave us.

I believe as our spiritual senses become more developed, we will find it so much easier to respond to a situation, instead of reacting to it.

When we react to the physical stimulus of sound and sights, we should also be cognizant of the spiritual senses as we plot our course. If someone hurts our "feelings", we can react in anger and end up fighting. Fighting is on the spirit of error list, so we have just been pulled into the wrong and sinful nature.

If we learn to listen with our *sense of hearing*, we will understand that our fight is not with flesh and blood, but with principalities, powers and rulers of darkness. Paul taught these principals so we would be aware of the spirits of error. Therefore, if we would take time to listen to the inner voice and let God reveal the truth when a person hurts us, we might better understand that person's pain or bondage. Rather than reacting negatively in the flesh, we should use our spiritual understanding and respond with forgiveness, compassion or an answer that could soothe, comfort or uplift. We would be implementing God's will and not giving our authority over to the devil.

Learn to ask and wait on God, when you see or hear something that causes aggravation in the physical. As you look to Him and use your senses of hearing and sight that are located in your spirit, you can become useful to God in setting captives free and breaking yokes of bondage that have held people captive, by using your P*ower of Speech*.

Those who do not know Jesus came to set them free will hear the good news. Let the love of God flow through you to those who are hurting. Use your spiritual senses as you pause and restrain from reacting in the physical realm. Implement discipline and ask God to give you the strength to stand in difficult circumstances. God's grace is for these trying times, and He renews His favor and grace towards us each day. Do not neglect His wonderful gifts.

Also use your senses of smell and taste. Spiritual discernment (the sense of smell) will alert you to the presence of evil or good, and the Bible teaches us to taste and see how good the Lord is. These are Gods spirits given to us for discrimination and discernment so we can choose between good and evil, because we *know* the difference.

Another spirit of God is that of procreations so that we may reproduce and enjoy sexual intercourse. This gift should be used appropriately and not be confused with the spirit of error of fornication.

Life is a spirit of God and we are created in His image. We are alive in the spirit and should learn to operate in that realm since we are His children and we desire life eternal with Him.

My most favorite spirit of God is the Power of Speech. How very important it is for us to learn to control our speech. God spoke and there was light. God creates with His word, and here we discover that God has given us the power of speech. I believe that we have power in our words; however, we can speak negative and positive things at the same time, thus rendering the power inactive. We must train our senses so that we respond with powerful words of life. I believe that God protects us while we grow into our spiritual selves, knowing that we must learn how to operate in the gifts of the spirit, before we can be turned loose to get everything we say! It is a matter of learning to be positive, walking in love, forgiving and using the spiritual gifts that God gave us to overcome the spirits of error that are also mixed in.

As we become aware of the spirits of God and the spirits of error, we should call on God to grant us spiritual discernment to make right choices. Spiritual growth is developed as we put our trust in God.

Take control of the words of your mouth. The Bible explains that out of the abundance of the heart, the mouth speaks. So, if you have trouble keeping your words pleasant, look deeper than your mouth to find out what is wrong in your heart. The heart is your spirit, and your mind is your soul. The soul is turned one way or the other, either towards the flesh and what it sees and feels, or towards the spirit and what it perceives and knows to be the truth from God.

It is all part of our journey, and the more we learn about our mind, body and spirit, the more opportunity we have to determine to choose the spirits from God and reject those from hell. Knowledge is power, and the more we know about our God given gifts, the sooner we can walk in the divine power that is in us. Remember Jesus defeated the ruler of this world, and by believing in Him, we receive the Holy Spirit of God, who will guide us through this spiritual growing and learning process. We cannot please God, unless we believe in His Son. The spiritual realm is there and always will be, but the door to the kingdom is Jesus, and there is no other way in. We must understand the importance of Jesus, before we start on a spiritual journey, or we could be led astray.

I emphasize that you make a mental note that "feelings" are not a spirit from God. Feelings are emotions that come from the physical realm, and they consist of such negative emotions as disappointment, confusion, defeat and guilt.

As we REACT to feelings, we construct walls of protection thinking that we will prevent the recurrence of the pain that we suffered from these blatant attacks of Satan and his principalities and rulers of darkness.

Unfortunately, as we subconsciously build walls of so-called protection, those walls isolate us from receiving the great and good things from God. A common wall that Satan causes us to construct quickly is that of unforgiveness. The devil never appears to us, so we are unable to see the real enemy. Of course not, the devil or spirits of darkness use real live people, and usually people close to us to cause us pain. They can disappoint us, lie to us, beat us, hurt us, and steal from us. And we being innocent and ignorant do not know how to RESPOND. So, the world teaches us the way of darkness.

We REACT in anger, hurt, guilt, shame, or other negative emotions. By succumbing to the world's logical way of dealing with these negative situations, we fall straight into sin. We think the person who sinned against us is the bad guy, but guess what? The devil has just sucked you into the dark world of sin by causing you to hate, be angry and hold a grudge, and the cycle spirals down into a worse situation. From those negative reactive feelings, the devil can now cause you to fall into complete depression with feelings of hopelessness, despair, and if left unchecked, can lead to suicidal thoughts! See, it worked didn't it. Now, you wish you were dead! That's just what he wanted!

So, how do we avoid these tragedies? How do we escape the prison of despair, defeat or just plain indifference?

I thought the answer was ridiculous when I was presented with it. It is called forgiveness. Yes, you will never step out of the black hole, until you learn to forgive the person who caused you the grief. If you are way down, it will take a while to come back. There is help, and it is Jesus. He can only help when you turn to Him. The only way you can turn is to let go of the ugliness and you do that by the process of forgiveness.

When I once sunk into a terrible depression brought on by an abusive situation, I sought the advice of a Christian counselor who gave me a slip of paper that simply read: "I forgive (Name) as an act of faith, in the name of Jesus". I thought the counselor must be nuts, but I needed help and this was all that had been offered. I would try anything to escape this misery. So I had to practice saying those words over and over and over. Of course, when I began saying them, I didn't mean it. It took a long time for me, because I had been beaten down for so long, that I had gotten way far off the track. You shouldn't feel that you are lying when you say these words, but understand that this is the countermeasure that we must use against the attacks of anger, despair, resentment and all the other ugly emotions that well up inside when we have been so badly beaten down. It is in this process of counter attacking the "feelings" that we take our eye off the situation, put our hope in God, and almost like magic, the forgiveness takes root in our spirit and eventually bring us back into the light and the land of the living. I vow and swear that forgiveness works. The time it takes depends on you alone.

By now you should have a better understanding of how the walls are built. The whole construction is based on our feelings. This is very important to understand;

because "feelings" are not a spirit that God has given us. The word "feel" is described as to touch, to perceive by sensation, to be aware of, an emotional REACTION. To appear, especially to the sense of touch. This "sense of touch" flies off the page and screams to me – NOT FROM GOD! To get a deeper, more meaningful understanding of the importance of this revelation, we must know the Spirits of God.

CHAPTER 6

WHY A TENT?

I have read many times about Jesus being transfigured with Moses and Elias appearing to Him when He took James and John and went up the mountain to pray. Every time I read the statement of Peter I wondered what he meant.

> And it came to pass as they were parting from him, that Peter said to Jesus, "Master, it is good for us to be here. And let us set up three tents, one for thee, and one for Moses, and one for Elias," not knowing what he said.
>
> St. Luke 9: 33

I decided it was time to investigate the meaning since it had piqued my curiosity. I began by looking up the meaning of the word *tent*. It is described as a portable lodge or shelter of skins, canvas or cloth, stretched and sustained by poles, used for shelter, especially for soldiers in camp.

As I pondered the definition of tent, I understood the parallel of our spirit man covered in skin, lodged in this world that God created as He stretched the world between the North and South Poles. As I wondered how this related to Peter speaking about the appearance of spiritual beings, I thought it was interesting that he wanted to immediately cover the spirits of Jesus, Moses and Elias with skin. He desired to change them into physical beings so they would not depart. He wanted to cover them with skin so he could see them and touch them and know they were present with him.

This goes to the very heart of our understanding spiritual matters. As humans existing in a physical body in a physical world, we can't seem to comprehend how life eternal in the spirit relates to anything we know. And, of course, spiritual matter does not equate at all to physical matter. So, here were Peter and James being made privy to the spiritual presence of Jesus and His friends, and Peter's best thought was to make them like us! How far off is this? Rather than trying to turn our spirituality into a physical condition, we should learn to become spiritual. Physical is temporary whereas spiritual is eternal. Our spirit man is waiting for us to find our self!

This reminds me of the time I was praying and meditating and the thought or inner voice conveyed to me that the Holy Spirit looks like me! It was such an exciting revelation! You look like me and sound like me because you are in me and have taken up your home inside of me. If we could realize that we are indeed the temple of the Holy Spirit, and that we don't just house the Spirit of God, we become one with the Holy Spirit. I believe that was what God was showing me when He conveyed that the Holy Spirit looked like me. Can you see the importance of this revelation? This knowledge can truly change the way we think about ourselves.

The world is cruel to us, and no wonder. The ruler of this world is none other than that fallen angel Lucifer, who was cast down out of the light into the darkness. The great angel of light was changed into a demon of darkness. His name was also changed and he is now called Satan, ruler of the darkness of this world.

Satan uses cruel tactics to keep us from the truth of God's love. He lies to make us believe we are unworthy of God's love. He is the one who condemns us and we fail to realize the sacrifice God made to redeem us and make us worthy. God knew our weakness in this physical state, and that is why only God coming into the flesh as Jesus could release us from this guilt. The shame of feeling shame is the lack of understanding that we cannot redeem ourselves! That is why God did it for us. He only asked us to believe Him.

When we understand who we are in Christ, and learn beyond any doubt that we are truly a child of God, then we can comprehend that we are worthy of God's love and God's best.

When you discover who you are in Jesus, then you can shake off the lies of the devil and say to him with authority in the name of Jesus: "Don't touch God's anointed!" Yes, when we have the Holy Spirit dwelling in us, we are God's anointed, just like Jesus is His anointed!

The devil condemned Jesus with lies, but Jesus overcame Satan and this world. We have been raised up on high with Him and share in His victory. Be not overcome with evil, but overcome evil with good!

As you discover the likeness of yourself to that of God, you will loathe condemning that likeness. God created us in His image, and we just cannot accept the devil's lies that we are anything less!

Getting back to the story of Peter wanting to put Jesus, Moses and Elias into tents, I realized how even Christ's disciples were so physically oriented to this world.

As we search for truth, we expect God to fit into our narrow knowledge of existence and manifest His great power into something we can see, feel or touch. That just can't happen. God is omnipotent, and to learn of God we must be awakened spiritually in order to perceive, rather than see, and to understand, rather than hear.

God did manifest Himself to us once on earth. He sent His Son Jesus, and look what the world did to Him. Some believed, but more didn't. Jesus existed and walked in the physical realm with us to teach us how to find the spiritual place in heaven where He returned to be with His Father. The teachings of Jesus as written in the Bible are for our spiritual enlightenment, and reading the Word of God awakens that spirit man that has been suppressed by this physical world and the deceptions that Satan has used to keep us turned in the wrong direction.

We are aware of the deep yearning and desire that we can't seem to define or understand, and it is this yearning that comes from our inner or spiritual man that leads us in the search for truth. We desire peace, contentment, success and love. The world has many avenues that seem to lead to the fulfillment of our desires; however, the world never succeeds in satisfying the desire of the soul.

Once we find the answer to our longing, we wonder how we missed it for so long. The answer is simple really, it is inner peace. The world teaches us to grab the gusto and leads us in many directions to achieve our heart's desire. The spirit leads us in but one direction and fulfills us with inner peace which is the satisfaction, success and joy that surpasses understanding. Peace is not as complicated as the world makes it seem. It is confusing, however, for, again, it is opposite of the worldly ways. You see, God fulfills us from the inside out; whereas the world tries to produce the same result by fulfilling us from the outside in. The way of the world is truly backwards to the way of God's kingdom living. The spiritual peace that our inner man is seeking cannot be found in material things that are passing away, but only in the eternal things of God

Chapter VI – Why A Tent? 192

Let us rejoice, Beloved,
And let us go to see ourselves in thy beauty.

Excerpt of The Spiritual Canticle
St. John of the Cross

CHAPTER 7

THE WALL BETWEEN THE HOLY AND THE PROFANE

Destroy this temple and in three days I will raise it up.

St. Mark 14:. 58

Jesus was referring to His body as the temple and indeed in 3 days he raised it up. The scriptures show us a pattern of the building of the temple and the things that are in it. This pattern is given to us that we might know the plan of God for man's salvation. Of course, that plan is Jesus, and the temple represents Jesus.

I read how Ezechial was given a reed to measure the temple and my eye was caught when he came to measure the courtyard.

The wall of the outer court of the temple is 500 cu x 500 cu to separate the holy from the profane.

Ezechial 40:20

Ch VII Wall Between the Holy and the Profane

This scripture is describing a wall that separates the holy from the profane. This to me is the separation between heaven and earth. The kingdom of God is the holy place that is separated from the kingdom ruled by Satan, the profane place.

I believe the measurement of the courtyard is significant in that it represents time. I learned while reading Nicodemus in the *Forgotten Books of Eden* that the measurement of the Ark of the Covenant was symbolic of the 5½ days until God would come to save Adam.

God had told Adam in another *Forgotten Book* that he would bring him back to heaven in 5 ½ days, and also explained that would be 5500 years on earth because 1 day in heaven is as 1000 days on earth. Therefore the Savior was expected to return in 5500 years after Adam was expelled from the garden.

The Ark is described in the scriptures at Exodus Ch. 25:10, as measuring 2 ½ cubits long, 1 ½ cubits wide and 1 ½ cubits high. The measurements added up to 5 ½ cubits.

Continuing in Nicodemus the story is told that Pilate visited the temple and demanded that the Jews explain what they really knew about the Christ that had just been crucified. They explained that they crucified Christ in ignorance and that they now knew him to be the Son of God. They looked up in their books and found this information about the Ark and determined that it was indeed, time for the Savior to come. These books are wonderful reading, and I believe there is a lot of information that has been lost, yet the story is still the same. The scriptures are not changed by any of these stories, but rather enhanced.

As I read about the measurement of the courtyard around the temple being 500 cu x 500 cu, I quickly did the math to understand the measurement of the courtyard equals 2500 cubits. I believe these 2500 cubits represent the years until Christ comes again. It would be the 2 ½ days that when added to the 5 ½ days equals 8 days or 8,000 years.

I find it difficult to explain, but I know that the restoration of the fall of Adam will take a week in God's time. Since, God created the world and Adam and Eve in 6 days, then rested on the 7th, so, too, do I believe that the restoration of mankind from the fall will be accomplished in another week – God's time.

This week represents 7000 years on earth and 7 days in heaven. The 8th day is significant of the new day, the beginning of the return to God where there is no more counting of time.

Therefore, we read where Paul exhorted us to endeavor to enter into the Sabbath rest. Further, he explains there will be a new day to enter, but it will be after the 7th – therefore it will be the 8th day. God spoke of this in the scriptures saying – "on the 8th day you must return it to me!" Therefore, I believe the end of time is the end of the 7th day. Then, on the 8th day, all that is of God returns to God.

The day and hour we do not know, however, we should be aware of the times. Remember, Jesus telling the people that they could read the sky, but they couldn't read the times!

> *You hypocrites! You know how to judge the face of the sky and of the earth; but how is it that you do not judge this time? But why even of yourselves do you not judge what is right?*
>
> St. Luke 12: 56

They knew that it was time for Messiah to come. The prophets had foretold the coming of the Lord, and they knew the time from God's testimony to Abel and Enoch that it would be 5 ½ days or 5500 years. The time may not have been exact, however, because Jesus testified:

> *For then there will be great tribulation, such as has not been from the beginning of the world until now, nor will be. And unless those days had been shortened, no living creature would be saved. But for the sake of the elect those days will be shortened.*
>
> St. Matthew 24: 21

Therefore, we do not know the day or the hour that He will come. But take heed to Jesus' warning that after 3 days he will destroy the temple and rebuild it again.

We are still talking about 5 and 3 days making 8. Depending on when and where God shortened the day, you should be able to read the times! It has been 2000 years since Jesus came, and the measuring of the wall would signify 2500 years, therefore with less than ½ a day until it comes down; if the day were shortened, how soon it must be until the end of the world that we know!

The holy is separated from the profane by a wall and this wall is measured and described by the prophet Ezechial. When I read this scripture, I was thrilled because I immediately realized this was the wall that God was giving me to write about. Yes, I started with the walls that we build within, but this is more than I had expected. This is the place that God brought me in scripture to show me why the title of this book is, *The Walls Came Tumbling Down!* This was the wall God was having me write about, the wall around the courtyard that separates the holy from the profane.

Today, I found another reference to the wall of the courtyard.

> *And there was given me a reed like to a rod, and I was told: "Rise and measure the temple of God, and the altar*

The Walls Came Tumbling Down

and those who worship therein. But the court outside the temple, reject it and do not measure it; for it has bseen given to the nations, and the holy city they will trample under foot for forty-two months. And I will grant unto my two witnesses to prophesy for a thousand two hundred and sixty days, clothed in sackcloth."

Apocalypse/Revelations 11: 1-3

The significance of this passage to me is the fact that the courtyard will be rejected. John is being told to measure the temple, the altar and those who worship therein.

I spoke earlier of change and how we can believe in Jesus and God, and think we are saved, yet if we haven't changed, being reborn in the Spirit, we are just frolicking outside in the courtyard. How horrible! Those in the courtyard are going to find themselves right smack in the middle of the tribulation when the walls come tumbling down. We must get into the temple in order to avoid this fate of tribulation. True, those who suffer in tribulation can be saved, but it will be through fire, and martyrdom and suffering!

I awoke to an urgent message one morning, a voice saying to me, "Come into the Glory!"

We can no longer straddle the fence or pretend to be close to God, when we have only made it into the courtyard. The handwriting is, indeed, on the wall. We must come all the way in!

The word "delay" stands out to me when I read about it in the scriptures. Paul explains that he was "delayed in order to spare you".

Ch VII Wall Between the Holy and the Profane

> *... there shall be delay no longer; ... the mystery of God will be accomplished as he declared by his servants the prophets."*
>
> Revelations 10: 7

God is patient with us and delays His coming in order to spare us. However, there are only so many days, there is an appointed time, and we must be able to read the signs of the times. He will not delay much longer, and we should be coming in droves to the kingdom; and we should come in rejoicing for it is a wonderful place to be.

A veil or wall of flesh has protected our souls from eternal darkness, and it is our choice to choose the holy or the profane. When the wall comes down, only those wise souls who chose to enter into the temple will be saved from God's wrath at the end of the world. Which side of the wall are you on? You can't straddle this fence any longer. You must get on one side or the other, and then after you leap over the wall, you must come into the temple. The temple is the place to be when the walls come tumbling down. This is where the counting of time ends on earth and everyone found worthy is established forever in heaven.

The temple is Jesus. Jesus is the door of the kingdom. To enter we must be born into the Spirit, because the kingdom is a spiritual place with spiritual beings. Just as we are spiritual beings that have been born into the world of darkness in the body of flesh, we must understand that the flesh is temporary until we return to our spirit. We are the ones who must choose the place of our eternal abode. Everyone knows that the flesh dies, and anyone who is conscious must be aware of his inner man. Our inner man is the soul and it is directed either by the flesh or the spirit.

As we grow up in this world and are trained in the way of the world, we are contaminated by the world and its sin. We know that Jesus died to deliver us from that sin, so that we can be reconciled with God. However, as long as we only use our worldly knowledge to determine our fate, we will always be convinced by the ruler of darkness of this world that we are unworthy. He spends his time convincing God's children that they are not worthy of God. The devil's mission is to destroy God's creation.

Do not let being found unworthy stop you in your spiritual growth. The old trick of the devil that seeks to kill and destroy mankind is to trap us in shame and feelings of unworthiness. And, of course, if we live in the world of the flesh and follow the god of this world, Satan, who was cast down and given dominion over this place, we won't be worthy!

We can never become worthy by our own merit. That is why God came down to earth, His word made flesh in the person of Jesus. He came to die for our sins and He became the sacrifice that we can't make, because we came into this world with the stain of sin. Jesus came from above, holy and divine and without sin. He is the Lamb of God, the only acceptable sacrifice. We cannot make a sacrifice for our sins. We must accept the forgiveness that Jesus won for us, because we can't do it! That is impossible. When we are born again, we give up this sinful fleshly life, and we become like Him.

We are born again or awakened into His kingdom of Spirit and life. Satan no longer rules us, but we are led by the Holy Spirit of God. It is a different life and it is not hard because Jesus did it for us. It is only for us to believe and accept Him as our Savior.

How can I explain it? It is like turning from left to right, front to back, as I explained in my first book. It is also like being turned inside out! There is a noticeable difference and there is a change! Now, instead of trying to satisfy ourselves from the outside in, we are fulfilled from the inside out! We discover that money and material objects are no longer our gods that rule and dictate how we should behave, and which we have learned to depend on in the world for our survival. We become richer than worldly rich. We become spiritually rich.

The things that God provides for us are established in the spiritual realm, and then manifested in the physical realm. Prosperity as described by God comes from trust and belief in Him as our Father and provider. He will not make you physically rich before He first makes you spiritually rich. God's riches can be manifested into the physical realm; however, there is a great difference in God's riches and the world's riches.

God's riches won't cause you to bow down to false gods. God's way of prosperity is completely opposite of the world's way. The world teaches greed – the spirit teaches giving. There is a different rule that comes with the two riches. The riches of the world can separate us from the love and trust of God, whereas the prosperity of God will delight our soul.

Worldly prosperity is usually the manifestation of wealth based on our physical ability to produce it. The world is not usually generous to us. We learn to eke out a living from this world, and thus we become greedy to hold on to what we have worked so hard for. In this vicious circle we are led and taught by the world's ruler and deceiver, and we end up making these material gains our gods. The job, the money, the home, the jewelry, the car, and all the things we worked so hard for in this world become the things that we pay homage to. The cunning deceiver has subtly changed our allegiance from God to material things. We don't even recognize it, until or unless we fall on hard times and we lose these things.

It is so painful for us to lose worldly things. This pain is caused by the fact that the flesh rules us and, thus, these things have become first place in our life – before God. I know most of you don't believe this, but if ever you go through a loss and you find it to be an excruciatingly painful experience, take heed, or you won't even understand that it was because you made these temporary worldly things into gods!

On the other hand, if God is truly where your allegiance lies, you won't suffer loss because you will have divine protection. There are two worlds and we are caught up in the flesh with the ability to choose. The world certainly has a tempting way of leading us in that direction, but a decision to choose Jesus Christ as our Savior will turn us around in the right direction.

Do not be fooled, the television evangelists are currently preaching on change. You can accept Jesus as your Savior, and believe that God is first place in your life, but if you do not make a conscious decision to change, you may never experience kingdom living. You may decide to continue in the ways of the world, straddling that fence. Those who don't go over the wall and come into the temple will sadly hear these words: "Depart from me – I do not know you".

Jesus told us that we must have eyes to see and perceive, and ears to hear and understand.

JESUS NAMES HIS WITNESSES

"If I bear witness concerning myself, my witness is not true. There is another who bears witness concerning me, and I know that the witness that he bears concerning me is true. You have sent to **John***, and he has borne witness to the truth. I, however, do not receive the witness of man, but I say these things that you may be saved. He was the lamp, burning and shining; and you desired to rejoice for a while in his light.*

"The witness, however, that I have is greater than that of John. For the **works** *which the Father has given me to accomplish, these very works that I do bear witness to me, that the Father has sent me. And the* **Father** *himself, who has sent me, has borne witness to me. But you have never heard his voice, or seen his face. And you have not his word abiding in you, since you do not believe him whom he has sent. You search the* **Scriptures***, because in them you think that you have life everlasting. And it is they that bear witness to me, yet you are not willing to come to me that you may have life.*

"I do not receive glory from men. But I know that you have not the love of God in you. I have come in the name of my Father, and you do not receive me. If another comes in his own name, him you will receive. How can you believe who receive glory from one another, and do not seek the glory which is from the only God? Do not think that I shall accuse you to the Father. There is one who accuses you, **Moses,** *in whom you hope. For if you believed Moses you would believe me also, for he wrote of me. But if you do not believe his writings, how will believe my words?"*

St. John 5: 31-47

Jesus named as witnesses: John and Moses, as well as His works, The Father and The Scriptures.

CHAPTER 8

THE TWO WITNESSES

The scripture about the courtyard that was discussed in the previous chapter is appropriate to continue in this chapter. First, I provide two scriptures about witnesses as a prelude to the information that I am about to share with you from my own personal revelation about the witnesses of Jesus.

> *And I will grant unto my two witnesses to prophesy for a thousand two hundred and sixty days, clothed in sackcloth."*
> Apocalypse/Revelations Chapter 11: 3

> *Behold, this is the third time that I am coming to you: "On the word of two or three witnesses every word shall be confirmed."*
>
> 2 Corinthians 13:1

These scriptures teach that two or three witnesses will always confirm God's word. I have had wonderful revelations about the witnesses of God's word. The word, of course, was made flesh and dwelt among us. The word of God is Jesus. So Jesus as God's Word will be confirmed by two or three witnesses. As I studied the scriptures, I found the witnesses and the story is a wondrous adventure from witnesses in heaven to witnesses on earth.

In St. Matthew we find the account of Jesus being transfigured on the mountain where he took 3 friends, Peter, James and his brother John. When he was transfigured before them, his garments became white as snow and his face shone as the sun, and behold there appeared to them Moses and Elias talking together with him.[1] It is also written in this account that Jesus said to them:

> *"Elias indeed is to come and will restore all things. But I say to you that Elias has come already and they did not know him, but did to him whatever they wished. So also shall the Son of Man suffer at their hands."*

Then the disciples understood that he had spoken to them of John the Baptist.[2]

I shared the above scriptural information in preparation of some new ideas that I have discovered from my studies and would like to share with my readers. While reading the story of Daniel and his three friends, I discovered this story establishes and witnesses to my personal revelation that Jesus was Abel. I addressed this belief about Abel and discussed the sources of this belief

---

[1] Matthew 17: 3
[2] Matthew 17: 12-13

in greater detail in my book, *Way Beyond the River*. However, as I was reading the Book of Daniel for the umpteenth time, I had this marvelous revelation that this was more than a story about Daniel and his friends; it was symbolic of the story of Jesus and Abel. This book gave more credence to my belief that Abel was the Son of God who returned to earth as Jesus. The story of Daniel is presented, so that I may discuss in depth the revelation that came to me as I read this portion of the book.

THE STORY OF DANIEL

The king told his chief chamberlain to bring in some of the Israelites of royal blood and of the nobility, young men without any defect, handsome, intelligent and wise, quick to learn and prudent in judgment, such as could take their place in the king's palace; they were to be taught the language and literature of the Chaldeans; after three years training they were to enter the king's service. [3]

Among these men of Juda: Daniel, Anania, Misael and Azaria. The chief chamberlain changed their names: [4]

NAME	NEW NAME
Daniel	Baltassar
Anania	Sidrach
Misael	Misach
Azaria	Abednego

---

[3] Daniel 1: 3-5
[4] Daniel 1: 7

CONTINUING FROM THE STORY OF DANIEL

To these four young men God gave knowledge and proficiency in all literature and science, and to Daniel the understanding of all visions and dreams. At the end of the time the king had specified for their preparation, the chief chamberlain brought them before Nabuchodonosor. When the king had spoken with all of them, none was found equal to Daniel, Anania, Misael, and Azaria; and so they entered the king's service.[5]

EXCERPTS FROM THE STORY

To Daniel the king said, "Truly your God is the God of gods and Lord of kings and a revealer of mysteries; that is why you were able to reveal this mystery." He advanced Daniel to a high post . . . made him ruler of the whole province of Babylon. At Daniel's request the king made Sidrach, Misach and Abednego administrators of the province of Babylon, while Daniel himself remained at the king's court.[6]

Daniel gave the king the interpretation and by order of King Belsassar: 'they clothed Daniel in purple, with a gold collar about his neck, and proclaimed him third in the government of the kingdom'.[7]

This concludes the story portion of Daniel. Now, I would like to share my revelation of Abel being Jesus, along with some other revelations of persons in the Bible who, I believe, had their names changed and were brought into the king's service.

---

[5] Daniel 1: 17-20
[6] Daniel 2: 46-49
[7] Daniel 5: 29-30

As Daniel was named "third" in the government of the kingdom, I realized this was significant of the fact that Abel was the third man in the history of God's creation of the world. There were Adam, then Cain and thirdly, there was Abel. I believe being named "third" is significant of both Abel and Jesus. Abel was the third man on earth, and Jesus is the third person of God in the Holy Trinity. Cain murdered Abel, and I believe God raised Abel up to heaven. I base this belief on my interpretation of Psalm 18. To me this Psalm describes Abel calling out for help.

> *The breakers of death surged round about me . . . In my distress I called upon the Lord and cried out to my God; from his temple he heard my voice, and my cry to him reached his ears. The earth swayed and quaked; . . . He mounted a cherub and flew . . . He reached out from on high and grasped me; he drew me out of the deep waters. He rescued me from my mighty enemy and from my foes who were too powerful for me. They attacked me in the day of my calamity, but the Lord came to my support. He set me free in the open, and rescued me, because he loves me. The Lord rewarded me according to my justice. . . . you indeed, O Lord, give light to my lamp; O my God you brighten the darkness about me, for with your aid I run against an armed band, and by the help of my God I leap over a wall. The God who girded me with strength . . . . who trained my hands for war and my arms to bend a bow of brass. You have stooped to make me great. . . . you made me head over nations . . . Therefore will I proclaim you, O Lord, among the nations, and I will sing praise to your name, you who gave great victories to your king and showed kindness to your anointed . . .*
>
> Psalm 18

The story of Daniel is a similitude of the story of Abel, and I have a good idea who his friends were. There are only two persons in the Bible who were taken from the earth and brought into the kingdom of heaven.

The first was Enoch of whom it is testified that he pleased God and was taken to heaven.[8]

The second would be, of course, Elias who was seen taken to heaven in a fiery chariot.[9]

Now, let's compare the story of Abel to the story of Daniel. Paraphrasing from above, and changing the characters, the story would go like this:

God, told the Holy Spirit to bring in some of the Israelites of royal blood and of the nobility, young men without any defect, handsome, intelligent and wise, quick to learn and prudent in judgment, such as could take their place in the king's palace; they were to be taught the language and literature of the heavenly hosts; after three years training they were to enter the king's service.

I believe that God first raised up Abel and then brought in Enoch and Elias to be trained as witnesses to the Son of God.

Likewise, just as Daniel and his friends had their names changed by the king, I believe Abel and his friends have also been given new names. The symbolism of the changed names is to denote a change from physical status to spiritual status. These are the names I believe were given them:

---

[8] Genesis 5: 23
[9] 4 Kings 3: 11

NAME	NEW NAME
Abel	Jesus
Enoch	Moses
Elias	John the Baptist

Continuing with the story:

God gave knowledge and proficiency in all literature and science, and to Abel the understanding of all visions and dreams. At the end of the time God had specified for their preparation, the Holy Spirit brought them before God. When God had spoken with all of them, none was found equal to Abel, Enoch, and Elias; and so they entered the king's service.

He advanced Abel to a high post and made him ruler of the whole world. At Abel's request the king made Enoch and Elias administrators of the His province, while Abel himself remained at the king's court.

Abel was clothed in purple, with a gold collar about his neck, and proclaimed third in the government of the kingdom.

You can see how this story is remarkable in telling how Jesus became our Lord and Savior. He was created by God's word when He spoke to Eve. Abel was truly the Son of God, and the Son of Man.

It just makes so much sense to know that our Savior was a man born both of the flesh and of the spirit. When he came as Jesus, he was born in the spirit and the flesh, coming down from heaven. My belief that Jesus was trained in heaven as Abel and then sent back to earth as Jesus is further testified to in the following scriptures:

> *"Behold, I come — (in the head of the book it is written of me) — to do thy will, O God."*
> Hebrews 10: 7
> *. . . and to Jesus, mediator of a new covenant, and to a sprinkling of blood which speaks better than Abel. See that you do not refuse him who speaks.*
> Hebrews 12: 24
>
> *Who has gone up to heaven and come down again — who has cupped the wind in his hands? . . . What is his name, what is his son's name if you know it?*
> Proverbs 30: 3-5

Beyond all imagination, the story of Daniel gives us insight to understand why Jesus was seen talking with His friends, Moses and Elias, when he was transfigured. Jesus also took with Him three friends who witnessed this spiritual vision.

I believe that Enoch and Elias were the friends that helped in the administration of this kingdom.

The Lost Books tell us that Enoch was given to write many books by God when he was taken up to heaven, and that he was able to give them to his children before departing forever to heaven. So who could have been better trained than Enoch to be sent to earth with the new name of Moses to whom it is attributed that he wrote the Pentateuch — the first five books of the Bible! It is even testified about Moses in scripture that "she named him Moses because she drew him out of the water".[10]

---

[10] Exodus 2: 10

Water is significant of spirit, and Moses was truly drawn out of the spirit into this world for God's purpose. It is also written of Moses that "He even drew water for us and watered the flock!"[11] Jesus called his followers his flock, and if Moses was watering God's chosen people, I believe he was imparting spiritual knowledge to them.

Of Elias the scriptures testify: *"Lo, I will send you Elias, the prophet, before the day of the Lord comes . . .".*[12]

It is further testified of Elias that he had a double spirit.[13]

I make note of the importance of Elias' double spirit, as I remind the reader that Jesus revealed to His disciples that John the Baptist was also Elias.[14] This testimony of Elias having a double spirit is significant for this reason. His spirit that re-appeared on earth as John the Baptist suffered death on earth. However, John the Baptist was just one of the spirits of Elias. Elias, himself, must return and suffer death in the earth.

I believe that Abel was taken up to heaven by God, and came back to earth as Jesus who was crucified.

I also believe that Moses was taken up to God, for it is written in the scriptures that:

"no one knows the place of his burial"[15] , and that

" . . . Michael the archangel was fiercely disputing with the devil about the body of Moses . . . ".[16]

---

[11] Exodus 2: 19
[12] Malachia 3: 23
[13] 4 Kings 2: 9
[14] Matthew 17: 13
[15] Deuteronomy 3:6
[16] St. Jude 1: 9

Therefore, according to my theory, it is necessary for Moses and Elias, who have not died in the earth, to return and die here.

The good news is that it is written that they will come again just ahead of the return of Jesus as King of Kings and Lord of Lords at the end times!

> *And I will grant unto my two witnesses to prophesy for a thousand two hundred and sixty days, clothed in sackcloth."* *These are the two olive trees and the two lamp-stands that stand before the Lord of the earth. And if anyone desires to harm them, fire will come out of their mouths, and will devour their enemies. And if anyone desires to injure them, he must in this manner be killed. These have power to shut heaven, so that it will not rain during the days of their prophesying; and they have power over the waters to turn them into blood . . . "*

Apocalypse/Revelations 11: 3-6

This scripture describes one witness as having power over the waters to turn them into blood. Remember Moses turned the water to blood when Pharaoh wouldn't let his people go. [17]

The other witness is said to have the power to shut heaven so that it will not rain during the days of their prophesying. Elias was the prophet in the Old Testament who stopped the rain for three years.[18]

---

[17] Exodus 7: 18-21
[18] 3 Kings 17: 1 and Ch. 18: 45

These are the powers that were given to Moses and Elias, and so we can understand that they are the two prophets who will come.

I also believe that they must return in order to die on the earth, for they have never died since being taken to heaven.

Remember we learned that Elias had a double spirit, and I have concluded that John the Baptist was Elias, for Jesus explained this to His disciples. Let me share some interesting scriptures about John the Baptist and Elias that explains other similarities they shared.

> *What manner of man was he who met you, and spoke these words? But they said: A hairy man with a girdle of leather about his loins. And he said: It is Elias the Thesbite.*
> 4 Kings 1: 7-8

> *But John himself had a garment of camel's hair and a leathern girdle about his loins . . .*
> Matthew 3: 4

John the Baptist was beheaded when Jesus was on earth. The scriptures testify that the *two witnesses* to come in the end times will also be killed. These are the witnesses I believe to be Elias and Moses.

> - : *And when they have finished their testimony, the beast that comes up out of the abyss will wage war against them, and will conquer them and will kill them.*
> Apocalypse/Revelations 11: 7

It is a wonderful revelation if you can accept it. And if you can't, it won't make any difference in the salvation story of Jesus. I just was so amazed by the turn of these events, that I couldn't help but share it.

We will all know all the truth when we get to heaven. God's ways are higher than our ways, and His thoughts are higher than our thoughts.[19] The more I study God's word, the more amazing things I learn.

My belief about these men of God being taken up to heaven and being returned to the earth is not at all a theory of reincarnation. If anything, this story negates and nullifies such a theory. The knowledge that I have learned about these men proves only that what is born of flesh must die of flesh.

The spirits that were taken to heaven had a wonderful, miraculous walk with God; however, they like all men suffered death, once and for all, before entering into eternity.

> *The visionary experience is one we all need if we are to fulfill our potential in God's plan. How shall we ever get through our Good Fridays if we are not buoyed up by the occasional vision of our own particular destiny in God? It must be a vision detached from the misfortunes and fortunes of life - for if we try to set up tents for our souls in the material world, the vision vanishes!"*
>
> - Jeane Dixon
> - The Call to Glory

---

[19] Isaiah 55:8-9. "For my thoughts are not your thoughts, neither are your ways my ways," declares the Lord. "As the heavens are higher than the earth, so are my ways higher than your ways and my thoughts than your thoughts."

CHAPTER 9

SIGNIFICANCE OF THE THIRD DAY

I wondered why the third day is mentioned in so many ways in the Bible. Whenever a passage of scripture stops me and grabs my attention, I have learned that God, through His Holy Spirit, is going to teach me something – if I listen and pay attention.

As I was reading a passage in the Gospel of John about the marriage feast at Cana, the fact that it took place on the third day seemed to stand apart. This was written at the beginning of this particular passage of scripture, so there hadn't been any discussion about a couple of days before to conclude that this party was now happening on the third day. The third day from what, I wondered.

Reading on I noted that the mother of Jesus was there. And the next sentence began with "Now Jesus too was invited to the marriage, and also his disciples."

Chapter IX – Significance of the Third Day

It seems *"Now"* must be important in that it was the third day and Jesus too was invited to the marriage along with his disciples. So, what had made it possible for Jesus and his disciples to come on this particular day, as opposed to any other day?

There must be a significant connotation about this third day, and I was going to learn about it. Let's look at the significance of the number three in the Bible. First, and foremost we know that God is in three persons, Father, Son and Holy Ghost. Another example of three came to my mind. We are composed of spirit, soul and body.

The third day, of course, is important to the Christian churches, for that is the day that Jesus rose from the dead, according to the scriptures. When Jesus was asked by the Pharisees to give them a sign, he replied that even as Jonas was in the belly of the fish three days and three nights, so will the Son of Man be three days and three nights in the heart of the earth. Here, again, Jesus was referring to his death on the cross and his resurrection on the third day.

My thoughts went all the way back to the beginning where God spoke to the serpent after he had deceived Eve in the garden, the prophetic words that a Savior would one day come to defeat the devil. He spoke to that serpent saying, "I will put enmity between you and the woman, between your seed and her seed; he shall crush your head, and you shall lie in wait for his heel."[20]

I have written earlier that my revelation in reading the Bible was that Jesus was Abel. My whole belief went back to these words of God, spoken right after the fall of man from paradise. Since, God creates with His word, it came to me that while he was speaking to the serpent, He placed the seed in Eve at the same time. And all the while the serpent was tricked into believing that God was only

---

[20] Genesis 3: 15

speaking to him. So, when God said he shall crush your head and you shall like in wait for his heel, the devil thought he was talking to him. But, to his downfall the devil missed the whole point from the very beginning. God spoke His word and placed that word in Eve. That seed was the word that would become flesh, the Son of God who would triumph over the devil.

I believe that Abel was the word of God made flesh the first time. I also believe that when Abel was killed by his brother, God raised him up to heaven in His spirit, and this was significant of the first resurrection. Abel being raised into heaven won the first victory over spiritual death.

Remember we are made up of body, soul and spirit, so there was the first victory to re-claim what the devil had stolen. He stole our spirit and it was left powerless and in darkness. We cannot live in heaven unless we are pure and holy.

God was on the move to restore us to our original state. He created us in His image and the light went out when Adam submitted to the devil, giving him the dominion over the earth and taking mankind into captivity. Adam had the dominion, but he gave it over to Satan. Now, God in His power and might must reclaim and restore mankind. This was no easy or ordinary task, but nothing is impossible with God! To Him be glory and praise forever.

The significance of the third day is becoming so clear. God has overcome the first death by His own Son whom He resurrected. Now, by that same Son, He has the plan in place to reclaim our souls.

He sent His Son who had been trained in heaven to bend the bars of brass and break the gates of iron. These bars and gates formed the prison that held the souls of men, and Satan had the keys. At least he did, until Jesus appeared again on earth. Here we see the fulfillment of those original words that God spoke to His Son who was in Eve's womb, and the devil thought God was speaking these words to him. The prophetic words being, "he shall crush your head, and you shall lie in wait for his heel."

All this time Satan was watching for the seed of God to crush his head as he lied in wait for his heel. The devil believed this because, first he was a serpent and his head was at heel level; and secondly, because he never knew that God had directed those words to someone else. That someone else was His Son. Satan was not unaware that Abel and Jesus was the Son of God, and Satan was ever in wait to destroy him. As spoken by God, Satan crushed Abel's head and murdered him through his seed, Cain. Smugly, Satan thought he had turned the tables on God, saving his own head. Stupidly, however he was fulfilling God's prophecy and plan.

When Jesus came into the world, Satan recognized Him again as the Son of God, and again plotted the death of our Lord. The scriptures confirm the words God spoke to the serpent and Eve about His Son.

Christ . . . having slain the enmity in himself.

Ephesians 3:14

He who eats bread with me has lifted up his heel against me.

John 13:19

God made a way for man to return to the Garden and His plan was perfect. It is continuing to be fulfilled this very day as we await the final and last return of Our Savior.

Just like the marriage at Cana happened on the third day, so will the final victory of Our Lord happen on the third day of His victories. The third day is significant of the final victory over the flesh, when our bodies will be glorified and brought to the marriage celebration that will go on for eternity as we are reunited with our God and Father in heaven.

We can enjoy a victorious life now as we await the final outcome. Jesus has given us the power to become children of the living God. The formula is easy enough; we just have to believe in Him.

When we believe in Jesus, the Holy Spirit of God comes to live in our heart which is representative of our spirit man, and Jesus comes and abides with us in our soul described as our mind. Now, we have the heart and mind of Christ, and we can enjoy the two victories accomplished by God through His only-begotten Son. Abel overcame spiritual death and Jesus redeemed our souls.

We are a three part being created in God's image. Therefore, God put into effect a most wonderful and mysterious plan to bring us back whole in body, soul and spirit.

The first victory was that of bringing Abel into the kingdom in spirit after Cain murdered him. Since Abel was the seed of God, He was pure and able to be brought into heaven. As God reclaimed the spirit portion of man, I believe this enabled Him to establish spiritual communication with us to give us instruction and teach us of His promise of redemption.

Jesus was that promise, the Son of God, returned to the earth. Again, the purity of the Son of God was key to the victory. Jesus, the Son of God, allowed Himself to be crucified in the flesh and his soul separated from His Father as it was taken into hell where Satan kept the lost souls that had fallen into his power.

Satan thought he had overcome the Son of God, but oh what a surprise when that old devil discovered the Son was pure, not ever having been contaminated with sin.

Chapter IX – Significance of the Third Day

Jesus entered into that place of darkness in the fullness of God's glory and light. He had the victory!

In this valiant and remarkable sacrifice, Jesus entered into that prison of darkness where Satan had kept all the souls of men since Adam. And as it is written[21], by the one man's obedience the tables were turned! Christ came out of that pit in victory, and he brought up every soul that Satan had kept locked up since Adam's fall from grace. And this story gets even better because Jesus being the same person as Abel went into that prison and brought out his father, Adam!

Our spirits can be reborn when we believe in Him and His resurrection. Jesus told us to believe in Him, and be reborn. When our spirits are born again into the light, our soul that has been held captive in darkness is set free!

At last I understand the significance of the third day and the marriage. The third day is when Jesus will bring the saints into heaven for the 1000 year reign and the marriage represents our spiritual union with Christ.

---

[21] Romans 5: 19: For just as by the disobedience of the one man the many were constituted sinners, so also by the obedience of the one the many will be constituted just.

CHAPTER 10

THE STORY OF EVE

One of the thoughts that I have brushed aside for too long is the story about Eve. I have heard evangelists teach that Adam committed high treason because God had instructed him not to eat the forbidden fruit, and Eve was not present at that time. So, while Eve was deceived, Adam committed an act of treason by disobeying God's command. I write this in order to present the following opinion that I have formed from my studies.

Ever since it was revealed to me that Abel and Jesus were one and the same person, I have thought that it only made sense that Eve and Mary were one and the same person and Mother of God. Eve became the mother of Abel, and Mary brought forth Jesus.

Let's look at the scripture before I continue with the explanation of my theory.

> *Then the Lord God said to the serpent: "Because you have done this, cursed are you among all animals, and among all beasts of the field; on your belly shall you crawl, dust shall you eat, all the days of your life. I will put*

> *enmity between you and the woman, between your seed and her seed; he shall crush your head, and you shall lie in wait for his heel."*
>
> *To the woman he said: "I will make great your distress in childbearing; in pain shall you bring forth children; for your husband shall be your longing, though he have dominion over you."*

Genesis 3: 14-16

This scripture has held my interest since my first reading of the Bible, and continues to keep my interest as many times as I have re-read it. I have written that I believe God planted His seed when he spoke. The scriptures say God is speaking to the serpent, however, I have come to the conclusion that he tricked the serpent by changing the direction of His word to Eve when he concluded with "and he shall crush your head . . .". Here is where I believe He spoke to Abel and as He spoke He planted His seed.

It also is evident from this scripture that Satan has planted a seed, because God is discussing his seed and her seed. Cain and Abel were in the womb, planted in a spiritual manner, before she and Adam came out of the garden into the world of the flesh. The word of God was fulfilled when Cain crushed Abel's head. The rest of the sentence that God spoke to His seed, "you shall lie in wait for his heel", was to be fulfilled in Jesus when he was deceived by Judas at the Last Supper. Jesus spoke these very words, saying:

> *"but that the Scripture may be fulfilled, 'He who eats bread with me has lifted up his heel against me.'"*[22]

---

[22] St. John 13: 18

Further reference to Judas is made in a prayer Jesus prayed for his disciples whom He had kept safe, and his prayer included the following:

"... *and not one of them perished except the son of perdition, in order that the Scripture might be fulfilled.*"[23]

Cain and Abel were destined to battle over the loss of Adam's soul and the fall of mankind from the time Adam departed heaven with Eve. You might as well know that I also believe that just as God's seed is to come into the world three times to save our threefold being of body, soul and spirit; I also believe that Satan's seed comes each time to do battle with Him. There was Cain and Abel who battled over the spirit of the Son of God. Then Judas and Jesus came at the same time to do battle over the soul. It is written that our Savior comes the third time as follows:

And I saw heaven standing open; and behold, a white horse, and he who sat upon it is called Faithful and True, and with justice he judges and wages war. And his eyes are as a flame of fire, and on his head are many diadems; he has a name written which no man knows except himself. And he is clothed in a garment sprinkled with blood, and his name is called The Word of God. And the armies of heaven, clothed in fine linen, white and pure, were following him on white horses.
And from his mouth goes forth a sharp sword with which to smite the nations. And he will rule them with a **rod of iron**, *and . . .*
And I saw the beast, and the kings of the earth and their armies gathered together to wage war against him who was

---

[23] St. John 17: 12

sitting upon the horse and against his army. And the beast was seized, and with it the false prophet who did signs before it wherewith he deceived those who accepted the mark of the beast and who worshipped its image. **These two** *were cast alive into the pool of fire . . .*

Apocalypse 19:11-21

These two, as written in the scripture above, are from Satan and are the opposites of Jesus and the Holy Spirit of God. Everything about Satan is the complete opposite of God. Just as God sent us His Word, Jesus, and His Holy Spirit; Satan sent the beast, his spirit, and the false prophet, his seed. This may be confusing to the reader, so I will try to explain in more simple detail. There is God, The Holy Spirit and the Son of God in the kingdom of light. Then there is Satan, the beast and the false prophet in the kingdom of darkness.

According to my understanding from studying the Bible, I believe that the Son of God appeared on the earth two times, and that the son of Satan also appeared each time to oppose Him. The Son of God won each victory. The battle of Armageddon is the final battle between these two and in that battle the beast along with the false prophet are overcome and thrown into the pool of fire.

This third time is significant of the marriage at Cana, because the saints will be brought into heaven with Our Lord, and will reign a thousand years with Him. During this thousand-year reign, it is further written that Satan, the ancient serpent, will be bound for a thousand years.[24]

I love the ending to this story, because when Satan is loosed at the end of the thousand years, he deceives the nations and gathers them together for the battle. And here the justice of God is revealed as it is written:

---

[24] Revelations/Apocalypse 20: 1-3

> *"And fire from God came down out of heaven and devoured them. And the devil who deceived them was cast into the pool of fire and brimstone, where are also the beast and the false prophet, and they will be tormented day and night forever and ever."*[25] *This is such an exciting end to the battle for our redemption, because God is the one who destroys Satan with the final blow! It is finished, it is over, and all who are found written in the Book of Life reign forever in heaven with God.*
>
> *Apocalypse 19: 910*

Well, I went a long way around the block to get back to the story of Eve. It seems that once I decided to write her story that the other pieces all fell into place. The story unfolded and the mystery was solved. Let me now tell the rest of the story of the Mother of God.

Eve did not disobey God's command, so the sin of Adam's disobedience did not contaminate her. She remained pure. I believe that is how God was able to bring His Word into the world untainted by the sin of the world. It was God's seed planted in the woman of purity that God used to preserve and restore man to the kingdom of heaven. I know that she came out of the garden with Adam because it is written in the scriptures that Adam had dominion over her.

> *To the woman he said: "I will make great your distress in childbearing; in pain shall you bring forth children; for your husband shall be your longing, though he have dominion over you."*
>
> *Genesis 3:16*

---

[25] Revelations/Apocalypse 20: 7-10

The scripture above has plagued my curiosity for ten years, and now I finally understand the words, *"for your husband shall be your longing"*. I have studied and studied about this longing of Eve for her husband. And, as I began writing about Eve and Mary, the answer came and it thrills my soul to understand at long last what meaning this scripture held.

First, of course, I looked up the word longing and that took me to the word yearn. The word yearn had a meaning of pity. Then, as I prayed and mediated about this scripture as I was unfolding the store of Mary and Eve, the answer came. Thank you, Jesus. You see, Eve pitied her husband because he had fallen out of God's grace. She had not. Look at the scripture of the angel addressing Mary that goes to the heart of this belief.

And when the angel had come to her, he said, "Hail, full of grace, the Lord is with thee. Blessed are thou among women."

Luke 1:28

Of course, you must remember that I consider Eve and Mary to be one and the same. And here is testimony to her status of grace. While Eve came out of the garden with Adam, she pitied him. Further, when Adam died his soul would have been kept in prison, while Eve being pure, never died! She never had to die in the earth, because she never lost the status that she had in heaven!

Eve was returned to heaven, where she remained until God sent her back as Mary, to conceive the Christ child! The belief in the Assumption of Mary that she was taken up to heaven, is the only thing that could have happened to her. She never had to die! She was taken up again on those eagle's wings to heaven.

So, as we read in the scriptures earlier about the marriage feast at Cana that took place on the third day, and the Mother of Jesus was there. It makes so much more sense now that I have such a vivid understanding of it. Of course, the Mother of Jesus was there. She never lost her right to be in heaven.

Not only did Eve bring forth Abel, it is written in Genesis Ch. 5: 3, that Adam *"became the father of a son in his own likeness, after his image, and he called him Seth."* You see, she also was the mother of the human race from which the chosen people descended. The testimony that Seth was in Adam's own likeness only confirms that the other two children were not. And, of course, they were not! They were in the image of God and Satan. Let's look at a scripture that sheds more light onto this situation.

In the same Book of Genesis, is the following vivid account of the birth of twins to the wife of Isaac, the son of Abraham:

> *. . . Rebecca conceived. The children jostled each other within her, and she said, "If this be so, why am I pregnant?" Then, she went to consult the Lord. He said to her, "Two nations are in your womb; two peoples shall stem from your body. One people shall be stronger than the other, and the elder shall serve the younger."*
>
> Gen. 25:21-28

This scripture speaks directly to the situation that Eve experienced when she gave birth to Cain and Abel. And, indeed, the elder shall serve the younger, for He is the Son of God! The description of the twins representing two peoples or nations also seems to coincide with Cain and Abel. Cain was the serpent's seed stemming from the empire of darkness ruled by Satan, while Abel was God's seed who would reign in the kingdom of light ruled by God. The battle between the two began in the womb.

Chapter X – The Story of Eve

The conclusion will be the battle of Armageddon!

Let's look at some more of the scripture in this chapter that witnesses to my conclusion that Eve is Mary.

"And the man called his wife, Eve because she was the mother of all the living."
Genesis 4:20

God said "Indeed! The man has become like one of us, knowing good and evil! And now perhaps he will put forth his hand and take also from the tree of life and eat, and live forever"! Therefore the Lord God put him out of the Garden of Eden to till the ground from which he was taken. He drove out the man; and at the east of the Garden of Eden he placed the Cherubim, and the flaming sword, which turned every way, to guard the way to the tree of life.
Genesis 4:21

In the footnotes of my Bible, it states that this passage about Eve being the mother of all the living must be misplaced, and suggests that this passage probably belongs in Chapter 4.

I think the passage is placed perfectly, because I believe that God planted His Word in Chapter 3 verse 15 where he spoke about her seed and the serpent's seed. This passage confirms that Eve was pregnant with the Son of God, before she came out of the garden.

And, as you read verse 21 above, it is evident that God was only concerned about driving the man out of the garden who had been contaminated, before he ate of the tree of life and lived in this condition forever! Since man had fallen out of grace and become contaminated with the impurity of the sin of disobedience, he was immediately cut off from God and heaven. Nothing impure could be contained in God's kingdom of light. That is why Adam had to be put out of the garden. God didn't seem to be concerned about Eve's condition. That further confirms my belief that Eve was pure and uncontaminated by the sin of disobedience that brought Adam under the jurisdiction of Satan.

Since it is my belief that Abel was the Son of God who returned as Jesus and will come again with a new name, it follows that the Mother of God, first being Eve who was not contaminated by the original sin, would be the same woman that would come as Mary to bring forth the child, Jesus. Jesus came into the world as the Word made flesh. I believe that Abel and Eve were taken up to heaven by God since they were able to enter by reason of their purity. The following scripture seems to confirm this idea about Jesus.

> *And no one has ascended into heaven except him who has descended from heaven: The Son of Man who is in heaven.*
>
> John 3:13

This scripture describes Jesus formerly Abel, the one who ascended into heaven after being murdered by his brother. Only Abel could have descended from heaven, being called the *"Son of Man who is in heaven"*. Abel was born in the earth to a man and woman, but He was the seed of God who was raised up in the spirit and brought to heaven with a perfect and pure soul. God brought Abel into heaven and trained him for the future victories He had planned to reclaim the souls of men and to restore us to our glorified bodies.

Since Eve would have been pure, I believe God returned her to heaven after the death of Adam. She could return since she was pure and untainted from the original sin in the Garden of Eden.

It follows then, that God returned her to the earth with a new name, Mary, and this time she conceived by the Holy Spirit of God and brought forth the Son of God. Jesus is called the Son of Man and the Son of God.

It just makes sense that the Word of God that was made flesh and called the Son of Man and the Son of God, being the same person, was also the same person who was called both Abel and Jesus. God raised Abel up in victory over spiritual death, and again, raised up Jesus in victory for the repossession of the souls of mankind that had been imprisoned by the original sin of Adam's disobedience that transferred man's dominion and control to Satan.

Satan never had a chance when Jesus came into hell to reclaim what belonged to God, because Jesus had never been tainted with sin. His soul had always been free, and that was how God was able to raise His spirit to heaven. The devil only saw Abel and Jesus as a man in the flesh. That stupid serpent didn't factor in the pure state of the soul and spirit of the Son of God and Son of Man.

The devil was tricked and duped into fulfilling God's plan to redeem mankind. Just as the serpent deceived Adam and Eve, he even deceived himself by his ignorant cunning in trying to destroy God's seed.

As I read earlier about the marriage feast at Cana, let's look at what was said in this scripture.

And on the third day a marriage took place at Cana of Galilee, and the mother of Jesus was there. Now, Jesus too was invited to the marriage, and also his disciples.

John 2:1

As I believe this third day marriage is significant of the third return of Our Lord to reclaim our bodies and bring us into heaven, I note that the mother of Jesus was already there. This is a future event, which means Eve, also named Mary in a later visit, was always with God in heaven. She is there now waiting for the marriage when Jesus will "now" at that time bring his disciples. Yes, everyone who believed in Jesus will be at this marriage. My point being that Mary was there, has been there, and is still there. Mary and Eve are one and the same, the mother of Jesus and the mother of Abel. The next time Jesus comes, He won't be born, but we will see Him coming on the clouds. That is because He has already been born twice in the earth, winning the soul and the spirit for mankind. His body has already been glorified and is in heaven. He is coming back in victory to glorify all of His saints and bring them home.

I found another interesting scripture just a few lines down after the Cana marriage scriptures that seemed to bear witness to Mary being Eve.

> *∴ . . . the mother of Jesus said to Him , "They have no wine." And Jesus said to her, "What wouldst thou have me do, woman?"*
>
> St. John 2:4

Every time I have read this particular question, I thought it sounded almost rude – to call His mother *woman*. However, since I determined that I would write the story of Eve, this question stood out to me in a more important way. When Jesus called her *woman*, my mind immediately took me back to scripture in Genesis. What did Adam call Eve? I looked back in amazement and confirmation as I read the following scripture in Genesis.

> *And the rib which the Lord God took from the man, he made into a woman and brought her to him. Then the*

> *man said, "She now is bone of my bone and flesh of my flesh; she shall be called Woman, for from man she has been taken."* Gen. 1:22-23

No longer did Jesus' question seem rude when he called his mother, *woman*. On the contrary, He was calling her by the name given her by Adam. She was Eve, she was Mary, and she was the mother of God!
Another reference to the woman is made in the final chapter of the Bible

> *And a great sign appeared in heaven: a woman clothed with the sun, and the moon was under her feet, and upon her head a crown of twelve stars. And being with child, she cried out in her travail and was in the anguish of delivery. And another sign was seen in heaven, and behold, a great red dragon having seven heads and ten horns, and upon his heads seven diadems. And his tail was dragging along the third part of the stars of heaven, and it dashed them to the earth, and the dragon stood before the woman who was about to bring forth, that when she had brought forth he might devour her son. And she brought forth a male child, who is to rule all nations with a* **rod of iron**; *and her child was caught up to God and to his throne. And the woman fled into the wilderness, where she has a place prepared by God, that there they may nourish her a thousand two hundred and sixty days.*
> Apocalypse 12: 1-6

> *And when the dragon saw that he was cast down to the earth, he pursued the woman who had brought forth the male child. And there were given to the woman the two wings of the great eagle, that she might fly into the wilderness unto her place, where she is nourished for a time and times and a half time, away from the serpent. And the serpent cast out of his mouth after the woman water*

> *like a river that he might cause her to be carried away by the river. And the earth helped the woman, and the earth opened her mouth and swallowed up the river that the dragon had cast out of his mouth. And the dragon was angered at the woman and went away to wage war with the rest of her offspring who keep the commandments of God, and hold fast the testimony of Jesus. And he stood upon the sand of the sea.*
>
> Apocalypse 12: 18

These scriptures only intensify my belief that Eve brought forth Abel, the Son of God, *"who is to rule all nations with a rod of iron; and her child was caught up to God and to his throne. And the woman fled into the wilderness . . .*

Eve disappeared for a time, and I believe that was because God brought her back into heaven. Then, we read *again* that the dragon was angered over the woman who had given birth to the male child. I believe this refers to the birth of Jesus, and this scripture then describes the dragon going away from the woman angry to wage war with the rest of her *offspring who keep the commandments of God, and hold fast the testimony of Jesus.*

I had been putting off and avoiding writing about Eve and Mary, until out of the mouth of babes, I was convicted in my spirit to pay honor to the mother of God. I was told that my great-niece, Amanda, asked her daddy the following questions.

"Daddy, who is the mother of God?"

He replied, "Mary."

She then asked, "Then, why don't the churches do something about it?"

Chapter X – The Story of Eve

After hearing her questions, I knew it was time to write what I believed to be true about Mary, the mother of God. And, so I have.

CHAPTER 11

HOW TO DREAM

Hereafter they will not be restrained from anything which they determine to do.
                              Genesis 11:6

This verse comes from the story of the building of the tower of Babel. I always wondered why God confused their speech to prevent them from building a city and a tower with its top in the heavens and making a name for themselves. As I pondered over this, I understood that we can't build a stairway to heaven. There is only one way we can get there from here, and that is through Jesus. The other words in that scripture that are significant are that they wanted to make a name for themselves. Obviously, they weren't going to give God the glory for their accomplishment, and so God sent a confusing spirit to confuse their language and separate them.

However, right after all of this takes place, God says:

'Hereafter they will not be restrained from anything which they determine to do'.

I looked up the word determine and found the following descriptive words: resolve, purpose, aspiration, desire, zeal. God is telling us we can have what we desire. He further reveals that the way to achieve the desires of our heart is to zealously pursue and aspire to that thing which we desire.

Now, somewhere else it is written that God gives us the desire of our hearts. This can be interpreted two ways. One, we can understand it to mean that whatever we desire, God will give to us. Or, we can interpret it to mean that the actual desire or ambition is given to us by God. I think the second interpretation is the best, of course. So, where do we find these desires of our heart? This is where the usefulness of dreaming comes into focus. Let's look at some words that describe dream. Mental image, hope, goal, aim, purpose and the word purpose brings us to the word determination! Yes, it comes full circle to what God said we could have – anything we determine to do!

Now, dreaming is not doing. The rest of the message God gave us was that we had to determine to do it. It is wonderful to have a dream of success in an area that brings joy to our hearts. However, sitting around dreaming about what could be, will never bring the manifestation of the dream. A dream is a hope, and hope is a God given gift. God didn't create us in His image without instilling His own creativity into us. We each have a creative spirit and to create is to bring into being. God gave us the ability to give birth to our dreams. God instilled His creative spirit within us and the word, create, means to give birth to, and how does a birth come about?

You become pregnant and expectant. That is exactly how you bring your dreams into manifestation.

First you become pregnant with an idea and then hopeful and expectant to receive it. There you have it in a nutshell. Dreams are fulfilled through hope and expectation. Throw determination into the mix and you are on your way to experiencing the dream that God placed in your spirit.

God does give each of His children a gift or gifts. He is never stingy. God is generous, kind and loving. The dream He has for us is to have abundant life, health, peace and joy. These gifts are imparted by the Holy Spirit of God into our spirit.

I believe dreaming is very important. God has given us many examples in His word about dreams. He sent angels to Joseph to announce the birth of Jesus and direct Joseph to safety in dreams. Daniel dreamed and prophesied great events into the future. Joseph, the son of Isaac, dreamed and became the 3rd highest official in the kingdom of Egypt, and he saved the Israelites and the Egyptians from famine. God will give you a dream, but it is important to learn how to dream.

I learned how to dream from a friend. She tells her own Cinderella story and who doesn't love a Cinderella story? My friend was a walking, talking testimony of the Pretty Woman movie and the Cinderella story. I met my friend shortly after she had been widowed, and she would tell me wonderful stories about her husband, the prince who came into her life in a long sleek Cadillac rather than on a white charger. She left a small town and abusive husband and came to the city with a baby son and $25.00 in her purse. She worked two jobs on her feet day and night to take care of her precious son. One day her prince charming saw her and fell head over heels for the beautiful lady. He flew her to exotic places on his private plane. He lavished her in beautiful furs and diamonds and bought her a new Cadillac.

They dated for nearly ten years before they married, because she had another love in her life, her precious son. Not until he was grown did she marry her prince charming and then they flew off to Hawaii for a honeymoon. They traveled the world to Amsterdam, France, England and more places than I can remember. She rode on the Orient Express, kissed the Blarney stone, and lived extravagantly. Oh, how I loved to listen to the many stories she could tell about her life with this wonderful man. Besides living in the lap of luxury, she had a man that was brilliant, humorous, loving, kind, and respected. Life just didn't get any better than that. She, in return, adored her husband and lavished him with attention and care.

This was a love story that surpassed anything I had ever been able to imagine. Here is the very first clue to dreaming. We have to imagine! Yes, as I was listening to all of her wonderful stories, my imagination would draw pictures in my mind and these pictures took root somewhere in my spirit. I had a dream of a man that I could look up to and respect. My previous experiences with men were disastrous. I never had met a man that I could respect, and so love never seemed to last for me. I seemed to always be searching for that perfect relationship, but it always eluded me.

Guess what? I found the perfect husband after I dared to dream about a take charge man that you could really depend on. He was that man that I could respect and trust to take care of me. I had never allowed a man to take care of me, and never really understood what role a man played. I had lost my father at a young age, and really didn't think a man served any useful purpose other than to father children. But, as I listened to the love story that my friend unfolded for me, I imagined this man that had come into her life, and longed for my own hero and that kind of romance.

Only after I hoped, dreamed and imagined such a person, did he actually materialize in my life. I found him and I love him so much. He has taken me around the country, but not the world. He may not be as rich as prince charming, but my life is as rich with him. He has my utmost respect, and he is the strongest, smartest, most adventuresome man. My life has been rich with travel and luxuries that I never could provide myself. If you can imagine it, you can have it.

If you don't have a dream, find one. Read a book, meet someone who inspires you, look around and you will find your dream.

One word of warning, however. Do not look to the dream or the person to fulfill you. My dream man came only after I had found my own self-esteem and happiness from within through the cleansing blood of Jesus and the tearing down of strongholds. One can never find their happiness in someone else. Until we discover our own happiness and self-worth, no relationship or prince charming will ever fill that void.

We must tear down the walls and fall on our knees and cry out for the help of Jesus. He will hear, and he will provide a way back, even if we strayed a long way from the path. Remember, God's mercy and grace make it all possible, and we get to God through Jesus.

Everyone loves a Cinderella story, that rags to riches story, like Pretty Woman. The reason these stories are so popular is simple. Each of us has a spirit that knows we were created in the image of God. Living in the world and longing to be in paradise is a longing that is imbedded in the heart and soul of every human being. As we discover our spirituality by believing and trusting in Jesus, the door to opportunity will be thrown open for us. We can have our own Cinderella story. Jesus is the champion prince on the white horse who comes to save us! It isn't fiction, it is a true story. Each of us is waiting for our prince to rescue us, and when we believe in Jesus, the story becomes real. He takes us into His kingdom of paradise where we live happily ever after. As we believe in Jesus, we are born again, not of flesh and blood, but into an enlightened spirit that can dwell in the protection and light of God, enjoying all of His promises.

It is in the pursuit of the promises of God that we discover obstacles or "walls" that could be hindering our spiritual progress.

One example that I encountered was recognizing the negative feelings that I had about pettiness. We must be alert to negative factors in our life, for these are hindrances to kingdom living. An act of pettiness could send me into a rage of anger. Stinginess or a begrudging act just made my blood pressure boil.

I prayed about why this trait bothered me so, and I was surprised by the reality of the answer. We, as children of God, are petty when we refuse to allow God, who has unlimited resources, to help us and provide for us. It reminds me of the difference between a small town – big city expectation. Let me explain this concept.

I was having a discussion with a girl in a small town who was going to go to beauty college. I told her it takes some time to build up a good clientele, but that once you do that it can be very lucrative. I was thinking of my own daughter's successful career as a colorist in the city. This girl was thinking about a small town shop with friends and family for customers. We were looking at the difference between a few clients and several hundred clients.

That is what I meant by the difference between small town, big city expectations. We can only see as far as our eyes allow. She saw the number of people in the country, while I was looking at the number of people in the city.

Our expectations are so limited by what we see in the world. The difference between what we can do in this earth, and what God can provide is such a vast, vast chasm that it hit me like a ton of bricks. I'm trying to tell this girl to expect more than a few clients – and what do you think God is trying to tell us to expect! Clearly, we should be expecting more than our limited worldly vision allows! God is bigger than the country, the city and the world. He is bigger than a mortgage, a career, or a snappy sports car! He's bigger than our debt. He's bigger than our imaginations!

The meaning of my rage over pettiness turned in on me, as I discovered I was petty in what I allowed God to give me! This was quite a revelation, and another breakthrough. Another wall came down with this knowledge and insight.

This is why we should learn to dream, and expand our imaginations to include those things that are impossible to us, but possible to God! ALL THINGS ARE POSSIBLE WITH GOD.

This goes right to the heart of the very popular Prayer of Jabez, when he prays, "Oh that you would bless me indeed, and enlarge my territory". Hear our prayer Oh, Lord, enlarge our territory and enlarge our vision that we may see to receive the great things you have prepared for us.

THE PRAYER OF JABEZ

And Jabez called on the God of Israel saying,

"Oh that you would bless me indeed,
and enlarge my territory,
that Your hand would be with,
and that You would keep me from evil,
that I may not cause pain."

So, God granted him what he requested.

                                        1 Chronicles 4: 9

CONCLUSION

I began this book because God gave me a title. God also showed me the walls around some people that I have encountered. This book is written for more than one purpose, because much later into writing the book, God revealed to me the walls of the courtyard, which I found to be significant of the times. I believe the times and the seasons are quickly pointing to the return of our Lord.

Christians believe that the return of our Lord will signify the end of this world as we know it, and the final destiny of our souls. We will either reign with God forever in His love and glory, or be separated from Him and His love forever.

The times are urgent for bringing all God's children home. There is a twofold purpose in this book; one is to save souls and the other is to save them in time!

I pray this book will reach out to those souls that are barricaded inside prison walls that separate them from God, and guide them on their journey home through believing in Jesus.

You may be deceived into believing your soul is well, when it actually is hiding away sins or hurts and unforgiveness behind a wall. We should be alert to our thoughts and actions, making note of negative emotions and finding their source. We can't be perfect, because Jesus was the only perfect man. Therefore, we must not be too hard on ourselves if we need a little clean up and refreshing now and then.

We are not perfect and we cannot be perfect while we reside in the flesh. However we are worthy, and never, never let the devil bring upon you condemnation and unworthiness. We must be confident in the cleansing blood of Jesus, quick to repent of sin and wash it away with the blood. Then, when condemnation tries to sneak in, shake it off the way Paul shook off the viper that bit and hung onto his arm.

Be confident and know that we are children of the living God. We are worthy and no demon in hell can take that away, because Jesus secured it. A most important factor in the forgiveness process is to remember to forgive yourself!

Earlier in my studies, I discovered I had forgotten this very important part of the forgiveness process. After forgiving all the people who had hurt me, I was still trapped in the shame that I had allowed myself to be abused. It amazed me when I discovered this wall that had been hiding a shame of so long ago.

Fifteen plus years had passed since that time in my life, and I was happy and knew I had truly forgiven the abusive person in my heart, when another issue that had been troubling me caused me to do some deep soul searching. How very surprised I was to discover that I had not forgiven ME!

It was a very real obstacle, but it disappeared as soon as I discovered it, prayed for my own forgiveness and believed that I received it. It set me free!

Do some soul searching of your own, and when you ask the Holy Spirit to shine His light into that inner area of your life, you may begin to discover areas that need repair or healing. We can run, but we can not hide from the eye of God who sees into our hearts. We should strive to have a heart that pleases God. We are His children and He loves us, and God's love heals all wounds.

As we search our soul through prayer, fasting and meditation, we will be able to discover the walls and tear them down. These walls are the strongholds that the ruler of this world has used to imprison our souls.

Before we can tear down strongholds, we must first understand the meaning of stronghold. It is a fortified place, a fastness, dissoluteness. Fastness is a state of being fast. Fast is a naval term for mooring, rope or chain. Here is a good clue that a stronghold is a form of bondage.

Dissolute is loosed from restraint, especially loose in morals and conduct; debauched. Debauch is to corrupt and lead away from virtue. Now, we see that being in bondage, we think we are loose. According to these definitions, we are loose from moral restraint and turned in the opposite direction of virtue.

That old devil never learns any new tricks. He continues to lead us turned the wrong way and causes us to build a stronghold where he can contain us.

I thought it was interesting and appropriate that one definition of the stronghold was fastness, because this is a nautical term. This fastness is a mooring or chain that when attached to an anchor, stops movement. A ship is described as a vessel and so are we. A vessel travels through water, and since water represents the spirit, our spirit man is the vessel that God can use, unless that old devil succeeds in putting a chain and anchor on us to prevent our movement.

This state of being anchored or trapped in a stronghold prevents us from moving in any direction. We are here to complete a journey in the right direction, and if we aren't watchful, that old devil will prevent our very movement in any direction.

You see, if the devil can't keep us turned in the wrong direction, he will attempt to anchor us and imprison us so that we no longer can travel the path to life. The devil has no power over us unless we give it to him. He only tempts us and lies to us. We do the actual damage of building walls or dropping anchor by believing his lies instead of God's truth.

Always remember Jesus died to make you worthy! Do not believe anything less and you will have smooth sailing.

The first meaning of stronghold was a fortification. A wall is a fortification. And the good news that Holy Spirit has imparted to my spirit is this:

"The Walls Came Tumbling Down!"

Be blessed.

BOOK III

DEDICATION

To Casey Allen Smith, my grandson, who believed in me. I dedicate this book to him for his great faith in me. I love you forever and look forward to our visits to New York City – remember the sky box is the limit!

Anne Urne

IT

CAME

TO

PASS

IT CAME TO PASS
CONTENTS – BOOK III

Chapter 1	252
Vehayah	
Chapter 2	265
Change	
Chapter 3	267
I've Walked in Those Shoes	
Chapter 4	271
Testimony	
Chapter 5	275
Forgive Him?!!	
Chapter 6	289
True Happiness	
Chapter 7	299
The Error of Omission	
Chapter 8	317
There'll Be Some Changes Made Today	
Chapter 9	333
Surprise!	
Chapter 10	343
Great Things	

Chapter 11	
Fairy Tales Can Come True	349
Chapter 12	353
The Eighth Spirit	
Epilogue	361

CHAPTER 1

VEHAYAH

I read a book on Jewish mysticism and Kabala, and while most of the information was much too complicated for my simple understanding, I found a most interesting fact about God's name. The letters of God's name are Veyhayah, and translated means "It Came To Pass". The Bible is so full of information, and I believe, that even if our understanding minds miss much of the information, our spirits are digesting the words just as our bodies digest good food. We become stronger in spirit, and eventually our understanding is made whole.

Holy Spirit, I feel your presence and your love. I begin this book with you, wondering where you will lead me this time. I am amazed at the wonders and signs that are manifesting in my life as I reminisce about the two previous books, as well as my first book that was more of a study guide and journal.

Chapter I – Vehayah

The first book in this Trilogy, *Way Beyond the River*, led me on a journey that turned me around from the direction of the world to the direction of the spirit. Oh, how wonderful to find the Way to the Promised Land. Then, book number two, *The Walls Came Tumbling Down*, helped me discover my own soul as the self-made walls of protection came down revealing my inner self.

As I begin this book, I am excited about the title that came to me the first weekend of February 2002 while I was at my favorite get-away, my retreat in Carthage, Missouri. It was there that the title was gently imparted to me as I prayed and asked if there would be another book, and if so, what would be the name of this book.

I believe the title, *It Came To Pass*, is truly my latest adventure with you, my wonderful counselor. It makes sense to me that as the first book turned me in the right direction to make the journey home, that the second book brought me into the kingdom where, upon arrival, the walls of my worldly prison came tumbling down.

Oh, how excited I am at the prospect of learning what is waiting for me in this book, *It Came To Pass*.

The title is your name, O God, Veyhayah! As I found over thirty instances where *It Came To Pass* was written in the Book of St. Luke, I learned that each time your name was written, there was a manifestation of your power.

It Came to Pass is found first in Luke Ch. 1:8 when an angel appears to Zachary announcing the birth of John the Baptist who will go before the Lord in the spirit and power of Elias. The second time is in Ch. 1:23, when Elizabeth conceives, and Angel Gabriel appears to Mary to announce the birth of Jesus. The last time is in Ch. 24:30, when Jesus opens the eyes of the men He had walked with and they recognize him when he breaks the bread, then he vanishes from sight.

In those scriptures where I found your name, there are appearances of angels, miracles performed by Jesus, healing and people being raised from the dead. I truly believe that I have arrived in the kingdom, the walls of my prison have come down, and that signs and wonders follow in your presence.

None of my books have been published, but I trust in you and I am never disappointed. I read about your patience, O God, and realize that it is not we who wait on you, but you who patiently waits on us. Since Jesus died on the cross, we have had access to you, your love, your power and your great grace. We are so foolish in the world, but when we let go and let God, we find you have been with us through it all. Until we let go of the worldly ways, thoughts and limitations, we are unable to receive the power you have imparted to us by your Holy Spirit.

As children we learn how to walk in your way, and it takes time for us to trust ourselves completely to you. To let go and give up our controlling thoughts and hidden walls of protection is a painfully difficult task. We know what works in the world, and we are without a clue that our flesh controlled thoughts inhibit the Holy Spirit who patiently waits for us to grow.

There is a passage from the flesh to the spirit, and the journey is wondrous as we step out in faith and see what God can do. As our trust develops, our faith deepens and, at long last, we are able to walk with you.

As we approach this passage from worldly control to heavenly freedom, we find that you were with us all the time as we made our journey.

We all know the story of Jesus dying on the cross for us. So, why is it so hard for us to understand? We come into the world with eyes and ears of flesh to see and hear what goes on in the world, and it takes a journey to find our spiritual eyes and ears in order to understand and perceive those things of the spirit. We begin by following rules – rules of the world.

We learn about our salvation through Jesus' death, but we have such difficulty understanding why he died. We are taught that he died for our sins. We know with a worldly knowledge and have such difficulty perceiving what actually happened. You see, He didn't have to die to get to heaven – He was God! He allowed His flesh to be crucified in order to bring us back!

How can we deny our inheritance and reject the sacrifice? Jesus placed our sin in his flesh that was nailed to the cross! When we see that He died so that we could be set free, it is imperative that we understand we are no longer under condemnation and worldly laws and rules. When our spirit is awakened, we can allow it to rule us, and we no longer have need for laws and worldly rules, because we have awakened to the love of God. We have been reconciled which is to be made acceptable to Him. We have the power of God in us by His Holy Spirit.

The world, ruled by Satan, would keep us in the dark as to our liberty. Jesus was the light that set the captives free. Satan was defeated that day on the cross! And, as long as we follow the rule of the world, we will be turned the wrong way, living in darkness and ignorance, when all the time the door to that prison was swung open and the Light, Jesus, was made available to us.

The key is believing! We can't work our way to heaven by good works because the only open door is the one Jesus opened. We already have the entrance into the kingdom. We are not in the dark, but we are looking in that direction. Just a turn and the light will be shining for us. The door is open, the light is on. Forget about trying to earn your freedom; you already have it. Believe that and you will not only escape the snare of the devil, you will walk in the power of God.

Turn around and leave the darkness that holds you with lies of condemnation, guilt, worry, unforgiveness, shame, fear and, especially, unworthiness. Forget about being worthy on your own merit; that won't happen. You are worthy for only one reason. That reason is Jesus died to make you worthy. How can you reject the sacrifice Jesus made to make you worthy? There is absolutely nothing that you can do to earn heaven. Only Jesus could do that, because He was God in the flesh. While you remain in the mindset of the world, you are blinded and prevented from living in the freedom of the spirit.

Only three pages into this book and I stopped, wondering what was next. I am serious when I tell you that my writing is led by the Holy Spirit, because I never know what, when or where the next area of writing will lead.

It's 4:30 a.m. and here I am! Many thoughts have been running through my mind, and I knew it was time to pour the coffee and begin putting these thoughts on paper.

I recalled Michelle's last visit. She commented that several people at her place of work were going on diets and some had become quite obese and this concerned her. I had also observed the same phenomenon. I knew of one beautiful girl who bloomed out quickly and had liposuction for Christmas! I told Michelle that I believed there was a spirit of fat around them, and I was serious about that. She then asked me if that was one of the spirits of error. I told her to look at the list in the back of my prayer book beside her.

Sure enough, she found the Spirit of Insatiableness! Yes, there is a fat spirit, and so we prayed and bound that spirit from operating in her place of employment.

"You nailed him!" I said to Michelle.

I knew the spirits of error by heart, yet I hadn't

matched the Spirit of Error, Insatiableness, with the fat spirit that I had observed operating in my workplace. We can be so blinded by this world, yet the spirit of truth will set you free!

Our discussion then turned to the title of my new book. I explained to her how I had learned that the Hebrew name of God, Vehayah, was the translation of the letters of His name meaning *It Came To Pass*. I continued to explain that when the name of God appears in scripture, His power is manifested in the earth by signs, miracles and appearances of His angels bringing good news.

As we continued to explore the significance of the title of my third book, I considered the books in sequence. The first book turned us in the direction of God to begin our journey. The second book brought down the walls that impeded our progress. This book, I surmised, was going to lead us into the deeper knowledge of God as we traveled into the spiritual realm of the kingdom. I believed this book was literally about stepping into the spirit and walking in the manifested power of God.

Considering the title, Michelle responded with the words "mountain pass". She had just recently returned from her first ski trip and the word pass brought this to mind.

I pursued her thought about pass and equated it to being on a high mountain ledge, and then leaping off into the love and protection of God in an act of faith. Michelle said, "We throw up a wall of protection, and that is why the walls have to come down."

I was thinking about her comment about throwing up walls, and I remembered Jesus being the door that is open, the only open door. And where would a door be, except through a wall!

I get excited as I discover that I am on track with this book. God is in control, and I am just at the wheel letting Him lead me to my destination.

Reflecting on her words *mountain pass,* I remembered how the Israelites were told to read the curses and the blessings from two different mountains as they *passed* into the Promised Land. A mountain pass, indeed! The mountains that we pass between are from the mountain of the curses to the mountain of the blessings! Oh, this is so good!

As I continued to replay our conversation, I remembered telling Michelle about just reading Paul's Epistle to the Galatians where he said, *O foolish Galatians!... Are you so foolish that after beginning in the Spirit, you now make a finish in the flesh?"*

I love to read the books of Paul, because he was so well versed in spiritual living. I learn new and different things every time I read through his books. Paul had an anointing and God spoke through him so that everyone could know about the life of the spirit. God has been speaking to us forever about His promises, and to receive them we must believe. Indeed, not works, but faith will put us over into that spiritual realm of promises that can be manifested in the world.

The promises of blessings that were given to Abraham and his seed are received by virtue of the spirit, and are then manifested into our physical realm. Only God can receive the glory for the things that He alone can do.

Here is the simplicity of faith! It is beyond our power and ability, and that is why we must let go of our control and throw all caution to the wind, as we trust completely and wholly in our God to perform that which He has promised.

Throwing caution to the wind is not a careless whim. You see, the power of the Holy Spirit has been demonstrated by wind. Remember the description of Pentecost?

> *"And when the days of Pentecost were drawing to a close, they were all together in one place. And suddenly there came a sound from heaven, as of a violent wind blowing, and it filled the whole house where they (the Apostles) were sitting."*
>
> Acts 2:1

This wind is the manifested power of God's Holy Spirit!

I had a dream recently in which I became aware of a family of people beside me in what seemed to be an alley. I interpreted this to be symbolic of a homeless family. As I became aware of their presence, I began to raise up as in flight over their heads, and as they were watching me in amazement, a strong wind began to blow over them. The wind was not a damaging storm wind, but a strong wind that was changing their condition. It was not something that I could see, but it could only be explained as something dingy being made bright or something drab being made shiny.

When the wind stopped blowing they were looking up and smiling brightly. They had been changed. I remember saying to the man who had quite a bushy growth of beard, that all he had to do was shave. Everything was well, now.

The dream ended, and as I recalled it upon awakening, I realized that it was that wind of God's manifested power changing lives and making people whole. I also realized that I had nothing to do with the miracle that took place, except for the fact that I got their attention. You see, God uses people to bring attention to His power. I love this part, because I can do nothing on my own, but I can do all things through Christ who strengthens me! It is so simple, yet we miss it! We try to become worthy on our own merit.

I couldn't help but stop and look up the word 'shave', since it was the predominant word in my dream. The second definition read: To make bare or smooth by cutting off closely the surface or surface covering of. The Colloquial definition read: Act of passing very near to so as to graze; as a close shave. Graze means to touch lightly in passing.

There is that word *pass* again! God is showing me that we must pass from the flesh to the spirit. Shave is described as cutting off the surface covering. This is yet another way of saying, "crucify the flesh"! To sum this up, I find it to be significant that we deny the lust of the flesh in order to enjoy the fruit of the spirit as the Bible teaches us this throughout the whole New Testament.

Jesus said we must be born again. That is literally changing from a flesh driven worldly direction, turning in the direction of the light, and following the gentle urging of the Holy Spirit. This seems very hard at times, but it is in this passing that we find our true spiritual self. We deny the dictates of the flesh, and follow the leading of the Holy Spirit. Through this obedience, we pass from this world into God's world. It is such a wonderful place to be!

Here again, I am reminded of Paul's exhortation. How foolish to begin in the Spirit and end in the flesh. That is what this book is about. We start in the flesh headed the wrong way, then we make a turn in the direction of God, the walls come down, and we find ourselves teetering on the edge of spiritual freedom.

"How foolish" indeed, to come this close to spiritual freedom, only to be frightened into throwing up a wall of protection! I now understand what that last wall is that we throw up for protection. This wall is called rules!

We make a start in the spirit only to end in a roadblock of rules that we create to control our flesh. Fear stops and prevents the passage into the spiritual realm of freedom. If you have ever read the Bible, you would know that God insisted that we DO NOT FEAR! So, you ask, what do you do? You trust God! You surrender completely. You let go and let God. Let go of the fear, fall on God's merciful arms, and let Him hold you, protect you and restore you in His power and love.

My understanding of this matter comes from my own experience. As we take off in the spirit, we discover the Holy Spirit who convicts us in certain areas as He teaches and guides us into our spiritual growth. We definitely have to make some changes if we are going to live in an opposite direction from the ways of the world. We begin by denying the cravings and demands of the flesh.

My personal experience was explained in my first book, when I had a huge conviction about alcohol. Now, let me explain my feelings in this area. You see I was raised in the Catholic Church where moderation in all things was the rule. So, drinking alcohol was not sinful to me, but drunkenness was the sin.

I enjoyed drinking red wine with my dinner in the evenings, and had made it a routine. Then, out of the blue, one day I got hit by a strong, undeniable conviction by the Holy Spirit that I should stop drinking it. Now, this was hard for me to understand. I was not brought up on Protestant Church rules, and I wondered why God was dealing with me in this fashion so I asked Him about it.

"God, I know drinking is not sinful, but if you show me that I shouldn't, then I won't."

So, in an act of obedience, not understanding, I gave up the wine completely. Later, I was able to partake of it again, however, in better moderation than before.

What I hadn't realized at the time was that even though I never got drunk, I was not the one in control of the wine. Instead the dictates of my flesh was the controlling factor. Now, had I not learned from this exercise in discipline that my conviction by the Holy Spirit was to put my spirit in control of my flesh; I could have very easily stopped my spiritual growth. I could have drawn the conclusion that drinking is a sin.

Stop right here and understand that the Holy Spirit convicts us of things to do and not to do, and this is a training session to put the flesh under in preparation of moving beyond the flesh into the spiritual realm of power. This realization made me aware of why there are so many religions and so many rules! Those who started out on a spiritual journey got convicted of something personal by the Holy Spirit, and believed that was where they should stop! They stopped and took what was a personalized program, and turned it into a rule that they tried to apply to all who would follow them! Here is the irony of beginning in the spirit and ending in the flesh. And how did they end?

They stopped at the ledge of spiritual freedom, and instead of passing over to the mountain of blessings, threw up a wall made of rules!

Being convicted by the Holy Spirit is useful for an individual to overcome worldly controlling factors that he or she is not aware of. These convictions by the Holy Spirit reveal to us the walls of our self-created prisons, which are hidden within us and preventing our spiritual growth. To make these rules apply to others is ludicrous! God made each of us different!

We each make our own spiritual journey. As we are convicted by the Holy Spirit, we discipline ourselves in the flesh so He can lead us out of the bondage of darkness into the realm of God's glorious light. We are tested at times to see if we will be obedient to God, but we pass each test and keep growing. It is foolish indeed to stop our growth and make a rule. Instead, we should grow past that obstacle and become spiritually stronger in an area where we were previously weak in the flesh. I can now drink wine and be in control of the consumption, being led by the spirit as to when, where and how much can be consumed. I learned to put the spirit man in control and instead of a rule I rely on temperance.

Spiritual ascendancy is about being led by the Spirit, not about making rules along the way. The Spirit becomes our personal guide, a spiritual trainer you might say, who strengthens our spiritual man so that we can break free from the control of our flesh. As we pass into this new way of living, we find that our submission and obedience to God is not something that we must suffer and dread. Instead it is the most freeing, joyous, jubilant experience that we have ever known.

If you wonder why you never seem to receive the promises of God, you should search your inner self for the walls that have prevented you from passing over. God gave us all the rules we need in the Ten Commandments. There are, indeed, rules for those who exist in the flesh, and that is where each of us begins our journey. The passage from flesh to spirit is where and when the rules change. Love takes over when we pass into the spirit.

CHAPTER 2

CHANGE

One morning I awoke and remembered dreaming that a man's voice told me I had a new last name, spelled U-R-N-E. I puzzled over this spelling and wondering if maybe I heard, "You Are In Me". I then wondered more about why there was an "E" on URN, because it doesn't spell a word with the "E" on the end. I thought about the fact that my name is Anne – with an E, and decided that the "E" was just keeping with the style of spelling my name.

I decided to look up the word URNE and, of course, there was only the word "URN" listed in the dictionary. I read in amazement that an urn is described as a vessel. My heart's desire is to be a vessel that God can use.

Another definition of urn was figuratively, the grave. Looking up *grave*, I found: *an excavation in the earth as a place of burial; a tomb; sepulcher; hence, death.* I considered this meaning and how it related to me.

I rejoiced as it came to me. The urn was significant of the fact that I had changed! I recalled one morning while I was praying very early that I heard a man's voice say to me: *Come into the glory.*

Oh thank you, Jesus, I will! I come in and I hide myself in you.

Yes, the urn in my dream was symbolic that I had died in the flesh in Jesus, and at the same time symbolic of a vessel that contains the Holy Spirit of God! I am that new creature created in Christ Jesus! What a wonderful revelation, to know that I am safe in the kingdom. I have died, crucified this flesh and am living in the kingdom! Praise God, for Jesus, my advocate, who died for me, cleansed me, and opened the door for me to enter into the glorious kingdom of God.

The Holy Spirit has convicted me recently about testimony. I read an interesting book in which the author shared the pain and suffering that he went through in his life, and I realized that my previous unpublished books were very shallow, as there was no information about the author.

I never had a desire to share my testimony. It was too personal and I preferred to distance myself from past sins and mistakes. This book, however, had impressed me that I needed to share my testimony if I truly want to send a message about change. I am jumping up and down with joy over my new life in the spirit, and that is the point of testimony. I no longer live in the shame of my past, for Jesus has washed me clean. I am a new creation.

How can anyone learn about the wonderful victory of this change, unless somebody testifies? I have now written my testimony with no holds barred. It is an interesting story of a very sad chain of events, but it has a fairy tale ending. There is a Cinderella story in all of us, and I hope my story will help you find yours.

CHAPTER 3

I'VE WALKED IN THOSE SHOES

What emotions have been evoked and memories dredged up as I listened to a friend on the phone describing her relative's irresponsible behavior. It reminded me of the behavior of the bona fide sociopath that I had married twenty years ago! If you have to ask, what a sociopath is, then you should read this book; if you know, then you could write it.

God had been showing me the word 'testimony' for the past few days, and I decided that what my books were missing was the part about the author that makes it credible. "I didn't just fall off the turnip wagon" – that's an old saying my husband uses at times. Well, how could anyone read something I had written and find it believable, if they didn't know the whole story?

I asked God, "What is my testimony? And, what does my dream about lots of shoes mean? I have heard the word shoes emphasized several times this week. Then, when I was reading a letter that came to the office, a sentence grabbed my attention that read, *until you stand in those shoes.*

That was it! After listening to a friend describe a person's irresponsible behavior and how she wanted to help, I wanted to scream at her – "Stop!" "Don't go there! That kind of help is not an act of kindness. You are being blatantly cheated."

I read some very good advice about that same time. Someone wrote to a newspaper columnist asking for advice. The person had taken in some relatives that were down on their luck. Only months later nothing had changed and they were still there! The adviser wrote that in a crisis situation, it is a Christian duty to help if you are able. He went on to say that if the situation is caused by a person's lack of responsibility and lifestyle, then it is not a crisis, and you are not helping when you assume responsibility for them. I memorized this advice, and now I use this as a measuring tool to determine if I am helping someone, or taking on their responsibilities. In short, is that person taking advantage?

My daughter has told me that I am an enabler, so I know that I have to be careful in judging certain situations. I could be described as a bleeding heart, so I have learned from a very painful experience that it is more important to make a wise decision, than to jump out on a whim, thinking you are doing the right thing. There isn't always a warning sign posted, and even if it is posted, we don't always heed the warning.

I learned a very painful lesson. We cannot take the place of Jesus! Sometimes our bleeding hearts are looking for approval or acceptance. It takes some serious heart and soul searching to find an answer, but take the time to know that you are helping the way God has directed you.

Do not be led by your feelings. Otherwise, you may find that you are getting in God's way. Read what Paul said about the widows – he was very careful to define those that required our help versus those that didn't. Just being a widow is not a qualifying factor. When in doubt or confused, this little advice that I read recently is very helpful in defining the fine line between helping someone or assuming their responsibilities.

I discussed the seven spirits of God in my other books, and feelings are not on that list! So, beware of feelings. I cannot over-emphasize this point.

An enabler actually aids and abets another person's irresponsibility! I do believe it is a well-disguised sin. Be on your guard, for it is a sin of pride that causes you to believe you can fix another person's problem. That irresponsible person could use your prayers and the help of God. Pray for them, but don't let them manipulate you.

First of all, we can't see the problem, but just the result of the problem. So, believe me when I say beware of getting tangled up with this tar baby, for it is a dangerous proposition! Read on and you will understand what I am driving at here.

As I recalled my phone conversation with the friend who was agonizing over the decision of again helping an ungrateful, unchanging loved one in trouble, I realized that I had found the mystery of the shoes! It was simple. I have stood in her shoes. That is why I must tell my story.

There is only one way to tell this story, and that is to begin at the beginning. I pray this blesses someone, for it is a testimony that I have of God bringing me back from a man-made hell on earth, to a joyful heavenly place that is also here on earth. We don't have to die to find heaven!

CHAPTER 4

TESTIMONY

I am half Irish and half English. Mostly, the Irish shows with red hair and hazel green eyes, being raised by my Irish Catholic Mom. Dad died before I hardly knew him. He was killed in a terrible collision by a semi-truck passing a car on a two-lane highway in the fog in 1952. I was four years old and had a two-year old sister.

Welcome to my world! Dad was the full-blooded Englishman, son of a brain surgeon father and a schoolteacher mother. The family was Presbyterian and very proper. I didn't get to know them well, as I was transplanted from Illinois to Oklahoma before I started to school.

Mom is a treasure, a gypsy at heart with beautiful green eyes and dark hair. She was very smart with an IQ of genius. She won an academic scholarship to a prestigious Catholic academy where she attended high school during the Depression.

She told stories about how she and a girlfriend, who weren't as financially well off as most of the girls attending this school, would draw pencil lines down the back of their legs to make it look like they were wearing stockings. This was a school requirement they couldn't always afford. Mom was an adventurer and lived a fascinating and interesting life. She could tell some stories. She worked for Dr. Kennedy at Washington University on the Manhattan Project. Yes, she worked with and for the men who invented the atomic bomb!

A few years after Father died, Mom fell in love with a man from Oklahoma. My new stepfather worked for a pipeline company which took us all over the United States, with our home base in Oklahoma. I once counted over thirty schools that I had attended. I was able to make straight A's, but as a shy, introverted, and very self-conscious girl, I found it very difficult to adjust to the many changes. I swore that when I grew up, I would buy a home and never leave it!

I have lived long enough to eat those words! My life growing up was obviously not a piece of cake. Mom was very strong in some areas, while emotionally fragile in others. She suffered a few nervous breakdowns, but overcame these obstacles as she left the hospitals and raised two daughters by herself. The stepfather was never factored into our relationship with Mom. She separated from him to move us away from the country and raise us in the city. Mother's love for me and my sister was primary in our lives. We never lacked for love. Mom was the "breadwinner and not a housekeeper". That's what she said, and was that ever the truth. She laughs now as she tells our friends at brunch, "I never pick up a vacuum cleaner, and Anne never puts it down!"

She laughs, we all laugh – it doesn't seem so important anymore. That's Mom and I love her immeasurably. I couldn't live in her house – and she couldn't live in mine. She says I throw away her newspaper, before she can even read it!

Growing up without a dad and being so insecure, I thought love and marriage would fix all my ills! I just married every time I fell in love – which was a little too often. My first marriage was to a high school sweetheart who had beautiful blonde hair, blue eyes and a turned up nose. That worked great for fathering my child, who is the most beautiful strawberry blonde with green eyes and the cutest turned up nose. Yes my pride and joy, she is the most gorgeous daughter that ever was born to a mother. I was a nineteen-year old mother and my husband had joined the Army. He served in Korea since his brother was already in Viet Nam. When he came home I discovered that he was now a hippie who was anti everything and didn't want to work! Well, not the father of my child – out he went! He went away and didn't pay child support. I can rightfully call her "my daughter" and, that's just the way I liked it. She was all mine and I never had to share her.

I landed my first job at an Air Force Base starting out in the medical department file room. I worked my way up from file clerk to medical transcriptionist and then on to become secretary to the chief of medicine.

During this stage of my life, I had another marriage to a strange fellow that only lasted a year. He was extremely jealous, mean and abusive.

Finally, the man of my dreams came into my life. He was a handsome policeman, with a southern Texas drawl. He could charm the birds out of the trees. He was also big, strong and carried a gun. He made me feel so safe and secure, and we were very much in love. We had the church wedding – my first church wedding. This one was for keeps; this was happiness. My daughter, Michelle was 3 when we met, 5 when we married and 8 when we divorced. This marriage ended when I discovered he was having affairs with what seemed like every girl in town. I was devastated and my heart was broken. I divorced him, even though I loved him so much I thought I would die without him. I had lost that special feeling. My trust had been betrayed and that special feeling was gone.

I steered clear of marriage after that for several years. I withdrew from feelings of love in order to protect myself from further pain and hurt. I did, however, date a man for four years. He had his home and I had mine. Life was ho-hum, safe and secure. I realized much later that I stayed in a relationship with this man for a long time because it kept me from falling in love and being hurt again. I cared about this man, and had lots of fun with him, but I wasn't mature enough to appreciate him. He was older and I was still in my late twenties to early thirties, thinking that love had to be some special exciting feeling.

Excitement? Yes! That is the word for sociopath! Enter the tall, muscular, blue-eyed, blonde cowboy in a Stetson hat, tight fitting jeans, manicured nails, clean cut, gorgeous – and my heart began to pound. How this episode occurred that changed my life forever amazes me. I was only going to stop by a nightclub because a girlfriend insisted that I come to her birthday party that night. So, there I sat when this Texan blew into town and into my life. He sat down in front of me and asked me to dance. He taught me how to two-step and asked if he could take me on a date later in the week! I felt like an excited teenager on her first date!

CHAPTER 5

FORGIVE HIM?!!

TESTIMONY CONTINUED

My life at this point was secure. I had a boyfriend for companionship, was comfortably settled in a fixed income existence, living from paycheck to paycheck. I had a nice 3 bedroom brick home. The grade school my daughter attended was right behind our house. There was a neighborhood swimming pool within a few blocks. Michelle's summers were perfect. She loved power tumbling and the coach at the grade school held summer classes in the gym every morning. During the summers while I worked, she tumbled all morning then rode her bicycle over to the neighborhood pool where she joined her friends. She could dive and swim and dive over and over all afternoon, and then play until dark. She never ran out of energy.

I became a pageant mom and took Michelle to dance lessons and every pageant that came to town. I loved to watch her dance and model her beautiful clothes. My life revolved around this child. Having little to no self-esteem as a child, I found my new identity in being Michelle's mom. Nothing felt better than this! I adored my beautiful girl. She was perfect in every way. She never required discipline which was a good thing, because I was not a disciplinarian.

Michelle hated pageants and ruffled dresses, preferring to be a tomboy to a beauty queen! She broke my heart when she announced going into the fourth grade that she was going to wear jeans instead of dresses! Oh, how I hated to spend fifty dollars on jeans that could have paid for a beautiful ruffled and lacy dress!

Then, when she was fourteen she told me she was not dancing anymore, because she was going into gymnastics full time. She loved her power tumbling that she had taken six years in grade school, and now she was throwing herself completely into gymnastics. She was on two teams and trained for 4-5 hours every day. She loved it. I used to beg her to let me sew sequins on her leotard!

Michelle competed on her high school gymnastics team, as well as studying under Bart Conner and his coach, Paul Zirt. Right after Bart won his Gold Medal at the Olympics, she was invited to go with him and a few other teammates to the World's Fair in New Orleans to do an exhibition. I was so proud of her, but I wasn't able to go. She did, however, tell Mom that when she came out to do her tumbling pass that Bart Conner announced her name, and said, "Here comes power!"

She had forgotten all about that, until recently when Mom talked about what he said. I believe it was a prophetic word that he spoke about my little girl.

Michelle and I were opposites in many ways. If we folded the laundered sheets she folded right while I folded left. No matter how we tried to coordinate this small task, it always made us laugh because invariably we turned the sheet in opposite directions every time. Regardless of our differences in taste and direction, we got along beautifully.

While married to the policeman, I had acquired some pretty expensive diamond jewelry from his parents who were in the pawnshop business. Also, my boyfriend after him had bought me a beautiful large solitaire diamond engagement ring.

I didn't drive a fancy car. On a secretary's salary, I could only afford an older used car. I was comfortably settled in that house that I was never going to move out of, so my daughter would never have to go through changing schools and leaving friends behind like I had. I would make sure that she had the best that my paycheck could buy. My life was just the way I wanted it. I was protected from the pain of marital disappointment. I didn't need a man to support me. I was in control.

Everything was just fine until I went to that birthday party. I fell head over heels for the Texas cowboy with those mysterious blue eyes who sat down in front of me and asked me for a date. I spiraled out of control and lost all sense when I fell in love with him.

My mom was suspicious of him from the time she laid eyes on him. She knew he was trouble, blowing into town in a new sports car, no job, and she observed that he knew too many card tricks. While I was falling in love, dancing and spending all my time with him, Mom was checking with people she knew in the police department. She called out of the blue one day to tell me the police were coming to pick him up. He had an outstanding warrant in Texas where he had jut stolen the sports car from his last girlfriend – after he had sold all of her furniture!

What in the world is happening? I can't comprehend this. How could this innocent looking blue-eyed charmer be a criminal? It couldn't be true. It can't be true. They can't put this beautiful person in jail! It must be some horrible mistake! I told him what Mom had said, and begged him to tell me that it was all a big mistake. Instead he told me it was true, but he put a much different twist on it. He couldn't get away from this girl and by the time he finished his story, it was all her fault. He, however, would do the proper thing so we could continue our love affair. He would drive back to Texas and turn himself in. And he did, too! I was impressed, and believed with all my heart that everything would be okay, now.

The song, *Why Do Fools Fall in Love,* comes to mind as I reminisce. Also, the behavior and cunning of a sociopath still boggles my mind. I later learned that when he reached the Dallas police department and jail that he walked up to a man just coming out of jail, handed him the keys to the sports car, and told him, "it's out front – you can have it." They never did pin that stolen car on him! He almost got out of the other charge of selling her furniture. He didn't get off completely clean though, he got probation for a first offense – and there I was at the courthouse to pick him up. We drove back to Oklahoma City, stopping in Gainesville, Texas only long enough to get married!

Mom and I had the worst fight of our lives, and we didn't speak for a long time; until I needed help. And then I couldn't find enough help.

How did it all begin? I have managed to put most of the ugliness of that six-year period of hell out of my mind.

God is merciful in letting us forget the painful things we go through. And, only God can turn the wrongs into rights, the pain into joy and the loss into restoration. That is what testimony is all about.

My new husband and I returned to my nice little house, and my nice little job, and he began looking for work. I knew life was going to be the happiest I had ever dreamed. He got some type of sales job and was going to make lots of money he explained to me. In the meantime, while we waited on commissions and sales, we were living on my paycheck. Before I met him, I barely had enough to pay the bills and buy groceries every two weeks.

Now, I had another mouth to feed, and he smoked too many cigarettes every day. That was so costly. Then, he wanted to take me dancing and I was paying for it! I had other obligations; Michelle's dance lessons and pageant clothes. I explained to him that he had to get some other type of job. Even minimum wage would help, if he would just bring in some money – instead of spending it all the time.

One day I answered the door to find a policeman was there to arrest my husband for writing hot checks! I can't believe my life is spinning so far out of control! I have always been a law abiding, decent human being. How can I be sucked into this lowlife cesspool of traipsing to jails, finding bail bondsmen and standing in lines for jail visitation! This is a nightmare – God what can I do?

Before I married this man, I told the doctor I worked for all about him and his exciting stories. My doctor told me before I ever married him that he was a sociopath.

What tales they can spin; they live in a make-believe world. He had me believing that he lived and grew up like one of the boys on the popular television show, Dallas. He had me believing that he was wealthy and well-to-do. What I didn't know was that he was telling me about the millionaire type life of one of the women he had hustled in the past.

I asked my doctor just what is a sociopath? He gave me a book. I read it and the last chapter stated that the consensus of the top psychiatrists in the nation was that a sociopath had no conscience, they could con a psychiatrist, and there was no cure. Their lives consisted of hustling and conning people out of money, going to jail, conning the courts to send them for mental health treatment, where they conned the psychiatrists that they were better, and the cycle continued.

These people are not stingy. They are very generous, usually because money means nothing to them. And why should it, they don't earn it. It is just something they get from conning people. They are extravagant, nice dressers, big spenders, and so they run with high rollers until they are discovered. They will make you feel like you owe them. They will spend a little on you – but they expect a whole lot more back. It is like playing a game with the devil – you can't win. They can read a person better than a book, and discover their weaknesses in a very cunning way. They know a sucker is born every minute, and if a person is greedy for gain – they are ripe for a sociopath to con them out of their money. They will laugh and say that's what they get for thinking they could get something for nothing.

The fool is the person who believes them. The sucker is the one who thinks the con will help him get rich quick. There is no such thing. The con man knows this – and the chump finds out the hard way.

No conscience the book said. They can't be cured the doctors agreed. I closed the book, and said to myself, "I can fix him!"

Famous last words. Six years later I was without my beautiful diamonds. I had no car, no job, no money, no self-esteem, and worst of all - no daughter! I fixed him all right! How low can a person sink? How miserably can you fail and how frightened can you become, before the darkness splits and the dawn at last shines into that corner of the world that has seemingly swallowed you up? I thought I would never smile again.

The hot check deal was only one of many. I tried so hard to explain to him how to handle money, how to not be so extravagant, how to manage on a budget. What was my response to this "trying to change him"? A black eye, a backhand across the face! Now, I'm not just trying to pay bills, I am trying to survive here! And, to make it worse I can't get away form this one. I would pray that he would find another woman and leave me; that I would be so broke with no food in the house, that he would have to go looking somewhere else – but he wouldn't go away! I managed to secure a divorce after 3 years, but he still wouldn't go away.

He did such horrible things. Once he pawned my daughter's roller skates and then yelled at her and grounded her for losing them. I later found the pawn ticket, but I didn't dare confront him.

That's a word to explore: *Confront.* We have to confront our fears – not be intimidated and cowardly. I have learned when we determine to confront a situation or a person, that we just ask Jesus to go and do the work, because He has already settled the matter – from the cross!

A confrontation is not an angry attack. It is standing up for what is right and expecting to be treated with respect and dignity.

The devil uses a variety of tactics to steal our self-respect and dignity and for very good reason. In doing this he causes us to feel unworthy and unlovable and, thus, manages to not only separate us from loving earthly relationships, he manages to accomplish his primary goal – keeping us from the love of God and the knowledge that we are His righteous children.

The sociopath was a very good teacher. Once you've dealt with a sociopath, you come out knowing that you were fighting with a demon. Anger and fighting are tools that play into the hand of the devil and keep us in bondage. We need prayer and then confrontation, God's tools, to keep us out of danger and bondage.

How low did I go? Well, my blood pressure went up to nearly stroke level. After being treated and released from the Emergency Room, I went home, laid down and prayed intensely because I felt my spirit lifting out of my body. Michelle was 12 years old when I got us into this mess, now she was 16, and I couldn't die now! God, I have to finish raising my daughter! My spirit returned as I lay on the bed wondering where I go now.

I resigned from my secure job at the Air Force Base. No longer a secretary, I had gotten promoted to a safety inspector position in an aircraft division. I had a good salary, great benefits and 14 years invested. I walked away giving it all up. I had been stressed to the max between this husband and a harassing female supervisor. The stress had landed me in that Emergency Room. The hardest thing I ever did was turn in my government badge, and walk away from 14 years of the only career I had ever known. That was the first big loss. Over the next few years my husband managed to pawn all my beautiful diamond jewelry. He even sold my furniture, but I discovered it in time to get it back. The most gut wrenching loss I suffered was the loss of my home. That secure place that I would never leave was gone. My husband had forced me to go with him to a sleazy loan company to put a second mortgage on my house to pay for his attorneys and fines for his hot check stunts. I made him promise that he would work and make the extra payment. So much for his promises! I was just able to sale the house ahead of the foreclosure! I no longer had a home, my secure place was gone!

We rented an apartment that cost three times more than my original house payment had been. How can things get so far out of control! We lived in a blur of places for the next few years, moving every time we got evicted for not paying the rent. The humiliation was horrible. One time he sent me into my neighborhood grocery store where I had traded for years to cash a check. The clerks said they were holding several hot checks on my account that he had written! How could he send me in there – knowing this! I couldn't understand – I just couldn't understand! How does this man think? It made no sense to me. I lived in humiliation. He would borrow money from doctors that I worked with. He stole from my daughter and her friends – and would lie when asked about the missing items.

When I quit my government job, I drew out all of my retirement money. I still believed this man would change. I put most of it down on a new home. At last I had a nice home again. I bought my husband a $1,000 lawn mower. He could at least get some jobs doing lawns. I invested the rest into a beautiful 2-carat pear shaped diamond. Later, I learned he sold the mower to the neighbor for less than $200! He pawned the new ring, too, and the house got foreclosed. We went back to the blur of apartments, and I still wondered how we ever got by the credit applications. He handled most of those deals, as he knew how to work any situation to his advantage.

I thought to myself that since I was not working and there was no more money, *he will have to go away*. But he didn't! Nothing I could do would help me escape this nightmare! We were completely out of food, and he walked to the convenience store and talked the cashier into giving him credit for cigarettes! We had no bread! I am the scum of the earth. Me, the granddaughter of a brain surgeon! What had happened to me?

Depression, helplessness and hopelessness overwhelmed me so greatly that I wished and prayed now for death. I can't go on – I can't go on like this. I was never suicidal because I was afraid that I might go to hell for it, and if hell could be worse than this, I couldn't bear it for an eternity!

My sister got me started watching a television faith teacher and his wife. Oh, how I prayed for a faith filled miracle that they taught about. Why? Because it would take a miracle and an act of God to get me out of this mess. They would teach on tithing, and I would put $5 or $10 in the collection plate at church or send it to them and then hope that God would return it ten or a hundred fold like the scripture said.

I worried about money all the time! I was in constant fear, dread and worry. Besides that, I was angry and resentful at the man who brought all this misery into my life. Well, miracles don't come to people who are wrapped up in the bondage of fear, worry and anger. These emotions are from hell for the purpose of keeping us in bondage. There is no hundred-fold return or miracles coming to someone tied up in a prison of darkness. It's not because God can't get it to us. The fact is we can't receive it!

I was consumed with fear, depression and every negative emotion that can be exuded through every pore of my being. I was completely hopeless and helpless. But now, I was reading God's word, I was listening to God's prophets, teachers and preachers. The word was getting into my spirit and it was beginning to grow.

There were times when I had out of body experiences. I believe I was looking for God so hard, my sprit just left to go find Him. I needed him so much. "Where are you my God? Where are you? I need you!"

One night at a Christian music presentation, I listened to a wonderful singer. Surprisingly, my husband attended church with me during this period of my life. Remember, he could fit in anywhere, although he even tried to con the preacher once, and almost did with some kind of oil well equipment scheme! I know God intervened for the man of God. Anyway, while I was listening to the music that night, standing and lifting my hands in praise, I closed my eyes and listened to the words as he sang, *I was there all the time!* My eyes flowed with unstoppable tears. I knew something had happened on the inside of me, I wasn't quite sure, but I knew God was there! I realized that He had been there all the time! When I felt so lost, alone, rejected, dejected and unworthy, He was there waiting for me to let Him in. I didn't have to search far and wide; He was with me all the while. I just couldn't see him. My spiritual eyes were blinded by my negative emotions.

My natural eyes were fixed on the problems, and I couldn't take them off the problem long enough to see the answer. Of course, the answer has always been and will always be Jesus. He is the door to our emotional freedom. He is our emergency exit from that dark scary prison of isolation into the light, warmth, freedom and love of God. The song, *Love Can Build a Bridge*, comes to mind. And what is love except God. God can bridge the gap that separates us from Him, but we have the power to choose or reject His love.

I went to buy the tape after the concert, and was surprised to find the song I had wanted to hear again was entitled *HE was there all the time*. That's not what I heard. He said to me, "I was there all the time!"

Somewhere in this blur of time, our wonderful pastor gave me the name of a non-profit counseling center that helped people free of charge. I put my name on the list and a year or two later I got a call.

I went to my first appointment, looking more for pity than help. I realized that my situation was hopeless, but at least I could tell somebody how awful this man had been to me. I understood that my counselor had a doctorate in theology and psychology. I expected an older man. I was in my mid-thirties by now, and to my surprise and dismay, this highly educated man was younger than I was! What did this kid know about life – and how could he help me? That was my attitude as I began my first counseling session. He was a very nice man, and he listened to me tell the whole sad story. Then he handed me a piece of paper on which he had written these words: "I forgive him as an act of faith, in the name of Jesus".

What is this – a joke? Forgive him? I hated him! I hated him with as much hate as I could possibly muster. And, being an Irish redhead I could muster up some huge anger and hate. But, I never openly displayed it, because he frightened me so much that I would go into convulsions when he raised his hand to me.

I was living in a hopeless and terrifying situation, and now this doctor hands me this note. Was he nuts?

Oh, all right, I'll try it. We talked and he explained how important it was to forgive. I had to chuckle a little though when he interviewed my daughter one time, because immediately after talking to her, he went out to the parking lot and chewed my husband out! The doctor lost his cool! That gave me some satisfaction. But, meanwhile back to the little scribbled note. He told me that every time I thought about the hate and resentment, I should counter that thought with these words. I had to say them so many times. I didn't mean it. I did it because I was desperate to find help, and this was all I had been offered. I did it over and over, and cried over and over, because of the hurt, pain and resentment. But, I kept countering with these words.

I can't tell you how long it took (months or years) – and maybe I never reached real forgiveness until he was gone. But, I can truly say that I have forgiven him. I can more happily say that I have been away from him for, oh my gosh, 15 plus years! Praise and thank you, Jesus!

The time went so slowly from the day I met that sociopath, quite appropriately on April Fools Day, until six years later when he ran off to escape going to prison for three felony convictions. Thankfully, I had secured a divorce before he left. I learned years later that they found him and he did serve time in prison. He tried to find me, but he made the mistake of trying to write to me at Mom's, and Mom knew the probation officer. He never found me, and I thank you and love you forever, Mom.

On this note, I must retell of God's words to me that I wrote about in another book. When I was praying to God over the anger I had over my sister's death and my niece's loss of her mother, God spoke these words to me so plainly.

I AM THE FATHER WHO CREATED YOU AND THE MOTHER WHO LOVES YOU". He said further about my niece, YOU DON'T KNOW HOW I CAN COMFORT HER! *TELL HER TO EXPECT GREAT THINGS.*

God then spoke one more line to me, only he used a different voice. In my very own mother's voice, God said to me: WHY *ANNE, I HAVE ALWAYS BEEN THERE FOR YOU!*

This was the only time I heard God's voice. I often hear the Holy Spirit, but only this one time did I hear the voice of God. I will never forget His words. He spoke so plainly, so emphatically, that there is no mistaking His words or their meaning.

Later, I realized that He used my mother's voice for a very good reason. I believe He wanted me to know for certain that He was my mother and my father, and in knowing this I should realize the Commandment to honor your mother and your father is so very important.

Our parents are the very pattern of our God in heaven. His love, however, is greater than that of our earthly parents. It is so much greater than the love we experience in the world. Everything here is but a shadow of the things to come. As we learn to love and be loved, we get but a glimpse of the love that is in God.

This Commandment further explains to honor your parents, so that all will go well with you. As I recalled God's words in my mother's voice, I was reminded of the significance of honoring my mother. He revealed to me that when I rebelled from her instruction and warning about the sociopath, I also rebelled against Him. No wonder I got into so much trouble!

God gives us so many important guidelines, and we should heed them. To go in another direction is more dangerous than we can ever imagine. The enemy does seek to steal, kill and destroy. I know. I lived with that enemy.

CHAPTER 6

TRUE HAPPINESS

Today, my life is wonderful. The things that I lost were restored. The most indescribable devastating loss was my time with Michelle. She shuffled from pillar to post to avoid living with us. I was in such a daze during those years I hardly remember her being gone. During that time she met her high school sweetheart who was 6'2 and my husband wouldn't mess with him. Jeff was her protector when I was taken away from her. She married Jeff at age 18, and had the most handsome son, Casey.

It was right after Casey was born that the sociopath went away. No wonder my Casey is such an angel to me. It seems when he was born the light came down from heaven and drove away the darkness from my life.

When he left, I was living in a one-bedroom apartment. I had given him our only car and all the cash I had to get him out of the state and out of my life. I had no job, no money, no jewelry, no house and no car.

I signed up with a temp agency and my first assignment was to do some typing for three days at the campaign headquarters of a young lady who was running for Lieutenant Governor. I reported to the office of this beautiful young woman, two years my junior, who had been in the Oklahoma House of Representatives and who had chaired the most powerful House Appropriations and Budget Committee. Two other girls and I were sent to her office, and on the third day as we were parading out of the office, the Press Secretary stood up, pointed to me and said, "Hold that girl!"

That was the beginning of a most wonderful new adventure in my life. At that time, I was bumming a ride to work and earning $6.50 an hour! But, I felt like a millionaire, because that was the most money I had seen in the last 6 years! Life was turning around, indeed.

It is to the glory and grace of God that I can report on the wonderful comeback and adventure that I have experienced since stepping out of the pit of darkness into the glorious light of God. My God justifies! My God reigns! My God lives! My God restores. My God turns the bad things into good things. My God is my protector and deliverer. My God is my all! He was there all the time, and now, I am truly aware of His presence and rejoice in it. Better than all the things He has done for me, the trust I have found in Him is the most precious treasure. Trust is so very important.

You have read about the tragedy, the loss, the bitterness, the misery and defeat that I suffered during those six long miserable years. Now, let me relate the joy and success that God has brought into my life. There would not be much use in telling the story of the misery, if not for the happy ending. And, I know it hasn't ended, because God goes on forever!

He has turned my hopelessness into hopefulness; my loss into gain; my misery into joy; my defeat into success, and my shame into glory. How big is God? He is bigger than anyone can fathom. How great is His love? It is greater than any human can imagine.

Get ready to jump off that mountain of curses into the arms of God's love and blessings. His love is who He is. His love is what He is. His love is all encompassing. Let me tell you what His love has been doing in my life.

Since that day when the press secretary called out "hold that girl" I have had many wonderful jobs. Remember, how the hardest thing I did was give up my secure government job. Well, I don't depend on the job anymore. I depend on God. I can walk away from any job now, at any time, because I don't put my trust in the job for my security.

My favorite thing to do now is temporary work. This world is temporary, and I want to be ready to go whenever the time comes for that place which is eternal. I aim at spiritual life, and no longer look to the temporary physical world to supply my needs.

You see a change happened when I came out of the darkness. I realized that the very things that brought me into that darkness and prison were the very things I relied on. The false idols of jobs, salary, house, car, diamonds and Me. Let me reiterate what I just said. These things, as well as my own self-control and self-will, are False Idols!

We take these things for granted and are blindly led down a dark path to destruction as we depend on false idols, mistaking them to be "the way we're supposed to do things". And worse than the false idols of job security, wages, insurance, retirement and material possessions, I found out I was indulging in self-idolatry by the very fact that the big "I" had to be in control of all my circumstances. That is pride! It is the sin that brought the downfall of the most beautiful, powerful angel of God.

Chapter VI – True Happiness

The sociopath that wreaked havoc in my life was aided and abetted by my own, unknowing sinful nature. How well trained we become in this physical world, being led away like sheep to the slaughter thinking we are on the right track! It is frightening to realize how far off we can be from the truth! So, back to the Cinderella part of my story.

I have had the distinct pleasure of working for two Speakers of the House of Oklahoma Representatives, a Chief Justice of the Supreme Court of Oklahoma; and enjoyed the excitement of working on campaigns for candidates for Lt. Governor, Governor and U.S. Senate. This sure does beat the old grind of civil service! The young lady who lost her bid for Lieutenant Governor also taught me to be a legal secretary when her campaign was over, and I worked for her many years, before going on to those other adventuresome jobs.

You see, God restored the job that I lost with abundant and exciting new jobs.

Michelle and Jeff divorced after several years, and she came to live with me while she attended a beauty college. Casey was 3 years old, and oh how I enjoyed those two. This was the most awesome restoration I received from God. The precious time that I lost with my little girl. I couldn't even imagine that God could do anything about that loss. But without my asking, because I couldn't even imagine such a thing, God gave her back to me for a time of healing and growing.

We grew together in God's love and learned together how to tithe, expecting God to take care of us. Yes, it was a quality time we shared with each other and with God. We were new at walking in faith, but we certainly knew we had nothing to fear anymore. We had already come through the most tortuous time together, nothing could frighten us now. We had God, and we were so happy. He can restore anything and He loves to please His children. He can turn the wrong turns we make into right turns, and our losses into gains.

Michelle and I learned a lot from our experiences and we know how to trust God, and God alone, for our safety, happiness and welfare. We lived together for about 5 years. Isn't that amazing? Then, in the same year we both remarried and have lived happily ever after.

I attended a funeral recently for a former co-worker from the Air Force Base where I had worked twenty years ago. I saw some of the doctors, nurses, and staff that I had worked with for ten years. It was so good to see them again. One was actually still working after all this time. They were older than me. I am now in my early fifties. They bragged that I hadn't changed a bit and looked great!

How high can God raise you from that low point! Another great evangelist teaches that we get double for our trouble! I like being in that doubly high place, and I know how high it is, because I know, too well, how low I had been.

I laughed later telling my mom and daughter how surprised the chief nurse was when I told her I had been happily married 10 years. As I thought about her surprise, I was reminded that during the 10 years I worked with them, I was married 5 times! No wonder she was surprised!

Oops, I gave it away. The fellow that I dated for four years, I married him on the rebound two months after my divorce from the policeman. I then had it annulled in front of the same judge who granted my divorce – on grounds that I hadn't waited the 6 months! We dated four years after the annulment. I guess it's all right to not count this one, since it was annulled.

I am certainly not proud of my track record. But, then we all go through so much in this short life on earth, as we try to discover who we are and how our life is supposed to be. It seems the stronger we are, the harder we fall. I was always an obstinate, have my own way, stubborn redhead! And, I had my way all right – all the way to the bottom of the pit – where I found my Lord Jesus who had been with me the whole time, and He raised me up on eagle's wings as we soared higher than the highest mountain.

   I am married to the only man in the world for me. He is twenty years older and has garnered my respect. He is of the greatest generation and he knows how to be a man. He is the strongest, kindest and the most humorous, handsome man that ever turned my head. However, he turned my head the right way – and now my life couldn't get any better than this. He has taken me around the country from top to bottom and east to west as he works as a catastrophe insurance adjuster. I am his helper and our work is very fulfilling as we help people who have just survived earthquakes and hurricanes. It is so wonderful to meet these heroes and hear their stories, to lend and ear and be there to help. Life is so good.

   I fell in love with my husband the first time I saw him. He was a county commissioner when I met him at a state wide meeting of nearly three hundred commissioners. He stood out in the crowd. He looked liked Clark Gable in the Misfits, with his Stetson hat, bushy black eyebrows, and twinkling brown eyes. We danced, and talked and fell in love.

   Later, he took me to visit his home in southwest Oklahoma and I marveled as I watched him wrestle tractors, plows and combines, ride horses and take care of the cattle. My favorite memory of those early days was when he took me with him to get a bull that had wandered off. He rounded the bull into a loading chute that was in the pasture and headed him into the trailer. Then, as he stood straddling the chute and reached out to shut the trailer door, it stuck! To my horror this bull turned around and was heading right for him. My heart felt like it dropped on the ground I was so struck with fear! Al didn't even flinch – he just kicked out his booted foot toward the bull's head, and yelled "get back in there!" And that bull turned around!

My heart fluttered, as I said to myself: "He *is* the strongest man in the world!" He is still that strong man for me today – ten years later. Life with my Al is one adventure after another – and I love to travel, now! He is my hero, and now I know what a real husband is all about. I waited six years after than horrible experience, but I tried it again, and this time it was right. God brought me the perfect mate – and I thank Him everyday for making my world so bright and wonderful.

Remember how I was never going to move out of that first house! It took a bulldozer to get me out of it, but look what God did once I got out! I love to travel, now. "Don't fence me in!"

After we married, Al brought me back to Oklahoma City after living in Southwest Oklahoma a couple of years. When we found the house we wanted to buy, my daughter came by to see it. She looked around and then said to me, "Mom, this house is exactly like the one you lost." I hadn't noticed that, but she was quick to see it. As I looked again, I saw it. The house even faced the same direction, and besides being exactly like the one I had lost, it even had the extras that I used to wish was in that first house.

I was astounded as I saw how God hadn't forgotten one detail in restoring those things that I had so painfully lost when I was in control of my life. He gave me back my time with my daughter, my house the way I wanted it, an abundance of wonderful jobs, my dignity and even the benefits that went with the first job! My husband has provided me with insurance and benefits under his state retirement that I lost when I gave up my federal job.

God is wonderful! He didn't forget anything! He gave me back everything I lost, and He gave it back to me bigger and better than before. And you know what? I have no control over it! And, I am so glad! Because I know how far out of control I can get, and now I have God in control and I am worry free!

As I was praising God and telling him how glad I was that He loved me, I was reminded of a vivid moment from my past. One evening as I lay silently crying over my hopeless situation, I remember sitting straight up and crying out, "I want my Daddy!"

The words that escaped from my mouth took me by surprise. It wasn't anything that I was thinking, it just roared up out of my soul! I remember wondering where in the world that plea came from. I could barely remember my father, so I couldn't imagine missing him or wanting him so much after all those years. He died when I was four years old.

Thinking about that now, I realize that I was in desperate need of a man who would protect me, save me from the monster I had married, and deliver me out of my hopeless situation.

As this thought quickly ran through my mind, I was reminded that I did have a Father in heaven that loved me, protected me and saved me from the misery and fear of death that stalks us in the world. God is our Father, our true and real Father, and it so wonderful to hide in His love and protection. He sent His Word, made flesh, crucified it, and delivered us from the kingdom of darkness and hell. All fear is gone, because Jesus overcame the world! He defeated Satan and took the keys away from him that he used to hold God's children captive! We are free indeed! God is my Daddy!

Now, is that a testimony or is that a testimony! Perhaps you might like to read the rest of the book that I have written about the things I have learned about God along my way. It's guaranteed to be true and I'm living proof that it works.

Believing and trusting in Him is the only way to survive as you find your way in this strange world. I discovered the hard way that I had false gods in my life, as I watched all of the material things disappear.

Those things had become more important to me than God. I looked to the money, job, house, car, and diamonds for my security. I was looking the wrong way – God wasn't in those things!

The most destructive and yet elusive idol that I worshipped then was myself! Yes, as I relied on my own self-sufficiency and control, I was taking my life out of God's hands and protection. I wasn't looking to Him; I was looking to myself as my provider. When I look back at the great things I learned as God rescued me from my wrong thinking, I can't help but smile, and say it was worth it all to have life, and have it more abundantly.

There is prosperity, and then there is prosperity. God's prosperity starts on the inside and manifests on the outside. The world's prosperity starts on the outside and rots the inside. We know by the fruit. God's fruit is peace, joy, contentment, happiness and everything that is opposite to the misery that I endured and suffered, until Jesus set me free! *Oh, lift up ye gates, and come in my King of Glory!*

CHAPTER 7

THE ERROR OF OMISSION

The title of this chapter reminds me of the errors and omissions insurance which my husband carries for protection in his work as an adjuster. Wouldn't it be nice if we had E&O insurance for our emotional protection? Emotional damage is caused by a smorgasbord of negative experiences which include rejection, abuse, loss and other actions that are usually and unfortunately dealt by a loved one. Our method of protection is something that needs to be discovered and examined and that is my plan for this chapter. God I need your divine help to get me through this one. There are captives that need to be set free, including my very own daughter.

The preceding chapters on my testimony were originally written for my second book. However, when I gave that book to my daughter to read and edit, she told me to take those chapters out. So, I did.

She said that reading those chapters were the hardest thing she had ever done. They brought up old memories that she had put away and never wanted to think about again. I deleted them from the book, regretting that I had brought back such painful memories for her.

It would be impossible for anyone to observe Michelle, her happiness and her lifestyle, and suspect that anything might be wrong. We didn't. She has had wonderful success in her career as a master hair colorist and her son is perfect in every way, of course. She has a great husband, lovely home, and a wonderful clientele. Just the other day someone at work told her that she was the most balanced person they had ever met.

One evening I spoke to Michelle on the phone and she confided that she was having difficulties and she just couldn't pinpoint the problem. While we were trying to figure out what was bothering her, she said she knew that she was emotionally detached. Well, of course she is! I am the one who showed her how! I wanted to protect her from the monster that had intruded into our lives so many years ago. Detachment was a form of protection!

No wonder she is confused! It has to do with emotional abuse and the way people deal with it. If you remember reading about my miserable six years with the sociopath, you will find it remarkable that little is said about my daughter. That is because our love went underground during this period. You see, I remember very well how angry and jealous this man became if I paid more attention to her than him. I even explained this to her, and told her we had to be careful to keep him from being mean and angry. To my horror, I recalled my role in throwing up this barricade in her childhood – to protect her!

We need God to reveal what it is she is dealing with in order to break the hold caused by that barricade. It has been there since she was 12-years old! And, this revelation is not just for her, but for every person that has suffered mental or physical abuse. Even though we get through the forgiveness process and begin to heal, some hidden barriers can lurk deep within.

The devil uses maniacal deviant attacks to prevent us from discovering and understanding our identity as children of God who can walk in His power. Not only does that devil stop our spiritual development during our pain, he also causes us to build invisible barricades. These can go unnoticed as we continue on our spiritual journey and then halt our spiritual growth years later.

We can obtain our forgiveness through Jesus and find protection in the arms of God, but that is only two-thirds of the way! We must next rid ourselves of mistrust and hidden inner barriers that we have constructed unknowingly. We are unable to reach the third part of our life, the spiritual realm, where miracles and wonders are manifested, until we can truly "Let Go and Let God"! This is what is going to happen in Book Three of the Spiritual Trilogy that God has given me to write.

As Michelle and I talked this matter over, we recalled how last week a person had just really irked her. She was a woman who had suffered sexual abuse as a child and she was still whining and crying about it. Michelle cannot tolerate weakness. You see she dealt with her mental abuse in a much subtler way. She became very strong both physically as a gymnast, and emotionally, as well. She built spiritual muscles that could hold back all tears and pain. This is what she is now dealing with. How do you get rid of such a powerfully strong barricade? One that contains the emotions which, she has discovered, result in her complete emotional detachment. She has made a safe place where nothing can hurt her. She can hide her love, her emotions and her pain; and that stronghold is coming down. God will show her the way.

On a Saturday morning a few days later Michelle called at 8 a.m. and told she was on her way over, saying that she had been up since 4 a.m. too!

"How did you know I had been up since then?" I asked her.

She just laughed, and asked me if I would fix her poached eggs.

Oh, what an interesting day we had, and I pray the Holy Spirit can re-create the whole turn of events as I marvel while I sit here writing this morning. That was what I was doing at 4 a.m. yesterday morning, by the way.
While talking with Michelle on the phone, I learned that she and her husband were having an argument. This didn't happen often, but Michelle was upset and knew that she had to deal with something going on in her life right now. She had to find out what the problem was and what to do about it. She was very upset, and that is unusual for her, because remember Michelle emotionally detaches from things like this. She knew she was definitely up against something, and she didn't know what it was. The obvious culprit was her husband.
Her journey is taking her into the spiritual realm, the realm of God's power; and there is an enemy trying to block the entrance. So, even though she is mad in the flesh, she also knows that she has to find out where the attack is really coming from in the spirit. Confusion has a grip on her and she has to see her way through to the truth.
Michelle and I talked this all over that morning over poached eggs before she went on to work. She asked if I wanted to go shopping with her later to look for a dress

for her brother-in-law's upcoming wedding. She said she would be finished working by 1 or 2 that afternoon.

I picked up lunch for us and met her at the salon that afternoon. While I was waiting for Michelle in the break room, a couple of ladies came in. They introduced themselves, and I told them I was Michelle's mom. (Still my favorite role.) One of the girls paid me a nice compliment and then asked if Michelle got her talent for coloring from me.

"No, she didn't get it from me. She must have gotten it from her father who was creative, even though she was never around him." I continued with the words, "I have absolutely no creativity."

Michelle came in and we left on our shopping expedition, which was really more of a brainstorming session over why Michelle was so mad at her husband. She was exhausted since she hadn't slept the night before and had gotten up at 4 a.m. She told me she was praying and fussing with God about her feelings and telling Him that He had to do something about them. She needed His guidance. She was in the grip of emotional turmoil. She needed His light of truth and understanding to bring her into peace and harmony.

We didn't come to any conclusions, and Michelle departed for home. She was going to try to grab a quick nap before going to an out of town ball game with her husband and son that night.

I ran the rest of my errands and arrived home a couple hours later. I had not even brought in all the groceries and sacks, when Michelle called and I discovered she was on her way over. Another explosion with the husband and she had left! This boil was really festering and she wasn't going to let it go much further.

She arrived and we watched some of the ball game on television. Then, we drove to her house to get some things in case she decided to spend the night. She also wanted some of her bible study materials, meditation book, prayer books and Bible. She was definitely on a mission to find the truth.

We went to my room and talked. I told Michelle that I had been fending off guilt and condemnation for the fact that she had gone through so much emotional trauma during my turbulent marriage. I also told her that I had given her to God a long time ago, and I had already prayed and reminded Him that He would fix her. I believed that with all my heart.

I wasn't going to fall for those old devilish tricks of condemnation and guilt. I knew that I had been forgiven. Even though I felt badly that my daughter hurt, I had given this concern to God, and I wasn't taking it back.

Michelle talked about the things that came to mind. She said the word Anaconda had been brought to her attention two or three times. The word had come to mind several times, and she even saw an Anaconda in a movie recently. The news was also reporting on the U.S. mission called Anaconda that was currently going on in Afghanistan. She described the enormity of this snake and told me it was so large it could blend unnoticeably into the Amazon River of South America.

Michelle and I brought out the dictionary and began what I jokingly call "our word game". We looked up Anaconda and it was described as a snake that crushes its prey.

As Michelle pondered this, she told me how she felt completely swallowed up by this huge snake in the fact that she was so emotionally detached. She was unable to see things around her because of this overwhelming feeling of being covered over, as if she were in the body of that huge snake.

She then proceeded to tell me of an encounter that she had with the sociopath when she was twelve years old. I was at work when her grandmother had come by to give her some money for her sixth-grade graduation. She hid the money somewhere in her clothes, so he wouldn't see it. He was a devourer and a thief that took everything and he also had a cunning ability to know things.

When she came back into the house he immediately confronted her about why her grandmother had come. She wouldn't tell him that she had some money, and defied him to bother her. She was my strong girl, not weak and afraid like me.

How it came about I'm not clear, but the part of the story Michelle relates is that now he has come into her room and is furious at her. She described him bending her over a bookshelf under her window. (I noted she was sitting under the very same window in the same room of this house that was identical to our old house.)

She continued, relating how he was screaming and cursing at her, pulling her hair and almost breaking her back. She told me that at that moment a huge feeling came over her and she cursed back at him. She frightened him and chased him from her room. She could feel the flame red in her face. She said something came over her and surrounded her, and it was so big that it frightened him. She remembers to this day, that he no longer messed with her, because she had protection. Good or evil she couldn't say, but she felt a power that she described as being so big that it frightened this evil man into retreat! She remembered he ran to the bedroom across the hall and stayed there.

Now we are talking about a spiritual realm that is unknown to natural man. Some people shy away from this realm and refuse to get involved in something that they can't see, feel or touch.

I only touched briefly on the fact that I had encountered out of body experiences. This is spiritual and we have a tendency to hide the unknown, not only from one another, but from ourselves, as well.

This book is not going to be the ordinary, but rather the extraordinary. While my first two books dealt with the body and the soul, this third book is going to deal with the spirit. Spiritual matters are indeed extraordinary because they are beyond the scope of physical senses. We understand our physical circumstances by sight, taste, touch and sound. Our spiritual senses of perception and understanding however require development.

As Michelle talked further, she remembered her gifts from God that had been taken away. For a period of time last year she had been overwhelmed by a spiritual gift of smell. She could perceive evil in her midst by the foul smell of it, and likewise, could perceive the presence of the Lord by sweet fragrances. She didn't know what to do with this gift, and eventually it just went away, much to her dismay. She prayed and asked why it was gone, and what it meant.

Michelle talked about visions she had in her life. The very first extraordinary encounter that Michelle had with the Lord was when she was about 14-years old. She was talking to her boyfriend, Jeff, her future husband. She told me this story when it happened and I wondered then what special plan God must have for her someday.

She described sitting with Jeff at his house when he began asking her questions about God, and she said that all of a sudden as they talked, she found she was looking through the eyes of Jesus and that she answered Jeff's questions, but it was not her that answered.

She described the beauty of seeing through His eyes. The colors were soft greens and blues, and they constantly changed almost like a kaleidoscope.

She then told of a picture that came to her in vision a few years ago that was so vivid that it gave her a desire to paint it. She has never been exposed to art or painting, because she was raised by her mother, the self-confessed uncreative one. So, this desire to paint must have been spiritually .imparted to her.

The first time that she described this picture to me, I became anxious to see it sooner than she wanted to paint it. She said that would be a hobby or something she would do after her son grew up and left home. He was only about 14-years old then.

The picture that she saw was the bottom portion of the cross and it was huge. The top of it went out of sight, probably into the heavens, the bottom portion showed the feet of Jesus nailed to the cross and the blood was pouring out like a river and splashing onto rocks surrounding it. The blood was a pure, vivid red and she could see it so clearly.

We began looking up words, and the revelation that played out as we did this is so remarkable! We began with the words that best describe Michelle.

Power: Ability to act; capacity for action or being acted upon. Capability of producing or undergoing an effect; as, to have the power, but not the will, to work.

Michelle thought about the last part of the definition 'to have the power, but not the will to work'. She surmised, "No gumption, detached." She thought about the fact that her creativity was something inherited from her father, and this not having the will also brought to mind her father who did not pursue his creativity. She gave me some relief for taking all the responsibility for the bad things that happened. She had inherited some of these traits of detachment and aloofness from him.

I had told Michelle that when the woman who whined and cried irked her I looked for the reason. I had explained to her that usually when we come up against something that causes us to react negatively, it is because our spirit recognizes it is a problem within us that has to be dealt with. My pastor that Sunday preached a sermon on becoming other-centered versus self-centered. He talked about persons who held onto their pain and wouldn't give it up by forgiving as indulging in idol worship of self. The fact was very blunt and to the point. He extended empathy to those who had suffered great affliction, but nevertheless brought home a vivid point.

Holding onto the pain makes you guilty of the same sin as the person who caused your pain. As the person who hurt you was selfish in thinking of his own desire and not the pain it would cause others; the one who is hurt has the same guilt of being selfish which is an engagement of idol worship, in not giving it up. I had related this to Michelle, and now she was seeing that her bottled up, covered up pain was not any different than that of the lady that had irked her. She just didn't express it vocally. She thought if it was hidden that it couldn't hurt. Right? Wrong!

We looked up more words:

Detachment: Isolation, indifference.

Michelle was uncovering things within that had to be dealt with. We had learned in our first study of antonyms that her natural behavior was that of being "indifferent" which she followed the meaning out to the word "death". We know by now only too well how that old devil tries to isolate us from God. So, too, in this spiritual uncovering, she found that "to not have the will" and to be "detached" was the same as "death".

Isn't it interesting that when we get to the core of our problems, the manifestation of them in our body is the result of what we find in our spirit?

Further discussion of the words "bring into being" brought us to look at the words create and creative. Michelle talked about how she saw creative people that seem to self-destruct. Creative people are the ones involved in the arts. They are talented people. One rock star she thought of has the power to capture an audience of millions and bring them to tears. His creativity is huge, and yet he keeps surgically changing his flesh, destroying it.

Michelle said she saw the creativity in her father when she met him, but he had just dropped out of the main stream. He did not pursue his creative talents and fell into that "lack of will" described above. She said her father could write beautiful lyrics, sing, play musical instruments and paint. She saw a great creativity going to waste there.

We continued our word search:

Create: To cause to exist; to bring into being.

To be creative we discover is to become like our Father, God, Himself. No wonder the devil is throwing up so many roadblocks and diversions. He surely doesn't want us to walk in our rightful inheritance and power as God's children. What a threat to that old demon we would be!

Our discussion went on as we searched for the things that we had wanted to create in our lives. My childhood had been that of a wanderer, attending many schools and being uprooted, so that as a grown-up I wanted a home that I would never have to leave – ever! That was my reaction to my childhood unhappiness.

Michelle on the other hand described how she felt out of place, almost embarrassed, because she came from a divorced home. She described her best friends as having two parents, and she didn't have that normalcy. I divorced her dad when she was only one. Then, at age 12 she lost me to the sociopath as I became helpless. She said that a friend or client had commented that her mother had done a great job raising her. She said she really had to think that one over, because she didn't have anyone there for her when she was growing up. The thought that she had done it herself immediately showed her the sin of pride and idolatry. That old devil will slip in something every chance he gets, that is why we must always be alert and in God's word and will in order to remain safe. She also remembers always "knowing" that she was protected, even though she didn't quite recognize what that force was or where it came from, she just always knew it was there.

She recognized the things that she needed to establish in herself as an adult to replace those things that were taken from her as a child. She needed: family, stability and a father. Where I had built my false idols out of material things, the house, job, car, and jewelry; Michelle had no need of these things. She had grown up watching these things come and go as we lived with the sociopath. She never had the time to grow attached to material objects. Her idolatry came with self-control! No one would hurt her like I had been hurt, she was strong and she exercised her strength fiercely in her pursuit of gymnastics, perfecting her muscle control, while at the same time developing her inner spiritual muscles. She married right after high school and even though the marriage was not right, she never let anyone know. She could detach and go on as if nothing ever happened, whether good or bad. She walked through anything and it never fazed her.

There were more words to look up in the dictionary:

Creative. Having the power or quality of creating.

Productive. Produce as work of thought or imagination, especially as a work of art.

We burst into tears on this word. It took us full circle back to Michelle's vision of the blood and the cross and her desire to paint that she was "putting off". That was why God took back her sense of smell! She wasn't using her gifts. She was supposed to be painting! The realization flooded over us both. I asked her if she could smell colors and she said, "of course". You see she mixes colors every day in her field of work as a "colorist".
She then began describing the difference in reds, and how the one in her vision was pure. "Like before oxygen touches it", she said. Ooh, what an implication! The oxygen in this world discolors the blood. The world contaminates that which is pure.
Michelle has had a major breakthrough! Her fight is not with her husband, it is with the deceiver who is trying to prevent her from using her creative God-given talent! It is flowing now, and I'm trying the best I can to tell it like it happened. I pray the order comes out right, because the way it came about was so absolutely astonishing, freeing and joyous!
The word "imagination" immediately brought us to a discussion of my sister, Marcia. Michelle told about how much she understood Marcia whom we lost a few years ago. Michelle said she suffered the same fears and feelings that Marcia had, and she learned a lot from Marcia, even though Marcia succumbed to her fears. We remembered

the legacy that Marcia had left us, and that was "imagination". So, we headed toward this word.

Imagine. To form a mental image of. To contrive or scheme, suppose or think to be, to form images.

Imagination. The act or power of imagining. The power to form mental images.

Wow, back to power. The word that best describes Michelle. The word Michelle relates to most is "power".
A description of the synonyms continued with: The power to form mental images of things not before one, or the EXERCISE OF THAT POWER IN LITERATURE AND ART!
Yes, Michelle was getting the picture! She needed to exercise her artistic ability. She must paint the image in her mind of Jesus and the flowing blood that is not only covering over the rocks, but splashing on the ones to the wayside. She talks about how important the words are that she read recently in her Bible, that every man, "every man" will be saved by the blood of Jesus!
We took a short break so Michelle could call her husband and tell him she loved him, and that everything was going to be all right. She would be home soon. She still had some things she was working on. She said he told her that he didn't know her. She told him no one did because she never shared her private feelings. She explained that she was working this out with her Mom, because I was the only one who had been there when it all began.
I came back into the room when she got off the phone and she asked me now to look up the word color.

Color. A quality of visible phenomena distinct from form and from light and shade, such as the red of blood!!!!!

How can we express the emotion that is erupting in this room as she is flooded with the blood and the revelation of her calling? Oh, I remember something I omitted much earlier on. Michelle said before we started the word search that her meditation book that she had opened up to between our two visits this day had talked about taking action, and not being passive or lazy! This whole session tonight is about taking action.

The action being shown to her is to use her creative God-given talent to paint the picture He has shown her. In a private divulgence, she told me she had seen this picture in her dreams on a wall in every church. She didn't say it with a sense of boasting, but rather a glimpse of things beyond her imagining. Remember, Michelle has never had a paint brush in her hand, nor has she ever had one iota of training in art. So, this is definitely a journey in faith!

Michelle also commented that three different women have witnessed to her about painting over the past few months. The first one answered Michelle's question, "do you have to be able to draw before you paint"? The woman told her you don't have to draw to paint.

A second and third woman each had given her information on painting, and one was looking up information on art classes she could attend.

Well, we had another word to check, so we continued:

Phenomenon. Any object known through the senses rather than through thought or intuition. The object of experience.

This is too much! Remember the seven spirits of God? Four of them are senses! The sense of smell, the sense of taste, the sense of hearing and the sense of sight. Confirmation, again, that Michelle's gift is from God and it is perceived by the spirits of God in the senses. At last, we were able to stop the word search at: *The object of experience.*

The object of the experience has to be what God can do when He turns the bad things into good things. The object is that we found our spirit and shed the body while releasing our soul from its prison. I hope this makes as much sense to you as it does to me.

Believing is receiving. Another good thing happened for me during all of this. While Michelle was marveling that she was surrounded by color, and her calling was shown to her as painting, she pointed out to me that I also was creative and had creative ability. My writing is an art and gift from God, and working as a secretary, I have been surrounded by words; just as Michelle working as a colorist has been surrounded by color. That made me feel very special.

Michelle also described how she could sense colors around her. She said the time she sensed them most was when she was in Phillip's arms, and that they were intense colors. They were the color of love! You might think I'm making up this next part, but I'm not. Michelle then showed me the next chapter of her bible study book that she hadn't started yet. Its title is "The Color of Love"!

We hugged good-bye. It was 1 o'clock in the morning when Michelle headed home and I went to bed saying thank you prayers, for Jesus took care of her just as I asked and expected.

Michelle and I covered a lot of ground in one evening as she discovered a passion to paint that had been buried along with her emotional pain of childhood. It was indeed a study of errors and omissions as she discovered the error of burying her pain that resulted in the omission of appropriate emotional responses.

There was one other word we looked up that evening. We looked up the word "art".

Art is described as skill in performance, acquired by experience. Give your experiences to God, and let Him turn them into a work of art.

Just imagine the possibilities!

"Must then Christ perish in every age to save those who have no imagination?"

> George Bernard Shaw
> From his tragedy, Saint Joan

CHAPTER 8

THERE'LL BE SOME CHANGES MADE TODAY!

I am about to write one of the most exciting chapters of all the books that I have written so far in the trilogy. I pray for guidance and direction in the flow of this work. There is so much to tell, it has begun to happen, and it must be told as it progresses because it is happening so fast. I don't want to leave out anything.

Where to begin? Obviously, I must go back to the beginning of this episode and carefully set down the series of events.

I earlier explained that I had been studying the Bible and writing for the past ten years, and only recently had the books started taking shape. I finished *Way Beyond the River* near Christmas of 2000. I didn't know what to do about publishing it, so I gave copies to friends and family.

Then, my second book, *The Walls Came Tumbling Down* was started in February of 2001 and I finished it on Christmas Day 2001.

Again, I gave copies to some close friends and family. Now, it is June of the following year and I have had a vision of the publication of all three small books into one book. I stopped writing on this third book for awhile because I understood that not only would this book be completed and published in a trilogy with the first two books, but there was no doubt that the ending would be about a breakthrough for my niece.

God showed me how He had told me to tell her to "expect great things" in the first book, and this book would not conclude until that promise was fulfilled!

God is never late, and His promises never fail. He has shown me recently as things are beginning to explode in the spiritual realm that I must believe. Believing and expecting are the catalysts that bring spiritual things into manifestation. So, let me say this again. You must believe in order to receive. If you believe it, you will receive it. If you doubt it, you will lose it.

The power of choice lies within us, and we are the captains of our ships. We steer the rudder that St. James described as our tongue. There is power in our words and there is power in our thoughts. The devil works tirelessly to direct our focus on physical possibilities where there are limitations and failures. It takes imagination to go beyond the circumstances that we see with our natural eye, and delve into the possibilities of the spiritual world, knowing, believing and expecting that all things are possible through Christ who strengthens us!

What foreboding obstacles emerge to discourage us from pursuing our dreams? Those who have failed to pursue their dreams know exactly what barriers manifest to dissuade and turn them around from the path that leads to success and achievement. These obstacles are real, and when you get right down to it, they are the product of fear.

Just as I am trying to explain how our dreams can be manifested by believing and expecting great things; I see that our failures are likewise manifested by our doubting and dread. You see it comes back down to choice. We make the decision based on what we see. Here is where we must distinguish between our physical and spiritual eyes. Determine if you are looking into the light or the darkness. The spiritual laws operate in either direction, so we must be sure we are going in the right direction.

To pursue the will of God in your life is to tap into the inner strength that comes from the spiritual man inside you. A word of warning is to never, ever pursue spiritual manifestation without being protected by Jesus. There are many books on spiritualism that will draw a person into spiritual darkness. Jesus is our protection because He won the victory over darkness and its inhabitants.

It is true that angels are all around us, but remember that one-third of them fell with Satan into darkness. It is even written that Satan can disguise himself as an angel of light. So, don't wander into unknown realms by using Ouija boards and other tools of darkness. Put on your armor of God, and take with you His Word and His Spirit. Just don't go there without Jesus as your savior.

We can be enticed into spiritual darkness, but we must choose to protect ourselves in Jesus who is the door into the spiritual light of God.

After I understood that Christy was still awaiting the manifestation of the great things promised her by God, I thought about her situation which is dire at present. No, I am not surprised. We all go through trials, and I am convinced that the greater the call of God on your life, the greater the obstacles that present to block you from receiving His gifts.

Christy and her family had to move out of their home this year when it became uninhabitable because of toxic mold infestation. She and her husband and three children have been forced out of their home, having to leave behind everything they owned. Christy prided herself on the fact that their home was completely paid for. There was no mortgage on the home and she and her husband had been totally renovating it with new cabinets, flooring and more when the toxic mold was discovered. As fast as they were working to turn this house into their country dream home, the mold was working against them as it devoured everything!

They are living with her in-laws while waiting for the outcome of their home insurance investigation, being unable to destroy the mold home or sell the property until a final determination is made. The mold was the result of water damage from a previous incident when a pipe broke and spilled water all over the floor, and unbeknownst to them ran into the heat and air vents that were located in the floor. That insurance claim was handled by an adjuster over the phone who only allowed floor covering replacement and the water in the vents went unchecked.

Mold was discovered much later when Christy became suspicious of it after her son had a terrible bout with allergies and an ear infection that caused his eardrum to burst. Since the discovery of black mold in their home the family has been waiting for months that have stretched into seasons while the insurance investigation drags on and on.

Christy actually handles the situation very well considering the devastation. She believes and knows that God will take care of them and that she must remain patient. I have talked to her on many occasions, and along with our whole family we pray and wait for her and her family to be restored to a normal home life.

In a recent conversation with Christy, I was disheartened when she told me that she and her brother believe that the great things are in heaven - not on earth! I can't explain how shocked I was to hear this from the lips of the girl that has such great faith in God!

Obviously, I disagree. I may not have stepped completely into the glory land, but I know it is there for me, and I pursue it vigorously. I have seen so many things happen that can only be attributed to God working in my life, and I have such a great expectation for so much more. I do believe that it depends on us to strengthen our inner man and submit this flesh to the dictates of the spiritual being that we truly are. We came into the world in the flesh, but we must overcome that limitation, and plug into the power of God through our spiritual man.

Through the spiritual sense I have been made aware of the power of "control" on people. God has directed my attention to this control operating in two important people in my life. Christy and another friend have been demonstrating the control they use in their lives, and whenever God shows me a problem, he always provides the answer.

It has been shown to me that controlling people are usually victims of some form of abuse whether verbal, emotional or whatever. The use of control is a tactic developed early in life for protection, and it lies hidden inside of a person, out of sight from them and those around them. It is a huge wall and barricade that separates them from the gifts of God and hinders them in experiencing the fullness of life.

In that conversation with Christy, I learned that as a youth she thought animals in the zoo were well taken care of and "secure". Her mother told her they were in a prison! She thinks that's the place to be - EGAD! I was flooded with emotion when I heard her say these things to me. How many others are living in self-made prisons in order to be safe?!

I used to be there myself! I had a home and never wanted to leave it. I was the one in control of all my circumstances when they spiraled into devastation. I explained to Christy how I had put my trust and security

Ch VIII - There'll be Some Changes Made Today

into a home and I lost it. Further, I replaced it, still believing that was my security, and I lost the next one too! I warned her that if mold had destroyed this home, don't expect the next one to be secure, because it could be destroyed or lost also. I knew it. I was speaking from my own experience. Another complication came to my attention as I talked to Christy about the possibility of renting a place until this matter is resolved. She surprised me when she told how she would never be able to spend money on rent, for that was throwing money away as far as she was concerned. She further explained to me how difficult it was for her to spend money on herself. She could spend it on her children, but she would become pale and sick to her stomach just thinking about spending it on herself.

I reminded her how worry over money drove her mother to an early grave, and it almost killed me. I told her she should seriously consider getting counseling. Her husband walked into the room about that time, and she told him Anne was saying she was crazy. Joe quickly quipped, "That's the pot calling the kettle black!"

We laughed and hung up, but I was on a mission to rescue Christy from her wrong thinking.

I began to pray earnestly because here I am expecting to write the end of my book as she receives great things, and she is telling me how adamantly she is opposed to receiving things! God, help us here!

Of course, I spoke to Michelle about the matter and we agreed Christy needed help. We weren't sure what, when or how; we just knew she needed help. We prayed and asked God for guidance and for Christy's deliverance from this emotional blockade.

As I was studying the next morning, I was continually bombarded by the word "control". I was being shown over and over this particular trait in both Christy and my friend, Barbara. I also believed they had both suffered abuse as children, and noted the common denominator as such.

I looked up the word control and was shocked to find the following definitions:

1. to keep within limits;
2. to test or verify by counter experiment; (counter meaning in the wrong way);
3. To exercise power over.
4. *Spiritualism.* A personality or spirit believed to actuate the utterances or performances of the medium.

Aha! Control is to verify in the wrong way. That tells me it obviously has them turned the wrong way. And, the spiritualism definition blew my socks off! It is a spirit! That is why I can sense it and feel it and recognize it! It is a spirit that is working through a person, exercising power over them and has them turned the wrong way. I had to look further into these meanings. So, I looked up the meaning of the word, medium:

A substance though which a force acts or an effect is transmitted.
A person supposed to be susceptible to supernormal agencies . . . as spiritualistic medium.

I knew pretty much that a medium is a type of psychic. However, I continued to read and found a meaning that just sucked the air out of me.

Biol. A nutritive mixture or substance, as broth or gelatin, agar, for cultivating bacteria, fungi, etc.

I stared at that word fungi and couldn't believe my

eyes! That is exactly what took over Christy's home - mold which is a fungi! It would seem that the mold was manifesting from the spirit of Christy! Now, I am looking up the word, mold:

Archaic & Dial.: The earth; hence, a *grave*!

A few days later a friend and client of Michelle's got in touch with her. Carla has been writing and researching for years about spiritual phenomenon. Michelle had lunch with her and they talked for four hours. Carla had gathered a wealth of spiritual information, and during the conversation, Michelle described her cousin as becoming very thin, isolated and withdrawn, and found it very difficult to communicate with her. Carla listened to Michelle and determined that Christy needed intercessory prayer. She also stressed that the prayer had to be specific. As they explored some of the events leading up to Christy' dramatic change, Carla explained that Christy seemed to have taken on the spirit of her mother who had worried so exceedingly about finances, and that if something wasn't done soon, it could kill her!

Later, Michelle shared this information with me. "Isn't it amazing how God answers prayer?" I commented. "We prayed for help, not knowing what to do for Christy, and out of nowhere your friend appeared whom you haven't seen or heard from in almost a year. She brought the answers we needed to help Christy!"

"Yes", Michelle continued, "It makes sense that the same spirit that caused Marcia's debilitating stress and worry over finances is blatantly working through Christy!"

As we discussed Marcia's spirit, we remembered how strong we had sensed her presence just a few weeks back.

I found one of my sister's favorite childhood books at an estate sale and purchased it. The book was *Fairy Tales from Grimm*. Marcia loved those stories, and she always had a great imagination. "Imagination" was the song that Marcia had wanted played at her funeral, and it was the legacy that Marcia left us.

I remembered thinking very much about her when I found the book. Several other things had reminded me of her that week.

"Michelle, I believe there is an important reason that we have been so aware of Marcia lately. Remember telling me about seeing Marcia's face quickly come and go while talking to two different women at about that same time frame?" I reminded her.

"I didn't know what to make of it at the time", Michelle said. "I asked Carla if you could pray for souls after death, and she told me 'yes'."

"Well, that settles it, Michelle", I concluded. "We must put together the specific prayer for Christy, and pray it together in agreement for her and her mother. I also believe that we should include my friend, Barbara."

You see I had a dream just a night or so ago, where I received a call from a man asking for Barbara. I got his name and it was Bob Sullivan. In my dream I asked Barbara if she had a brother named Bob, and she told me no, that would be her father. Her father is dead!

When I woke up and thought about the dream, I realized that I had not gotten any message from her father. But, as I recalled this dream, I understood the message that was conveyed through my spirit. Bob and Barbara need the same specific prayer!"

Ch VIII - There'll be Some Changes Made Today

I was being flooded with information, as I tried to relay it to Michelle. "Isn't it wonderful how much information is being conveyed to us through spiritual awareness and understanding!" I exclaimed.

"It all adds up and makes so much sense spiritually, even though to our natural senses it would seem ludicrous. I am so excited about this deeper knowledge!" I explained to Michelle. "All of these thoughts and messages are pieces of a puzzle that are coming together to form the perfect, specific prayer that must be written and prayed for the salvation of souls held captive! There was the fleeting glimpse of Marcia's face, her favorite book, the call from Barbara's father, and then remember the beaver and frogs?"

"Yes" Michelle recalled, "I saw a huge dead beaver while running around the lake one morning a few days ago. I felt sorry for him lying there dead, and I just couldn't get over how huge that beaver was. He was as wide as he was long, and he was so huge that his tail looked small in comparison."

"And," I continued, "Do you remember how you described Christy to me just last week when we talked?"

"Of course!" Michelle remembered. "I saw Christy as a stagnant pool with water that couldn't flow out. That beaver must represent the dam builder that has been stopping up the flow from Christy. It is a witness of the spiritual sense I had about her!"

"Yes!" I interrupted, "and my attention was drawn to frogs in a most exaggerated fashion. Last week Barbara's friend, Cheryl, sent me a thank you card with a note to the "princess", my new nickname from Barbara, along with a bottle of wine. The bottle had a frog standing tall on the label. It was obviously symbolic of the frog and princess *fairy tale*. Later that same day, I went to the doctor, where the nurse gave me an Augie Froggie sticker for being good. It was a big green frog sticker! Then, I swear, I watched a TV program that same night about a town in Oklahoma named 'Frogville. Can you believe all this attention to frogs in one day?"

I continued my story about the frogs as Michelle patiently listened. She is so good to indulge me, because I realize I do go on and on with detail at times. I believe I learned that trait from my husband as I used to listen to him tell story after story as we drove down the country roads where he grew up. He could even tell stories that would last on a trip that started in Los Angeles and ended in New York!

I just knew that my attention had been held captive by frogs for some reason, and I was going to find out why! I went into my room and pulled down the *Grimm's Fairy Tale Book* thinking the frog and princess story would surely be there. As I opened the cover, I was not even surprised that the very first page had a picture of the princess looking at a frog in the pond. The picture gave the page number of the story, so I turned and read it.

The frog had been under a curse placed on him by a witch. He was really a prince, and after the princess agreed to allow him to come into her palace and eat from her plate, the frog turned into a prince.

Michelle and I discussed all these peculiar happenings and realized that the people we were going to pray for were under a curse, and we must come against that curse in prayer to break its power, and to set the captives free. We must prepare a prayer and pray it together.

I got up very early on Sunday morning and did my

usual Bible study and prayers. Then, I began writing the following prayer for Michelle and I to pray together:

THE PRAYER

In Jesus Name we put on the armor of God, plead the blood of Jesus over us and those we are praying for and draw a circle of light around us. We come against the curse of abuse and the spirit of control that has held Marcia, Christy, Bob and Barbara captive in darkness and bondage. Forgive them, Jesus. We command a legion of angels of God to surround and protect us and do battle with the enemy.

We raise the banner of Jehova Nissi. Our victory in Jesus is manifested in all of our lives. Marcia, Christy, Bob and Barbara are set free from the curse of the Law and the curse of abuse. We cancel the power of the spirit of control that has worked through them. They are delivered by the power in the Name of Jesus from the spirit of control that has held them captive. They are no longer mediums for unclean spirits. BE LOOSED IN JESUS' NAME! We command the legion of angels of God to minister to the souls of Christy, Marcia, Bob and Barbara. Now, in the Name of Jesus we speak healing and deliverance to them, rejoicing in Jesus our deliverer. Come in O King of Glory, and bring them out of the darkness and into your light and healing.

Shalom! Be made whole. Be restored. Be ye citizens of the kingdom of God. SET FREE in Jesus' Name! We claim your victory over death and hell, over all principalities, powers, rulers of darkness and spiritual wickedness. We give Marcia, Christy, Bob and Barbara to you, Jesus. We bring them into your presence with praise and thanksgiving. Thank you, Jesus, for their deliverance, healing and restoration to the Kingdom of God. In Jesus' name we agree. Amen.

Michelle called me as the prayer was finished, and we prayed it together over the phone. Afterwards, we felt really good and were excitedly happy. We knew the prayer had worked. We believed it!

After praying, I mentioned to Michelle that Christy was down in the country camping out this weekend. Michelle asked me where, and I told her in a town in southeast Oklahoma. Michelle then wondered if they might be at *Beavers* Bend which is in southeast Oklahoma. I told her I thought *Frogville* was also in that part of the state. I got out my computer map and checked. We found that Christy was 73 miles from Beavers Bend and 72 miles from Frogville!

We just knew that the curse, symbolized by the frog, had been canceled, and the dam, symbolized by the beaver, had been torn down. The captives were set free! The prayer had worked! It was too emotionally powerful not to perceive! This was a jump up and down shout-for-joy victory! God leads us in mysterious ways, but if we practice using our spiritual senses, we can know so much more than what is visible to the natural eye.

This is such a wonderful demonstration of the difference between the physical senses and the spiritual senses. It goes to the heart of perceiving, instead of seeing, and to understanding rather than just hearing.

Michelle also told me about an earlier dream where she was fighting with a snake that was biting her, and her husband wouldn't help. She said she fought as it wrapped around her and kept biting her hand, but she finally succeeded in throwing it off. In her dream she was going up in an elevator with her husband next, and wondering why she hadn't died from the snake bite. She survived.

This dream represented another story in itself about spiritual victory over attacks that can come against a marriage. Her husband wasn't helping her because it was her own struggle, not his. However, they both rose above the problem as symbolized in the elevator ride.

During Michelle's four hour visit with Carla, she related this dream to her. At that same time she noticed she had two small bruises on the inside of her arm. She showed them to Carla and said, "That was probably from fighting with the snake."

Her friend asked aghast, "Are you manifesting your dreams?!"

It was this comment that reminded me of the definition of medium being a substance that grew mold. It was yet another insight and witness to me that the mold growing in Christy's home was indeed a manifestation of the death and decay that was building up in Christy's spirit. The mold was manifesting into her surroundings.

Thank God, she has been set free! I don't know if Christy or Barbara realize what has happened, but God has shown me that the power behind receiving is believing. God has shown me the importance of believing it, and I do beyond all doubt.

I heard a sermon yesterday on the radio about a message God gave to a man who cried out to Him that his prayers were never answered. The reply was that there are two such powerful spiritual laws, that even unbelievers can use them. The first is giving and receiving. The second is the power of the word. Many people who doubt, voice that doubt and it manifests. On the other hand, believers voice their belief and bring those things into existence.

I am convinced that the souls of both the children and the parents that we prayed for have all been set free. I believe that Michelle and I had our attention drawn to Marcia for the specific purpose of praying for her and Christy, and my attention was drawn to Barbara and her father for the same purpose.

The specific prayer was formed as the result of a sequence of meaningful coincidences. There was an amusing assortment of messages that ranged from frogs and beavers to princesses in fairy tales! The messages were conveyed through dreams and unlikely messengers which brought our attention to the discernment of the spirit of control. This was an elaborately orchestrated and divine intervention!

You will recall that Barbara's friend, Cheryl, gave me a bottle of wine with a frog on the label. This was significant of the *fairy tale* about the *frog* and the *princess*. Barbara had nicknamed me Princess; Marcia loved fairy tales and my attention had been drawn to frogs. I found this amusing episode to have been part of that divine supernatural plea to intercede for Barbara and her father and Christy and Marcia. What a joy to be able to intercede for God's children and our loved ones and to learn that the power of prayer, specific prayer, can set the captives free through the victory of Jesus!

Yes, there have definitely been some changes made today! I saw Barbara and she is calmer. I used to see her as formidable, now she appears petite, happy and approachable.

I talked only briefly to my niece. She told me she had a dream that she was fighting with me, and that I had her and a boy in a dungeon. She could look out two windows; one had a view as if from the top of a skyscraper, the other was at ground level. She peeled away some layers and got out. The boy wanted to go with her, but she told him he had to stay there.

Hmmm - now doesn't that sound like a soul that has been set free? Who is the boy? Does he represent the spirit of control? I think so. Why was I in the dream? Do you suppose it had to do with my part in the prayer? I do. And, I believe *IT CAME TO PASS!* VEHAYAH.

Ch VIII - There'll be Some Changes Made Today

AND IT CAME TO PASS, while they were wondering what to make of this, that, behold, two men stood by them in dazzling raiment. And when the women were struck with fear and bowed their faces to the ground, they said to them, "Why do you seek the living one among the dead? He is not here, but has risen."

St. Luke 24: 4-6

CHAPTER 9

SURPRISE!

My journey has taken me on a wonderful series of discoveries and surprises. From the beginning of my journey which began over ten years ago when I first read the Bible and experienced the power of expectation, to the present when I am rejuvenated by the wonder of surprises, I realize that the mysteries of God are a continual feast for the mind and soul that delights the spirit.

It is with great difficulty that I approach the ending of this book only because the nearer I get to the end - the farther away it becomes. The surprises do not stop nor do the discoveries cease to delight. It isn't any wonder. After all God created life and there is no end!

We are destined to live in the light of God for eternity and the journey that takes us through this world to the heavenly kingdom beyond is exhilarating. Only when we turn in the wrong direction toward the darkness does life seem to stop. The tragedy in this is that it doesn't. If your journey is not leading you onward and upward you desperately need a turn in the right direction.

Chapter IX – Surprise!

My latest surprise began subtly, then exploded into a realization that rocked me to the depths of my soul while simultaneously propelling me into the highest jubilation of knowing that I had yet to experience. It was such great news that I could hardly wait to share it with the world.

As I pondered revealing a most personal and profound truth, I wondered is it too much too soon? Can I really expect the world to accept such an idea as this? Then came fear! That old culprit was staring me in the face, defying me to open the doors to my soul! His weapons were significant as he threatened to not only discredit me, but worse to discredit the work that I was about to publish in fulfillment of the desire of my heart!

Recalling the knowledge that I had gained in my journey and the exhortations I had proclaimed all through my book, I made the decision to proceed with this chapter trusting the truth to make itself known on the pages that follow.

With the help of a friend I am encouraged to relate the incidents that lead up to the most wonderful surprise of my life. It began with subtle coincidences which brought back memories that exploded into a knowing that only I could understand.

In the pursuit of a deeper spiritual knowledge I have read many books on the subject. A recent book was about Christian mystics. To my surprise, I found this book consisted mostly of saints. Being a Catholic from my baptism as an infant, I was delighted to see my journey was taking me back to where I had begun. Over my lifetime I had ventured into non-denominational churches where I enjoyed great spiritual worship, became an avid student of our great modern day faith teachers and evangelists, and over the course of my writings was attending a Methodist Church. I found all these religious experiences to be enlightening and fulfilling on my spiritual journey.

My attention was riveted when I came to the section that was written about St. Therese of Lisieux who is also called the Little Flower. She is the one I chose for my patron saint when I was confirmed in the Catholic Church when I was 12-years old. Therefore, having chosen her name made it that much more interesting for me to I read about her. She was described as one of the more modern mystics. The mystics of old were contemplative, whereas St. Therese was described as a modern mystic who was both contemplative and active.

My very own initials are ACT (Anne Urne is my new name). These initials have been an encouragement to me in my pursuit of truth. St. Therese being described as an active spiritualist touched my heart. With fascination I learned that she had written a famous book, *Story of a Soul,* that was the most widely read book of spiritual seekers. I couldn't wait to read it!

I found a copy at the library and read the most riveting story I had ever encountered. I recognized some similarities between our lives. She lost her mother at age 4 - I lost my father at the same age. Therese had a very strong will - oh how I recognized that trait! As I read her Story of a Soul I found my own soul falling in love with this wonderful saint.

The past weeks had brought my attention to St. Therese more than once. I began to recognize a pattern of coincidences developing and they were meaningful coincidences which is the trait of a spiritual experience.

My mother told me one day that she had ordered me a rosary from Our Lady of the Snows. A week or so later she showed me that instead of the rosary they had sent this beautiful porcelain statue of St. Therese. So when I got a copy of her book to read, there she stood on my nightstand right beside me as I read her book.

I already had a picture of her on the wall in my dressing room - right next to a picture of Jesus. I remembered how I found that picture of her at a flea market at the Rose Bowl[26]. My husband had taken me there one weekend while we were working on the Northridge earthquake in 1994. I liked the picture very much and it was the very same picture that Lilly, who was like a second grandmother, had in her home when I was a child. It was probably that very picture of the beautiful little nun holding a crucifix of Jesus and a bouquet of roses that had inspired me to choose her as my patron saint and take her name at my Confirmation.

I didn't know that much about my chosen saint, but she was special to me. It seemed she had made herself known to me since I was a child in subtle "little ways". That was Therese's doctrine - her little way.

As I was reading the last words that Therese wrote in her manuscript from her death bed: *"through confidence and love"* the following words made me gasp: 'Here the pencil which has replaced the clumsy pen falls from Therese's hands. The manuscript shows evidence of wavy lines and illustrates the strong will of Therese who cannot finish her work'.

In that very instant a memory exploded into my consciousness that rocked my soul! The word *pencil* took me back to an incident that happened over twenty years ago, and it was one of those mysterious events that you just don't talk about. Only my sister knew and experienced the phenomenon that I am about to tell and she is no longer with us. Two other persons have been privy to this information and they are Christy and Michelle.

---

[26] Only after proof reading this chapter many times did I notice that the picture of the little saint who is famous for her love of *roses* was waiting for me at the *Rose Bowl*. Another surprise!

Now comes the step of faith as I place my credibility on the line in order to explain my extraordinary belief that St. Therese has been helping me for a very long time.

It was in the early 1980's when I was suffering with intense depression and feelings of hopelessness because of my marriage to a sociopath. One of my co-workers was a self-professed psychic and medium. I visited with her on occasion and listened with curiosity as she told of her ability. I believed that she had the talent; however, I was cautiously skeptical. What bothered me most was that she only believed that Jesus was a good man and teacher. She explained that she always prayed light and angels around her when meditating, but I wished more than ever that she would profess Jesus as the Son of God.

One day I was in her office and she told me that I had a spiritual guide who was a woman with dark hair. She explained that she would guide me. She also told me that I had a very bright light within. On another occasion she told me she saw me without my diamonds. I had some beautiful large and expensive rings and I knew I would never part with. Just for the record - they are gone. The sociopath didn't miss a thing in divesting me of all material goods along with my dignity.

It was on that day that she told me I had a spiritual guide that I pondered who this might be. My grandmother who died when I was very young had dark hair. Could it be her? I returned to my office that day and was so very sad. I didn't know which way to turn or how to ever get out of my hopeless situation. I thought about it for awhile and then I prayed. I prayed for my spiritual guide, whoever she was, to please help me. I remember sitting at my desk, all alone in my office, with a yellow tablet and a pencil in my hand. As I prayed and meditated I held the pencil to the tablet and to my astonishment it began writing without my assistance! I will never forget the words that appeared that day on my tablet:

LOUSY WORLD BETTER LOVE NOW

These words exploded into my consciousness as I read that Therese dropped the pencil! At last I knew beyond any doubt that Therese was the one who had guided my *pencil* and wrote that message on my tablet so many years ago! She was indeed my spiritual guide.

This explosion of knowledge came to me in waves as I recalled Therese's vocation was *love* and her message to me was to *love now*. Another quote of St. Therese jumped up from the pages of her book: "I am not breaking my head over the writing of my 'little life'. It is like fishing with a line; I write whatever comes to the end of my pen." Therese has been guiding the writing of my book!

I realized she has always been with me and now she is making herself known to me as I near the publication of my book. The reason she has come to help me are written in her very own words. She is quoted talking to her sister, Mother Agnes, saying:

> "*After my death, you must not speak to anyone about my manuscript before it is published; you must speak only to Mother Prioress about it. If you ACT otherwise, the devil will lay more than one trap to hinder God's work, a very important work!*"

Therese knew a hundred years ago that the devil hinders the work of God and it is not without wonder and awe that I recall my very own journey that lead me to the Lost Books. I believe my saint is here to keep this book from becoming lost as well. Her very warning 'to *ACT* otherwise' invoked my initials.

The coincidences have not subsided but are continuing. I was having some difficulty with a few women at a new job and I was praying about it early one morning when these thoughts came to my mind. I was asking for help from St. Therese who had written in her book about expressing her love to a sister that annoyed her and from whom she would have preferred to distance herself. Therese taught how to go beyond the person and love the soul that contained Jesus. As I was going over this in a drowsy and sleepy state just before waking up, I was lead to look at the girls in my office as flowers. I then began going from office to office and depicting each girl as a rose of a particular color. Oh, I thought it would be nice to give each of them a rose in their own color, but I didn't have that many vases. Then, I remembered the earlier revelation about my vase.

In an earlier chapter I explained how I was given the new last name of Urne. It was many, many months later that God showed me a similitude that depicted me and my new name in a wonderfully symbolic way. He showed me how I was like my beautiful crystal vase which is kept in a lighted gold cabinet that takes center stage in the living room. My name is Anne Urne, an urn – a vase. He revealed to me as I looked at that beautiful crystal vase sparkling in the light that I was that vase. I am abiding in the light of Jesus and His light is abiding in me. The illustration of the light over, in and through the crystal vase made the words of our Lord so perfectly clear when he said, *Abide in me and I will abide in you.* Up to this time I couldn't quite grasp how I was in Jesus and Jesus was in me, but now as I looked at the vase in the light and saw the light passing through the vase, it became crystal clear! As the light abides in the vase so, too, does the vase abide in the light. Jesus is the light and I am the vase! It is so simple when God shows you a picture that you can see and perceive. If you ever wondered why Jesus spoke to his disciples in parables, this explains it. We are no more able to comprehend the spiritual with our physical abilities, than we can talk to a dog in dog language. There is more

Chapter IX – Surprise!

than a language barrier between us and God, there is a body barrier. We are flesh and God is spirit. Not until we get the understanding into our spirit do we actually hear what God is trying to say to us.

Now, as I thought about the many colored roses at my office representing the girls I worked with, God showed me that I was the vase and they were the flowers! I visualized placing each one of those roses into the beautiful crystal vase and offering it as a sweet smelling bouquet to the Lord. Now, that could be none other than my very own Little Flower St. Therese guiding me into another one of her "little ways". It worked too! My flowers are now lovely to work with.

Another coincidence that I noted as I read St. Therese's book was that it was divided into three manuscripts. My book *The Spiritual Trilogy* also consists of three manuscripts!

Another remarkable incident occurred within a week or so of finishing the Story of a Soul. I departed on a short trip with my husband to see the Rockettes who were performing in Branson, Missouri. On the trip home my husband decided to take me to Eureka Springs and give me a quick tour of this quaint little tourist town. First he took me to the Crescent Hotel which is on the historic register and he especially wanted me to see the church just behind it where you enter through the bell tower because of the hills. It was St. Elizabeth's church and it was also on the historical register. It was a beautiful small stone structure and as I entered the large wooden doors guess who was waiting in the entry! A life size statute of beautiful St. Therese smiling at me. I knelt and lit candles and thanked her for all of her help.

I would now like to acknowledge the very special person, saint and friend who has been with me for more years than I realized because I only became aware of her presence as I neared the end of the trilogy. I am humbled, amazed, awed and spiritually ecstatic about recognizing and finding my spiritual sister and friend, none other than my patron saint who has mystically manifested her presence to help guide me as I approach the publication of this book. It is none other than the beautiful, mystical and loving St. Therese, the Little Flower of Lisieux, who vowed to come back to save souls. On July 17, 1897 a few months before her agonizing death from tuberculosis she predicted:

"I WILL RETURN!" "I WILL COME DOWN!"

On her deathbed St. Therese made her now famous prediction:

I feel that my mission is about to begin, my mission of making others love God as I love Him, my mission of teaching my little way to souls. If God answers my requests, my heaven will be spent on earth up until the end of the world. Yes, I want to spend my heaven in doing good on earth.

Story of a Soul
St. Therese

Chapter IX – Surprise!

On that day the deaf shall here the words of a book and out of gloom and darkness, the eyes of the blind shall see.

Isaia 29: 18

CHAPTER 10
GREAT THINGS

    Many years I have pondered the words God spoke to me when he said, *"Tell Christy to expect Great Things."*
    As I conclude this trilogy, I am still struggling with the complete understanding of the *Great Things*. There are two instances of the word GREAT in the scriptures that come to my mind every time. The scriptures are from words spoken by God to Eve and by His messenger to Mary. They both involved the birth of a child. As I write this I realize it was the child that I have known as the Lord in both instances, the firstborn being Abel and to me his second appearance on earth when he was born into the world in the holy name of Jesus.

> *To the woman he said: "I will make* **great your distress** *in childbearing; in pain shall you bring forth children . . ."*
>
> Genesis 3:16

And the angel said to her, "Do not be afraid, Mary, for thou hast found grace with God. Behold, thou shalt conceive in thy womb and shalt bring forth a son; and thou shalt call his name Jesus. He shall be **great** *. . .*

St. Luke 1: 30-32

And Mary said, ". . . Because he who is mighty has done **great things** *for me,*

St. Luke 1: 46-49

I spoke to Christy recently and told her how I was nearing the end of my book and that I knew it would not be complete until I had written about her great things that God had promised her. I had finally given her the most unusual chapter in this book to read that dealt with abuse, frogs and princes. My hope was that it had not insulted her, but as she talked to me about reading it, I realized she was holding back something. She told me she thought it was pretty funny as far as the animals go, and that she knew there had been a spirit of abuse involved. Then she abruptly stopped and had a look that I perceived to be of disapproval.

"Have I hurt your feelings?" I asked referring to the abuse. "I would never want to write anything that would hurt you," I continued still thinking the abuse thing was too intimate to discuss publicly in a book.

Then she surprised me by saying, "If that is how you see it, that's fine. But you just don't understand! You see my brother and I both *believe* in great things, we just don't expect them to be here." "When Mary received great things, she was talking about the birth of salvation into the world by her son Jesus! How can anything compare to such a great thing as that?" she finished.

We discussed that great things from God cannot be compared to material things, fame or fortune which are the measure of great things in the world. I understood what she meant, but the complete meaning had still not been revealed to me. As I awoke this morning, I understood it was time to begin writing about the great things. I could no longer put off the end of this book, and Christy wasn't going to write it for me. So, today the study of great things along with my expectation of understanding is put into action.

The study must begin in the word when God spoke to Eve that she would suffer great distress in child bearing. This is a suffering in the flesh which brings about a birth. The words must have more meaning, and I searched scripture, employed the dictionary and intoned prayer for guidance in my pursuit of truth.

First, I referred to the scriptures which revealed to me that Great Things to Mary was a birth and Great Distress to Eve was childbirth. Hence - Great Distress births Great Things. This shines a brighter light on the words Jesus spoke when he said we must be born again.

Now, to the dictionary for interpretation of certain words in the scriptures, and here are the definitions that I found had meaning that correlated with the truth I was searching for.

Great	Majestic
Majestic	Royal
Birth	Beginning
Thing	State of Being or Existence

GREAT THINGS, therefore, can be described as royal existence in the kingdom of God to which we are brought in by a birth. It is a new beginning or existence into a better place. This study is painting a picture that is beginning to make sense. I believe the understanding will come.

This is the time to employ the power of prayer for understanding and guidance as the pursuit of divine truth is like searching in a dark place for an exit and at last a glimmer of light is glimpsed in the distance that beckons the weary wanderer to it. Oh, thank you Jesus for your light in this dark world.

Suffering great distress in this world such as the childbirth described to Eve is a similitude of the difficulty we suffer when being born again into the kingdom of God. It is a comparison of natural birth to spiritual birth. Jesus explained it to his disciples when He said:

> *With difficulty will a rich man enter the kingdom of heaven. And further I say to you, it is easier for a camel to pass through the eye of a needle, than for a rich man to enter the kingdom of heaven. . . . With men this is impossible, but with God all things are possible.*

Now, I recognize the difficulty that I have had with my understanding of *Expect Great Things*. I have not focused upon the "expecting" part of it. Christy knew all along that she was happy, content and safe with God. She *expected* God to take care of her and her family through the distress, and this brought her the *great things* which were peace and trust through her very difficult process of losing every material object that her family owned to toxic mold. The *Comfort* which God had spoken of at the same time was with her through the whole process.

Another way to understand the comfort is to look back at the words of the angel spoken to Mary: '*for thou has found grace with God*'. Comfort can then be recognized as the grace of God that makes it possible to pass through great distress and enter into the great things of God.

My belief that we can have it all here on earth is more clearly defined. It is only when we can give up the false securities found in this world and put our complete trust and faith in God that we finally and completely achieve the high life of a child of the king. Great things can be manifested in the earth when we are born again in the spirit. How we develop our faith and trust in God is an individual process and no two persons use the same process. Just as we develop into our unique personality, so do we uniquely find our way back to the Father. There is such a fine line that runs between the riches of the world and the riches of God. It is described as a veil in the scriptures, and only when the veil is lifted do we gain the understanding and perceive the truth that sets us free. Yes, God has promised great things, we just fail to perceive and understand that they are manifested not man-made. The greatest thing is indeed the salvation of a soul.

The process of saving a soul begins by its birth into the flesh of the earth. It is finished by its birth into the spirit of the kingdom of God, b*ecause He who is mighty had done great things.*

. . . the power of God, which is called great.

The Acts 8:10

CHAPTER 11

FAIRY TALES CAN COME TRUE

It was only yesterday that I wrote the chapter on the great things in an attempt to finish this book. Now, it is early morning and I must tell of the dream I just had. I awoke early and remembered it vividly. As I remained in bed, I recalled the dream while wondering what it meant as I replayed it in my mind.

THE DREAM

I was at Michelle's house alone, when someone knocked at the door. I opened it to find an older graying gentleman, dressed impeccably in a gray suit, white shirt, tie and beautiful black full-length wool overcoat. He was dressed to the nines and looked like a high-polished banker. He had a powerful aura and was immensely lovable. He was a man who commanded respect and I was completely drawn to him. Instantly, I recognized him even though I had never met him. It was Harry! Yes, I was standing in the same room with Harry, himself!

WHO IS HARRY? Why he is none other that the role model I chose for my ideal mate. I wrote about him in the second book of this trilogy. The chapter was entitled, *How to Dream*. He was the Prince Charming in the Cinderella story about my girl friend. Her husband was Harry! He had all the qualities of intellect, maturity, kindness, strength, humor, love, caring, compassion and generosity that I desired in a husband for myself. It was after I learned to dream and recognize the traits that I wanted to find in a mate that I found my own Harry, my dream man, and married him. Harry represents my dream come true!

My thoughts turned again to the dream. In it I was taking Harry to the airport and there was an urgency to get him to Gate 25 for his departure. We made it.

As I recalled this part of the dream I began asking about its significance, and as quickly as I asked the understanding came. Number 25 represented the year 2025 and that was the number of the departure gate. *Could this be the rapture year?* I wondered. *Could it be the year of my own departure?* I recalled the timetable I had constructed and remembered the year I had approximated for the rapture was 2036.

Contemplating the possibilities, I realized that 2025 could possibly represent my personal departure date, but I knew better. I have had one of those *know that you know* feelings about my end being one of flying away, so much so that I laugh at the thought of making funeral preparations. It's just one of those things I have always known. My husband occasionally asks me about my funeral plans. He wants to at least know my religious preference for a service and the town I wanted to be buried in. My answer always flusters him when I say, "I'm going to fly away just like the song: *I'll Fly Away - Oh Glory*. Then I would tell him that I knew he wanted a quiet place in heaven, but I was going with the rowdy crowd that would be playing horns, waving tambourines, marching and singing: ♪ *"Oh, When the Saints Go Marching In, Oh when the saints go marching in; Oh, yes I want to be in that number --- When the Saints Go Marching In."* ♪

As I thought about the discrepancy in the dates, I recalled reading that we had passed the millennium several years prior to the year 2000 due to counting errors over the centuries. That could account for the difference in my calculated end time of 2036 and the year 2025 signaled in my dream. Between God's shortening the days and our discrepancies in counting time, it would be impossible to pin down the date. That is why we are told to be watching and ready as we won't know the day. The times, however, we should understand.

Again, the realization of the full meaning of my dream rocked me. My prince had come on his white horse and carried me away to his castle. The spiritual marriage of my soul to the bridegroom is consummated.

"My dreams have come true!"

THE END?

The Prince took Cinderella upon his horse and rode away.

The Story of Cinderella
Fairy Tales from Grimm

CHAPTER 12

THE EIGHTH SPIRIT

My plans for The *Spiritual Trilogy* did not include finishing this chapter. After starting it I became frustrated by this vague and elusive eighth spirit, so I just excerpted this information completely from the book. I decided to address the topic in a later book.

While bearing down on publication, however, my attention was unmistakably drawn to the operation of this spirit and I knew it was time to hear what the Spirit was saying.

I have known about the eighth spirit for years. I learned about it at the same time I discovered the seven spirits in *The Testament of Reuben* in the *Forgotten Books of Eden*. These spirits were discussed earlier in this book, so my concentrated effort was not focused on the portion of testimony that discusses the eighth spirit of God and the eighth spirit of error.

> *Seven spirits therefore are appointed against man, and they are the leaders in the works of youth. And seven other spirits are given to him at his creation that through them should be done every work of man.*
>
> Reuben 1: 12-13

Chapter XII– The Eighth Spirit

The Eighth Spirit of God:

Besides all these there is an eighth spirit of sleep, with which is brought about the trance of nature and the image of death.

Reuben 1:22

The Eighth Spirit of Error:

And with all these the spirit of sleep is joined which is that of error and fantasy.

Reuben 1:31

The eighth spirits are difficult to discern and both are described as spirits of sleep. The differences must be established. A quick check of sleep surprisingly brought up the word rapture. I believe this eighth spirit has been difficult to recognize because it has been waiting for the end time to appear.

God's eighth spirit brings about the trance of nature and the image of death. Trance is described as a passageway. God's very name, Vehaya, which means *it came to pass,* is a significant coincidence of the occurrence of the word *pass* as I see it.

The eighth spirit of error is described as the spirit of sleep to which error and fantasy are joined. Looking up the word *error*, I found: belief in what is untrue or departure from truth. Fantasy is described as an illusory imagination which is further described as a deceitful illusion; an unreal or misleading image presented to the vision, and a deceptive appearance and false impression.

Fantasy and error point to the mission of this eighth spirit of error which is to cause man to depart from the truth by using a misleading image.

> *And I saw another beast coming up out of the earth, and it had two horns like to those of a lamb, but it spoke as does a dragon. And it exercised all the authority of the former beast in its sight; and it made the earth and the inhabitants therein to worship the first beast, whose deadly wound was healed. And it did great signs, so as even to make fire come down. And it leads astray the inhabitants of the earth by reason of the signs, which it was permitted to do in the sight of the beast, telling the inhabitants of the earth to make an image to* **the beast** *. . . And it leads astray the inhabitants of the earth . . .*

The Apocalypse 13: 11-14

The pursuit of this eighth spirit continues to point to the last chapter of the Bible.

> *The beast that thou sawest was, and is not, and is about to come up from the abyss, and will go to destruction. And the inhabitants of the earth – whose names have not been written in the book of life from the foundation of the world – will wonder when they see the beast which was, and is not. And here is the meaning for him who has wisdom. The seven heads are seven mountains upon which the woman sits; and they are seven kings: five of them have fallen, one is and the other has not yet come; and when he comes he must remain a short time. And* **the beast** *that was, and is not,* **is moreover himself eighth, and is of the seven***, and is on his way to destruction.*

Apocalypse 17: 8-11

There it is. The eighth spirit of error is the beast! This is such a gripping revelation as I recall my analogy earlier of the Father, Son and Holy Spirit to the opposing forces of Satan, the false prophet and the beast! The beast is Satan's unholy spirit. The realization that the eighth spirit is operating in the world right now is mind boggling. That means we are in that part of prophecy that describes tribulation and end times!

The mystery is sublime and the answer is divine. As my journey progresses, the direction and speed propel me into a new understanding that is very exciting.

Who is God, but the Alpha and Omega; the beginning and the end. Just as the end of the Bible describes tribulation, the beginning of the Bible describes the plagues that Moses brought upon the Egyptians. The beginning and the end somehow blend into the same story. It is a full circle and in reaching the end we find the beginning. The two meet at the intersection of the same place.

While reading the very first pages in the Book of Genesis last week my attention was riveted on the word *separation*. When God created the world it was described as separating light from dark, dividing the waters above and below, separating the earth and seas, and separating day from night.

This observation of creation in separation was being pointed out to me in the scriptures, while at the same time recognizing that Jesus was described as making the two one by virtue of His death. God in the spirit created the two, and God in the flesh made them one again. God is our wholeness. The creation in separation, I believe to be significant of our separation of flesh and spirit. Creation means birth, and we here again see that a birth in the spirit is essential and it is effected by our separation from the flesh.

We know that God is truth and Satan is a liar. The answer to the mystery is found when the deception of Satan is revealed.

> *But none of you shall go outdoors until morning. For the Lord will go by, striking down the Egyptians. Seeing the blood on the lintel and the two doorposts, the Lord will pass over the door and not let the destroyer come into your houses to strike you down.*
>
> Exodus 12:23

The story of God striking down the first-born is beyond our comprehension. We don't understand how a good God could destroy.

Our concept of Satan from the beginning of time has been that of a destroyer because his mission is to steal, kill and destroy. So, how can we explain the scriptures that describe God as the destroyer? We look at the words.

Create: Conceive, to bring into existence, begin.

Destroy: End, to bring to naught by putting out of existence.

The understanding came when God showed me that He was the creator and the destroyer. How could that be? It was the deception posed by the eighth spirit of sleep being joined in error and fantasy.

The error and fantasy was believing that the destroyer was Satan. This very lie set the stage of our journey in the wrong direction because we lost the correct perception of God also being the destroyer. Satan's mission to usurp God's position of power was defeated when God cast him out of heaven. Satan now operates in the earth being stripped of his power by Jesus.

The deception of Satan being a destroyer was an attempt by Satan to imitate God! The error was in the illusion of death, and the fantasy was that the destroyer was a killer. This fear of death was instilled in man from the beginning, and Satan used this fear to lead us away from God.

Again and again I return to the descriptions of the eighth spirits of sleep. God's spirit is the trance of nature and image of death. Death then is only an image of the flesh, while the soul is being caught up to heaven.

In the eight spirit of error we find the real meaning of death. For to this sleep is joined the error and fantasy which is the belief of a false illusion. The false illusion is death, because there is no death!

Thus, believing the eight spirit of error we are fiendishly drawn off course by our fear of death, and if not checked, the soul will pass out of this world into eternal darkness. The lie is to keep us turned away from the light of Jesus, our truth! Darkness is the closest thing there is to death. The reality, however, is worse. It is the eternal existence in darkness without love!

Our power to choose determines the destination of our soul. When we end in the body of flesh, we are born into a spiritual body being translated into the spiritual realm. In this realm exist two rulers, the God of Light and the ruler of darkness.

Our destination is crucial to knowing Jesus as the true light. To miss Him is the fatal error that determines our eternity! Ironically, the ruler of darkness by his eighth spirit of error cunningly leads away souls into eternal death. If death was indeed a reality, the struggle of our souls would be in vain.

In the flesh Jesus said, "It is finished." In the spirit God says, "It Came to Pass."

The conclusions drawn from this study are simple when put into perspective. The eight spirit of error has been identified in the scriptures as the beast. My studies showed the beast to be the unholy spirit of Satan. With all things being on a level field, we can then understand that the eight spirit of God is none other that His Holy Spirit.

Only by awakening to our spiritual senses can we find the truth. Jesus is the truth and He beckons us by His word in the scriptures, and the Holy Spirit who calls out, urging us to turn around and find Jesus.

So much hinges on that little turn. At last we can discover the meaning of life.

THE END AND THE BEGINNING

EPILOGUE

Christy is our beautiful dreamer, like Joseph and his many-colored coat. She had a dream while I was writing this book and she has graciously permitted me to share it.

CHRISTY'S DREAM

God came to her and gave her a gift wrapped in gold and in a specific shape. As she handled it and tried to open it, the shape kept changing and she couldn't get it back to the way it was. God took it from her and told her He would fix it and bring it back. He then went up a mountain. She waited a while, but God didn't come right back as she had expected Him to. So, being tired of waiting and wanting her gift, she went to the mountain to find God. She could see Him at the top, playing golf and laughing. He was having a good time. She encountered a man at the foot of the mountain who advised that he was God's brother and he could take her there. She didn't want to be bothered by this man, and didn't want his help. So, she went to the other side of the mountain, where a woman got right in her face. She was a sister to God, and told her she couldn't get there from this side.

Christy reminded me how once I had difficulty understanding or relating to who God was. She told me she never had a problem understanding who God was, but she couldn't comprehend Jesus. After this dream she clearly understood who and how Jesus fit into the picture. He was, indeed, the only way to God. She learned that God could come to us anytime He desired, but we could not go to Him, unless we went through Jesus, the man at the base of the mountain. The woman who flew into her face – that was the Holy Spirit.

The gift? Now, that is another story.

Consider your soul as a castle made out of a single diamond or of a transparent crystal, in which are many rooms, just as in Heaven there are many mansions . . . Some of them are above, others below, others on both sides; and in the midst, in the centre of them all, is the chiefest of them where many things most secret pass between God and the soul.

St. Teresa of Avila
The Interior Castle
Published in 1577

Toward the end of writing the third book of the trilogy, my attention was dramatically and repeatedly drawn to the word *crystal*. Noting that it was a source of energy, a ball used by some to foretell future events and discovering myself as the crystal vase were just a few of the ideas that passed through my mind as I kept running into the word.

How wonderful as I finish this book that I should stumble upon this quote from the Mystic of Mystics, St. Teresa of Avila.

> *Consider your soul as a castle made of . . . a transparent crystal.*

Indeed! Not only will I consider it, but I will find that book and devour it!

I have discovered the crystal of my soul and I have become one with the music. I have flowed in it and with it as it resonates to the east. New insights continue to enhance and enlighten me. The circles of knowledge and truth continue to expand and widen into a kaleidoscope of new perceptions and understanding.

There is one wonderful encounter I had one morning with God and I would be remiss to omit it from this book. As I awoke one morning and reached over to touch my husband's shoulder as he slept, I felt the strength in his arm. At that same moment I told God that I knew He was much greater and stronger than my husband, and that I should love Him first, but I admitted, *Oh, God, I just can't feel your strength and closeness like I do his.*

I then got up and went into the living room and began reading my Bible. It was very early and the most wonderful thing happened. God shook the room where I sat - - and I felt his POWER and strength! Oh, how wonderful our God is!

Just as God is described as the beginning and the end, so our spiritual journey continually reaches endings that are only new beginnings.

ACKNOWLEDGEMENT

My special thanks go out to my new found friends of the Sisters of Benedict. Their kindness, acceptance and encouragement meant more to me than words can express. A very dear sister confirmed that my spiritual experiences were indeed authentic. It seems I have bumped into a bevy of Benedictines at this juncture of my journey. I look forward to a new learning experience as the Lord takes me to new spiritual heights. A Benedictine rule is to *listen*, and my response is: *Here I am Lord.*

Another Benedictine that I must acknowledge is a Benedictine monk from California. His magnificent book is the latest jewel added to my collection and it was given to me by my daughter's friend, Donna. It is entitled: *Second Simplicity* by Bruno Barnhart.

Donna brought the book to Michelle with a note that I read in amazement:

Hello Michelle's Mom. You have inadvertently repeated Bruno's words verbatim . . . He lives in a perpetual vow of silence. I'd say we need to visit. If not, enjoy his work.

Donna is a writer and Michelle had given her a copy of my manuscript to read months earlier. When she brought the note to Michelle, she explained that she had tape recorded a seminar he conducted for the Benedictine sisters who took her as a guest. This monk only breaks his vow of silence to conduct these periodic seminars. It was from this recorded message that she found the verbatim words in my manuscript.

BIBLIOGRAPHY

Anne Urne used only one Bible for her study. It was the Catholic Bible given to her by her beloved Lilly who took care or her and spoiled her as a child. Anne was amazed that she still had this book in her possession more than thirty years later when she decided she would read the Bible. It has been retired as it became threadbare, but she keeps it in a special place as it is a very special Bible. She still reads the same Bible as she replaced it with an exact copy.

As Anne studied and traveled the path of her spiritual journey she found that books with answers to her questions came to her in an almost magical fashion. The books listed are those used in her spiritual quest for truth along with the books that she has written, including the one that was written after the Trilogy: *Trust Me - the Untold Story of Mary Magdalene,* by Anne Urne.

New American Catholic Edition The Holy Bible
Douay version and Confraternity of Christian Doctrine.
    Imprimatur: Francis Cardinal Spellman,
    Archbishop of New York, NY, June 8, 1961
    His Holiness Pope Pius XII - Urges the Study of
    the Sacred Scriptures
    Holy Father Pope Leo XIII - Encyclical Letter
    © 1950, 1958, 1961, by Benziger Brothers

- 1961 Author given this book by Lillian James in Decatur, IL
- 1993 Author first read entire book on 2/24/93 in Walters, OK and continued reading from cover to cover 19 more times through 5/10/96 while traveling around the country

The Forgotten Books of Eden
   © 1980 by Crown Publishers, Inc.; BELL, 1981 Edition
1993   Author found this book on a shelf at antique store in Citrus Counties, FL

The Lost Books of The Bible and the Forgotten Books of Eden
   © 1926 & 1927 by Alpha House, Inc., Published by The World Publishing Co.

1996   Author found this book at an estate sale in Oklahoma City

A SPIRITUAL TRILOGY
   ©2003 by Anne Urne, BOIS Publications
   2011 2nd Printing

2003   *First published book by, Anne Urne; included were her first 3 books written and completed in:*
   2000 Way Beyond the River
   2001 The Walls Came Tumbling Down
   2002   It Came to Pass

The Call to Glory Jeane Dixon Speaks of Jesus
   ©1971 *Jeane Dixon, Published* by William Morrow & Company, Inc.

2000   Author borrows this book from her mother to read and it is signed "Blessings" Jeane Dixon

The Da Vinci Code
    © 2003 by Dan Brown and Published by Doubleday

2003   Author reads book believing the purported marriage is blasphemous, falls in love with the story and is overcome with the desire to learn the truth

Holy Blood, Holy Grail
    © 1982 by Baigent, Leigh and Lincoln, Published by Delacorte Press

2003   Author must now read this book - and it is right there in her closet waiting for her

The Gospel of Mary Magdalene
    © 1997 Original French Michael Albin
    © 2002 English by Inner Traditions International

    2003   Author discovers the existence of this book while nearing the end of her own book about Mary Magdalene

TRUST ME
The Mystical Story of Mary Magdalene
    © 2004 by Anne Urne and Published by BOIS Publications

2004   2nd published book of this author, Anne Urne

TRUST ME

The untold story of Mary Magdalene

By Anne Urne

And coming soon Anne Urne's next book to be released and featured June 2012 in the IWPA Booth at the Chicago Printer's Row Literary Festival, entitled:

COMMUNION OF SAINTS

www.ingramcontent.com/pod-product-compliance
Lightning Source LLC
Chambersburg PA
CBHW070717160426
43192CB00009B/1219